"HER DECK ONCE RED WITH HEROES' BLOOD."

Gun deck of "*Old Ironsides*," 1931.

On the Decks of
"Old Ironsides",

BY

ELLIOT SNOW,

REAR ADMIRAL, C.C., U. S. NAVY, RETIRED,

AND

H. ALLEN GOSNELL,

LIEUTENANT COMMANDER, U. S. NAVAL RESERVE

NEW YORK

THE MACMILLAN COMPANY

1932

PRINTED IN THE UNITED STATES OF AMERICA
NORWOOD PRESS LINOTYPE, INC.
NORWOOD, MASS., U.S.A.

PREFACE

FEW books have been written giving such a complete and keenly interesting history of the United States Frigate *Constitution*. In *On the Decks of "Old Ironsides"* the authors have undertaken and successfully presented a most comprehensive history of life in the Navy during the period of "Iron Men and Wooden Ships." No one can read this volume without having a feeling of pride and gratitude for the ship and men that did so much in helping to lay the solid foundation of this country and its Navy. The authors have done a great service to their fellow countrymen.

No ship that sails the seas is so old as this, and none, old or new, has so glorious a history, no ship has trained more officers and men. You will read this book with pride. What we are *"Old Ironsides"* helped to make us; without her we, as a people, might not have continued to be. The men that commanded her, sailed her, and fought her are here today only in spirit. But they are here, and they will be here as long as the United States lasts.

The brave relic of brave days, *"Old Ironsides"* is not only a ship but a challenge. She represents the problems of a young, sparsely peopled country fighting for its life; we appreciate the idealism and strength that built her, manned her, and fought her. We realize our immense indebtedness to the past that lived and died that we might be, as we are, free, powerful, a leader among nations. She is part of what America has been, is, and will be.

She was built when this nation, now deemed the most powerful on earth, was young in years, poor in developed resources, inexperienced in the practice of a new and then truly revolutionary form of government, and uncertain, in consequence, of a lasting place among the world's political entities. She was built, together with other ships less famous, not for belligerent attack without provocation or for mere maintenance of an already strong national position, but for desperate defense of our violated rights on what was then the high road of our hopes for continued existence and augmented strength—the sea.

The United States then lived both literally and figuratively by the sea. Maritime commerce was the country's life blood. Industry was in the offing, but yet held no lively promise of prosperity, and indeed what little there was could not hope to survive or to enjoy foreign markets unless the United States should establish itself securely among the nations of the earth by successfully asserting its right to the freedom of the seas.

It was this one ship, magnificently named the *Constitution,* that had most to do with establishing that right. The debt we owe to her designers, her builders, her officers and crew, is one of profound gratitude and respect. If one were to select a solitary symbol for America's adolescence, it would be this majestic Frigate that rides the seas today.

This volume is replete with tales of her speed and staunchness as a sailing and fighting ship, and of the courage and skill of the men who manned her.

How many, young or old, grasp the full significance of the fact that she was the product from truck to keelson of hand labor, skilled to the point of artistry in crafts now rarely practiced. The bolts that fastened her timbers and the copper that sheathed her hull were hand fabricated in the shop of Paul Revere, patriot and metalsmith extraordinary. The live oak and red cedar that went into her were hand felled and hand hewn by men now unknown. Her innumerable fittings were forged by others whose names have not come down to us. And thus she was a product, not of machines, but of men, and therefore characteristic of her time.

Likewise she was sailed, towering majestically a white cloud above the blue deep, by men as familiar with her vast expanse of canvas and complexities of rigging as we are with the innumerable devices of the machine age. They too were craftsmen, skilled in a typical American lore.

No one can read this book without experiencing a feeling of patriotic gratitude to its authors for their thorough comprehensive treatment of a subject dear to all true Americans. *On the Decks of "Old Ironsides"* is a task "well done."

LOUIS J. GULLIVER,
Commander, U. S. Navy,
Commanding U. S. Frigate *Constitution*

Wilmington, N. C.,
November 26, 1931

INTRODUCTION

This volume is composed principally of material which has not been within reach of the general public except to a negligible degree. The average date of publication of a great percentage of these records is nearly a hundred years past. They have been in process of collection over an extended period by Rear Admiral Elliot Snow, C.C., U. S. Navy, Ret., whose association with the U. S. S. *Constitution* has been a long and close one. The best known period of the frigate's service was from 1804 to 1815. The reader of these pages, however, will realize that she led an extremely active and eventful career also from 1821 to 1881, as well as prior to 1804. In order to give here the complete story of the ship, her famous engagements have been included, even though comparatively well known. However, in these chapters also, the tale is presented through recently uncovered first-hand writings.

Even in the case of a ship as active in war as was *"Old Ironsides,"* the time spent in the presence of the enemy is, after all, but a few hours. The ship's *life* is lived in between battles. We can learn of this life by reading of the experiences, the viewpoints, and the sensations of her various officers and men themselves. We can follow the ship through storms and pleasant weather, through battle and threats of battle, and through anomalous and unheralded strife.   The varied events cover many decades; and their telling brings out not only the character of each writer but also the outlook and even the literary style of the times.   In order to retain the valuable authenticity of these records, each has been reproduced with as great a degree of exactness as possible.   Only about a half dozen words have been altered where palpable errors were detected.

So, by the work of their pens, we are enabled to accompany through their sailing and their fighting, a long list of *"Old Ironsides'"* associates: Schoolmaster George Jones, Midshipman and Lieutenant Charles Morris, gun sponger Moses Smith, merchant skipper Orne, Lieutenant Chads, R. N., the old tar "Oceanus," Professor of Mathematics Dow, foretopman Mercier, Captain's Clerk Benjamin Stevens, and Lieutenant Very.   They are the very soul of the ship.

H. A. GOSNELL

Princeton, N. J.,
September 14, 1931

THE MACMILLAN COMPANY
NEW YORK · BOSTON · CHICAGO · DALLAS
ATLANTA · SAN FRANCISCO

MACMILLAN & CO., Limited
LONDON · BOMBAY · CALCUTTA
MELBOURNE

THE MACMILLAN COMPANY
OF CANADA, Limited
TORONTO

ON THE DECKS OF "OLD IRONSIDES."

CONTENTS

Contents

ILLUSTRATIONS

xiv   *Illustrations*

"OLD IRONSIDES"

Ay, tear her tattered ensign down!
  Long has it waved on high,
And many an eye has danced to see
  That banner in the sky;
Beneath it rung the battle shout,
  And burst the cannon's roar;—
The meteor of the ocean air
  Shall sweep the clouds no more.

Her deck, once red with heroes' blood,
  Where knelt the vanquished foe,
When winds were hurrying o'er the flood,
  And waves were white below,
No more shall feel the victor's tread,
  Or know the conquered knee;—
The harpies of the shore shall pluck
  The eagle of the sea!

Oh better that her shattered hulk
  Should sink beneath the wave;
Her thunders shook the mighty deep,
  And there should be her grave;
Nail to the mast her holy flag,
  Set every threadbare sail,
And give her to the god of storms,
  The lightning and the gale!

OLIVER WENDELL HOLMES, 1830

CHRONOLOGY

1794–1797	Building at Hartt's shipyard, Boston. Authorized March 27, 1794; launched October 21, 1797.
1797–1798	Fitting out. Act passed March 27, 1798, to complete her. First moved under sail July 2, 1798.
1798–1801	Cruised against French along Atlantic Coast and in West Indies waters.
1801–1803	In port at Boston.
1803–1807	Flagship of Mediterranean Squadron under Commodores Preble, Barron, and Rodgers. Engaged in War with Tripoli, 1803 to 1805.
1807–1809	Overhauling at New York.
1809–1811	Flagship of Northern (Home) Squadron.
1811–1812	Special Service cruise to Europe.
1812–1815	Engaged in War of 1812.
	1812, July 16–19—Escaped capture when chased by British squadron of seven vessels including four frigates.
	1812, August 19—Under Captain Isaac Hull, captured H. M. S. *Guerriere*.
	1812, December 29—Under Commodore William Bainbridge, captured H. M. S. *Java*.

1813, —Overhauling at Navy Yard, Boston, for ten months.

1814, February 14—Under Captain Charles Stewart, captured H. M. S. *Pictou*.

1814, April 3—Escaped capture when chased by two British frigates.

1814, —Blockaded in Boston for eight months.

1815, February 20—Under Captain Charles Stewart, captured H. M. S. *Cyane* and *Levant*.

1815, March 12—Escaped capture when chased by three British frigates.

1815–1821   Repairing and in idleness at Navy Yard, Boston.

1821–1823   Flagship of the Mediterranean Squadron; back to Boston.

1824–1828   Mediterranean Squadron.

1828–1831   At Navy Yard, Boston, in idleness. Condemned by Naval Commissioners and ordered to be broken up and sold. Public sentiment, aroused by Oliver Wendell Holmes' poem, saved the frigate.

1832–1835   Repaired for service. First ship to enter new dry dock—June 24, 1833.

1835   Special Service cruise to Europe.

1835–1838   Flagship of Mediterranean Squadron.

1839–1841   Flagship of Pacific Squadron—based on Callao, Peru.

1842–1843   Flagship of Home Squadron.

1844–1846   Special Service cruise to Brazil, the East Indies, the Pacific, etc. Around the world from west to east.

1846–1848   Idle at Boston.

1848–1851   Flagship of the Mediterranean and African Squadrons.

1851–1853   Idle at New York.

1853–1855   Flagship of the Mediterranean Squadron for the last time. Captured American slave schooner *H. N. Gambell*.

1855–1860   At Portsmouth, N. H. In idleness and fitting out as school ship for the Navy.

1860–1871   School ship for the U. S. Naval Academy at Annapolis, 1860–1861; Newport, 1861–1865; and Annapolis again, 1865–1871.

1871–1876   In ordinary; hauled out and rebuilt at the Navy Yard, Philadelphia.

1877–1878   Training ship at Philadelphia.

1878–1879   Last cruise to foreign waters. Carried to Havre the U. S. exhibits for the Paris Exposition. On way home, ran aground but was pulled off by British tugs.

1879–1881   Last active cruise. In service as training ship for apprentice boys.

1881–1883   In idleness at New York.

1883–1897   At Navy Yard, Portsmouth, N. H. In idleness and serving as receiving ship.

1897   Towed to Boston for her centennial— October 21, 1797–1897.

1897–1907   Laid up on exhibition. Repairs authorized,

February 14, 1900, but no funds raised. Recommended in 1905 that she be used as a target.   Nation wide protest prevented this action.

1907–1908   Partially restored to extent of $100,000 appropriated by Congress.

1908–1925   Laid up on exhibition.

1926–1931   Rebuilding at Navy Yard, Boston, through funds raised principally by popular subscription.   Total cost, about $800,000.

1931   July 1—Went into commission completely restored.

1931–1933?   Towed to various American ports for exhibition purposes.

ON THE DECKS OF *"OLD IRONSIDES"*

CHAPTER I

CRADLE DAYS

WHO could have foreseen that the settlement of a family of Welsh Quakers in Haverford, Pa., in 1682 would have a far-reaching effect on our early navy and on the destinies of our nation? It was from this family that Joshua Humphreys sprung. He was born in 1751 and the date was June 17—not long afterwards to become "Bunker Hill Day." Joshua Humphreys was the man who designed and made the molds for the U. S. Frigate *Constitution,* the grand old ship of war endeared to millions and, since 1812, known familiarly as *"Old Ironsides."*

In his youth Joshua was indentured to a ship carpenter in Philadelphia by the name of Jonathan Penrose. The death of the latter "gave young Humphreys his time" before he was twenty years of age. He thereupon engaged in business with his cousin John Wharton. Within five years he was building and equipping many fine vessels for service against the British. He was commissioned by the "Committee of Safety" of Philadelphia to build a galley. He was further employed by "The Marine Committee" to fit out a fleet of war vessels—the fleet which sailed in 1776 under Commodore Esek Hopkins. Before the end of the Revolutionary War he became recog-

3

nized as the ablest and most skillful naval architect of his
day.   He was "read out of meeting," no less, by his fellow Quakers because of the aid which he gave to the Colo-
nies!   He died where he was born—in Haverford—on
January 12, 1838, at the ripe old age of eighty-six.   What
a magnificent monument he erected to his own memory
many years before his death when he laid out the U. S. S.
Constitution.

For many years after the United States became a nation
the disgraceful procedure was followed of paying ransom
and tribute to the semi-piratical Barbary States who
preyed upon our commerce.   This method was used as
an ineffective substitute for the protection of our ships
and citizens by armed force.   Finally in Congress there
was kindled a spark of self-respect sufficiently bright to
cause the authorization of six naval vessels.   The act was
approved on March 27, 1794.   There were strings attached to the bill but it brought about the start, at least,
of the *Constitution* and five other frigates.

Joshua Humphreys, of course, had long since given
much thought to the whole proposition.   As early as January 6, 1793, he had written to Robert Morris:

'Southwark, January 6, 1793.
'Robert Morris, Esq.:

'Sir,—From the present appearance of affairs I believe
it is time this country was possessed of a Navy; but as that
is yet to be raised I have ventured a few ideas on that
subject.

'Ships that compose the European navys are generally

distinguished by their rates; but as the situation and depth
of water of our coast and harbours are different in some
degrees from those in Europe, and as our navy must for
a considerable time be inferior in numbers, we are to
consider what size ships will be most formidable and be
an over match for those of an enemy; such Frigates as in
blowing weather would be an over match for double deck
ships, and in light winds to evade coming to action, or
double deck ships as would be an over match for common
double deck ships and in blowing weather superior to
ships of three decks, or in calm weather or light winds to
outsail them. Ships built on these principles will render
those of an enemy in a degree useless, or require a greater
number before they dare attack our ships. Frigates, I
suppose, will be the first object and none ought to be built
less than 150 feet keel to carry 28 32-pounders or 30 24-
pounders on the gun deck and 12-pounders on the quarter-
deck. These ships should have scantlings equal to 74's,
and I believe may be built of red cedar and live oak for
about twenty-four pounds per ton, carpenters tonnage including carpenters bill, smiths including anchors, joiners,
boat-builders, painters, plumbers, carvers, coopers, block
makers, mast makers, riggers and rigging, sail makers and
sail cloth, suits and chandlers bill. As such ships will cost
a large sum of money they should be built of the best ma-
terials that could possibly be procured, the beams of their
decks should be of the best Carolina pine, and the lower
futtocks and knees if possible of Live Oak.

'The greatest care should be taken in the construction
of such ships, and particularly all her timbers should be

framed and bolted together before they are raised. Frigates built to carry 12 and 18-pounders in my opinion will not answer the expectation contemplated from them, for if we should be obliged to take a part in the present European war, or at a future day we should be dragged into a war with any powers of the Old Continent, especially Great Britain, they having such a number of ships of that size, that it would be an equal chance by equal combat that we lose our ships and more particularly from the Algerians who have ships and some of much greater force. Several questions will arise whether one large or two small frigates contribute most to the protection of our trade or which will cost the least sum of money, or whether two small ones are as able to engage a double deck ship as one large one. For my part I am decidedly of the opinion the large ones will answer best.

'I am very Respectfully
'Joshua Humphreys.'

Not such a bad exposition of naval policy! When the new navy was authorized, Humphreys' ideas prevailed. On April 12, 1794, he was directed by the Secretary of War to "prepare the models for the frames of the frigates" proposed by him. These models, or "molds," were not ship models. The practice of constructing small models of projected vessels seems to have gone out of fashion a few years before this date. The *Constitution* was built according to the "sheer half breadth and body plans" from which Humphreys prepared the molds. Her "lines" were —and still are—beautiful to look upon.

Construction was commenced at Hartt's shipyard in Boston under the direction of Colonel George Claghorn. The master mechanic was a Mr. Hartley, and he must not be overlooked when praise is parcelled out for the building of this ship. When the time came to lay her keel there was no red cloth stop-water material at hand to place in the scarfs and garboard landways.[1] There is a very pretty tradition about the solution. Though unverified to date, it has all the earmarks of being founded upon fact. The story goes that Joshua Humphreys' daughters each possessed a long handsome full red cloak —as the fashion of the day demanded. Now, here were the garboard strakes ready to be laid and not a bit of suitable red cloth to be had in Boston. No garboard strake was ever laid in those days unless, in the white lead along the rabbet, was laid also a piece of red cloth. This was usually flannel like that laid under the copper sheathing in that period of ship construction. Now the *Constitution* just *had* to be a "lucky ship"; so each girl sacrificed her red cloak, tore it into strips, and placed the strips along the garboard strake landing.

The work progressed. The length of this ship is 175 feet, beam 43½ feet, draft 23½ feet, and depth of hold 14½ feet. According to the method of measurement then in use her tonnage was 1,576, her displacement (normal) being somewhere around 2,200 tons. A very great

[1] The "scarfs" are the notched joints where the lengths, or "strakes," of outer hull planking join together. The lengths next to the keel are the "garboard strakes." These notch into the keel on each side. The projecting "land" or "landing" of the strake fits into a "landway" or groove in the keel known as a "rabbet."

percentage of all the construction work on a wooden sailing ship is performed before the launch. The *Constitution's* spars were shaped out in the yard which lay between Hartt's shipyard and Comey's wharf. Paul Revere furnished the copper bolts and spikes, and a Mr. Thayer made the gun-carriages. The anchors were forged at Hanover, in Plymouth County, Mass. Her sails were made in the old Granery Building where Park Street Church now stands. The carvings and ornamental fittings were the works of Skillings Brothers, of Boston. These included her figurehead—the first of several. It was a figure of Hercules, holding a club overhead in the act of striking. The first battery mounted on the frigate was purchased from the English. It comprised twenty-eight long 24-pounders on the gun deck and ten long 12-pounders on the quarter-deck.

Construction went on apace. The great day of launching approached. The "magnificent spectacle" was set for September 20, 1797. Colonel Claghorn unburdened himself in the Boston Herald in the following manner:

'Navy Yard Boston, Sept. 18, 1797

'The Contractor, having extended to his fellow-citizens, all reasonable gratifications of their laudable curiosity, during the progress of the building, believes he may with propriety, make the following requests and suggestions, on the operating of the launching of the *Constitution*.

'That (except the President of the United States, the Governor, Lieutenant Governor, and their respective suites, and those specially admitted who will be comparatively few) no persons will in any way attempt to pass into the navy yard.

'The reason of this request is obviously to prevent interruption, or intrusion, which might be injurious or ruinous to the act of launching, under the most favorable conditions, and indispensably requiring perfect silence and obedience to orders. Independent of this conclusive reason, the dangers of encroaching spectators would be imminent, from the occasional and abrupt falling of bodies, used in the construction of the ship, a conformity therefore, to this request is earnestly solicited.

'It is suggested that as the tide would be full, that it would be necessary to the safety of the spectators, especially women and children, that they do not approach in crowds too near the margin of the contiguous wharves, as the sudden entrance of so large a body as the frigate will occasion an instantaneous swell of the water, the height of which cannot be easily calculated, and against which therefore, discretion of the people ought to amply guard.

'It is regretted in this instance, that the yard and the place around it, are too contracted for the occasion, and will probably excite too much desire, in which all the citizens have so much interest. It is therefore, submitted to those who can conveniently make arrangements to place themselves in vessels or water crafts at due distances on the profile side of the frigate, but by no means too near, either in a right line or otherwise, as the agitation of the water, even at a considerable distance, may be somewhat hazardous.

'It is also recommended that those who erect platforms

to accommodate spectators, that they have them also secured in every respect as the loss of life of a single citizen
would mar the satisfaction and pleasure that the constructor would otherwise enjoy of building and constructing for the ocean a powerful agent of national justice
which hope dictates, may become the pride and ornament
of the American race.
                                        'George Claghorn.'

Alas, the famous frigate received a most inauspicious
start in life. This may be learned from the letter which
the Colonel was constrained to write six days later to the
Secretary of War:

'Navy Yard, Boston, September 24, 1797

'Sir,—Having before stated to you my intention of
launching the frigate Constitution, on the 20th inst., the
necessary preparations were made to that end; and at the
appointed time all the blocks and shores were removed,
with full expectation of her moving gently into the water.

'She, however, did not start until the screws and other
machinery had been applied; and then she moved only
about twenty-seven feet. Concluding that some hidden
cause had impeded her progress, and the tide ebbing fast,
I decided it to be most prudent to block and shore her up,
and examine carefully into the cause of her stopping. I
found that the part of the ways which had not before received any of the weight, had settled about half an inch,
which, added to some other cause, of no great importance
in itself, had occasioned the obstruction.

'The next day, after due preparation, the ship was raised
two inches, in fifty minutes, by means of wedges; her bilge-

ways were then taken out and the apparent defects removed. All things being in order, a second attempt was made on the 22d inst., and upon the removal of the supports, she moved freely for about thirty-one feet and then stopped. On this unexpected event, as she was somewhat advanced on the new wharf, which was built for her to pass over only, and not to rest upon, I judged it advisable to suspend any further operations, although it might have been possible, with the machinery previously prepared, to have pressed her into the water; but if she had been constrained twenty or thirty feet farther, and then have stopped, her situation would have been critical, on a foundation by no means solid; accordingly she was perfectly secured in her new situation.

'On examining the ways erected on the new wharf, I find they have both settled abaft about one and five-eights of an inch; which circumstance, as it could not have been foreseen, the descent of the ways was not calculated to overcome, and which solely occasioned her to stop.

'I had formed the inclined plane upon the smallest angle that I conceived would convey the ship into the water, in order that she might make her plunge with the least violence, and thereby prevent any strain or injury; I must give the ways more descent, which will remedy the defect occasioned by the settling of the new wharf; and I am fully confident that the next trial, at the high tides in October, will be attended with success; in the mean time I shall proceed in completing the ship on the stocks.

'I am, very respectfully, your humble servant,

'George Claghorn.

'Hon. James McHenry, Secretary of War.'

In view of the remarkable record achieved by the *Constitution* subsequent to her unpropitious debut, superstitious old salts should revise their estimate of the disasters portended by the sticking of a ship on the ways.

Several weeks sped by.   The work on the ship and her fittings was delayed but little, however, by the fact that the vessel was still in her cradle.   Captain Samuel Nicholson was placed in command.   On October 20, the day before the actual launching, he had a rather unfortunate public squabble with Claghorn.   The following account of it is taken from *Old Landmarks of Middlesex,* by Samuel Adams Drake: [2]

'In consequence of the narrow limits of Hartt's Yard, it had been agreed that no spectators should be admitted on the day previous to that fixed for the launch, without the permission of Captain Nicholson, Colonel Claghorn, or General Jackson.   While the workmen were at breakfast Colonel Claghorn had admitted some ladies and gentlemen to view the ship, but when they attempted to go on board Nicholson forbade their entering.   This was communicated to Colonel Claghorn.   In the afternoon of the same day some visitors who had been denied an entrance to the ship by Nicholson were admitted by Claghorn, who, however, was not aware that they had been previously refused permission.   The captain, who was furious when he saw the men he had just turned away approaching, exclaimed to Claghorn, "D—n it! do you know whom you have admitted, and that I have just refused them?"   The latter replied that he did not know that

[2] Roberts Brothers, Boston, 1876.

circumstance, but, having passed his word, they might go on board. The whole party being assembled on the Constitution's deck, Colonel Claghorn went up to the captain and desired, with some heat, that he might not treat these visitors as he had done the ladies in the morning; to which Nicholson replied that he should say no more to them, but that he had a right to command on board his own ship. To this Claghorn rejoined that *he* commanded on board the ship, and that if Captain Nicholson did not like the regulations, he might go out of her. Upon this the parties immediately collared each other, and Nicholson, who carried a cane, attempted to strike his adversary, but the bystanders interfered and separated the belligerents. The affair was settled by mutual apologies.'

The grief of the skipper was not yet ended for, on the following day, another incident occurred: [3]

'It had been the intention of Captain Nicholson, a somewhat pompous old martinet of the 1776 school, to reserve for himself the honor of hoisting the national ensign over the new frigate, and when leaving the yard to obtain breakfast, on the morning of the 21st, promulgated an order, directing that no flag was to be raised or displayed on board until his return. But the captain was fated to lose the honor he coveted, while an humble artisan gained the distinction of being first to throw the stars and stripes to the breeze over the powerful frigate. Could he have

[3] "The History of the U. S. Frigate 'Constitution,'" by Captain Horatio D. Smith, U. S. Revenue Cutter Service; *United Service Magazine,* 1891. The same anecdote is recounted in Rear Admiral George Henry Preble's *Origin and History of the American Flag,* 1872.

looked into the future and foreseen the grand career destined for the vessel, his disappointment would have only been equalled by his wrath.   A workman, named Samuel Bently, a calker, actuated by a spirit of reckless mischief, and secretly bearing no goodwill to the straight-laced naval veteran, took advantage of his absence, and, watching his opportunity, slipped on board, seized the halliards, to which the ensign was already attached, and the next instant rustling folds of brand-new bunting, representing the "flag of the free," waved over the structure.

'When Captain Nicholson returned, and beheld the flag fluttering in the damp, chill air, his anger burst forth with characteristic energy; but the mischief had been done, and the flag was not hauled down.'

This was the famous flag of fifteen stripes and fifteen stars.   The *Constitution* was the first frigate to display at sea an ensign of this design.   She flew one before Tripoli and in all of her engagements in the War of 1812. Her whole original store of bunting was the handiwork of the celebrated Mrs. Ross of Philadelphia.

The third attempt to launch the frigate was completely successful, though the day was cold, cloudy, and raw, with a stiff east wind.   A contemporary account of the event follows:

'THE LAUNCH
'A Magnificent Spectacle!

'On Saturday, October 21st, last, at fifteen minutes past 12, the frigate "Constitution" was launched into the adjacent element, on which she now rides, an elegant and superb specimen of American Naval Architecture, combining the unity of wisdom, strength and beauty.

'The tide being amply full, she descended into the bosom of the ocean with an ease and dignity, which while it afforded the most exalted and heartfelt pleasure and satisfaction to the many thousand spectators was the guarantee of the safety, and the pledge that no occurrence should mar the joyous sensations that every one experienced and which burst forth in reiterated shouts which rent the welkin. On a signal being given from on board, her ordnance on shore announced to the neighboring country that the CONSTITUTION WAS SECURE.

'Too much praise cannot be given to Col. Claghorn for the coolness and regularity displayed in the whole business of the launch; and the universal congratulations he received were evidence of the public estimate of his skill, intelligence and circumspection.'

The *Boston Centinel* gives a more full description in its issue of October 25, 1797:

'THE "CONSTITUTION" LAUNCHED

'The spring tides the latter part of the last week gave the workmen in the naval-yard an opportunity to complete the ways for launching the frigate "Constitution." Colonel Claghorn, anxious to give as early information of the intended operation as possible, directed a gun to be fired at daylight on Saturday morning last, as a signal that at full sea he should move her into her destined element.

Before noon a very numerous and brilliant collection of citizens assembled at the spectacle, and at fifteen minutes after twelve, at the first stroke at the spur shores, she commenced a movement into the water with such steadiness, majesty, and exactness as to fill almost every breast with sensations of joy and delight, superior by far to the mortification they had before experienced. Such was the regular obliquity of the ways that she came to anchor within two hundred yards of them without the least strain, or meeting or causing the most trifling accident. And she now rides at her moorings in the harbor, a pleasing sight to those who contemplate her as the *germ* of a naval force, which in no remote period of time will protect the flag of the *United States* from the depredations of piratical marauders.

'As soon as the enlivening burst of gratulation was heard from the ship, her ordnance on shore replied to the shout, and, joined with the huzzas of the citizens on the adjacent shores, demonstrated the lively interest the great body of the people took in her safety, and evinced the popularity of the government by whose direction she was built.

'The best judges have pronounced the "Constitution," like her *archetype,* to be a perfect model of elegance, strength, and durability. And every individual employed in her construction appears to pride himself in having assisted at the production of such a *chef-d'oeuvre* of naval architecture.

'To Colonel Claghorn the meed of general approbation of his skill, prudence, and intelligence has been freely bestowed. And the United States are under obligations to *General Jackson, Captain Nicholson,* and *Major Gibbs* for their indefatigable care and attention in the superintending of the various departments necessary to her equipments. If the well-deserved fame of *Messrs. Skillings,* as carvers, could receive an addition, we should pronounce their workmanship, which decorates the frigate, a masterpiece of theirs. Indeed, no part of the work in the hull or rigging can for strength and beauty be exceeded, and the eulogiums of foreign naval gentlemen have been warm and explicit in her favor.

'May the "hoary monarch" of the element, on whose bosom she now reclines, protect her with his trident; and whenever her departure into the waste of his realm may be necessary, may propitious breezes waft her to the haven of peace, or aid her to hurl the vindictive thunder of national vengeance on the disturbers of our country's repose, or the depredators on the lawful commerce of our citizens.'

The foregoing flowery effusion changes most abruptly; the next and concluding sentence, in a most trenchant though unconscious shot at the future, observes:

'Though rated only as a forty-four, she can be made conveniently to mount sixty-four guns.' [4]

[4] Sixty-four guns mounted at one time would be barely within the realm of possibility. She has, however, mounted as many as fifty-four.

CHAPTER II

FROM REVEILLE TO TAPS ON THE "CRACK SHIP"

"Six days shalt thou work as hard as able;
On the seventh, holystone the deck and over haul the cable."

BEFORE hearing of the experiences and deeds of the *Constitution* and her crew it is fitting that the reader should learn something of life aboard a man-of-war in days gone by. A certain George Jones was Schoolmaster and acting Chaplain of *"Old Ironsides"* from 1826 to 1828 when the ship was on the Mediterranean station. Fortunately he left us a record of his cruise.[1] From this book is taken the following outline of daily routine on board ship a hundred years ago.

'The week days are all alike; so one day will answer for the whole. At day light, the drums are ordered up, for the reveillé; but the slumbers of the sailors are first broken, as it is meet they should be in such a place, by the reports of guns. They are the night guns of the sentries, which are fired off at the first tap of the drum: the reveillé succeeds; and by the time this is over, the boatswain with his mates, are stationed on the gun deck, close by the main hatch: he gives a long pipe, which they

[1] *Sketches of Naval Life,* by A "Civilian"; 1829. Afterwards Jones was regularly commissioned as Chaplain.

18

answer by similar ones: a long one succeeds, repeated also: and then is the cry, "all hands, ahoy," echoed by the mates, in deep and lengthened tones. Then comes another long pipe; and their brazen voices are heard, "all hands up hammocks, ahoy." The men spring from their hammocks, lash and carry them on deck, and stow them away in the nettings: twelve minutes are allowed for this. The boatswain reports the main deck clear, to the lieutenant of the watch; and a similar report is made from the officer of the birth deck. The starboard watch now spread over the spar deck: the larboard, over the next below; while the birth deck is occupied by the cooks: the holy-stones are produced; water is pumped, or drawn at the bows, and passed aft; and a general scouring of the decks takes place. Boats' crews are excepted, as they have to clean themselves, and look after their boats. After the holy-stone, comes the *squill-gee;* a wooden instrument like a hoe, but with a face, broad and flat, and lined with leather: the decks are partly dried with it; and the operation is completed by the *swabs,* articles formed by tying a number of loose yarns together, now dashed, by their handles, with violence about the deck. Twice a week, before cleaning decks, and on the same days, there is a general scouring of clothes through the squadron: hammocks are scoured, in summer, once a month. While the rest are washing decks, the carpenter's gang scrape the combings of the hatches, and their gratings; and the quarter gunners clean the match tubs, shot boxes, gun carriages and guns. When all is over, the boatswain is rowed ahead to square yards; the carpenters go around the ship, to see that all is clean, on the outside; the rigging is hauled taught, and laid in order; and boats are lowered from the ship's sides. The ship now presents order and symmetry, in all her parts; and there is an interval of leisure for a few minutes.

'At six bells—but I have forgotten: you do not know what six bells mean. The twenty four hours, I have already said, are divided into six equal parts: the sentry, at the cabin door, has charge of an half hour glass, or time piece; and reports every half hour to the quarter master on deck, who sees that the bell is immediately struck. He reports, however, not the hour, but the number of bells; and thus we count time on board. Half past twelve, is one bell: one o'clock, two bells; and, in this manner, we proceed, increasing by one, every half hour; till we come, at the expiration of the watch, to eight; after which we commence again. Six bells, in the morning, then, are seven o'clock: and at six in summer, and eight in winter, the men are piped to breakfast, with the same ceremonies that were used, in calling them from their hammocks. About twenty minutes previous to this, the cooks are sent to the galley, for tea-water; and they now appear on the decks with their black painted table, or more properly, deck cloths, and utensils for breakfast. It consists of tea, ship's biscuit, cold meat; and in port, sometimes also potatoes, dried fish and such articles. The last they procure from the bomb-boats, which are suffered at meal times to be along side, and with which they exchange bread dust, rice, &c.; for of money, they have none. None can be paid them, by the purser, without an order from the captain; and this is given only when they are permitted to

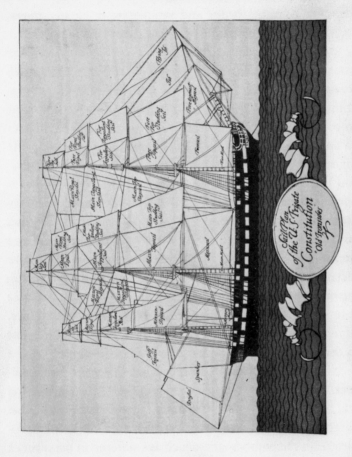

Sail Plan
of the U.S. Frigate
Constitution
"Old Ironsides"

"SHE'S A GREAT VESSEL, SIR! TREMENDOUS SAILS!"

go ashore. The decks are swept down after each meal. One hour is allowed them for breakfast; at the expiration of which time, all hands are called, and they go about their work. Then also, at drum roll, the ensign is run up, the guards in undress are succeeded by those in uniform; and the band is ordered to the quarter deck. We have a company of about twenty, most of them excellent musicians; and they help to wile away many an hour. The officers, at this time, make their appearance. Those in the steerage and cockpit, are aroused by a midshipman from the watch at six bells: their hammock boys lash their beds, and stow them on deck; they have breakfast, and now come up to take the fresh air, and promenade, while their rooms are holy-stoned and cleaned: at nine, we have school.

'You ask how we find employment for so many men; and I will answer, by leading you through our ship. We commence on the starboard side of the main deck; and leaving the school room, come first to the carpenter's gang. It consists of six or eight men; and is provided with complete apparatus, and furnished, by the ship or officers, with constant employment. Next is the turning lathe; and this also is seldom idle. We pass a gun; and, in the next recess, find the cooper, with an aid or two, at work; next, the shoe-makers; and, just beyond them, come to a little man, a Hindoostanee—the ship's barber: he has usually an assistant; and a general overhaul of the men's chins, twice a week, with a round among the officers, every morning, furnishes them with sufficient business. We now advance a few steps; and, perched on a huge beam, just forward of the main hatch, find the tailor, with a mate or two.   Directly forward of them is the galley, a huge stove, with its satellites, mostly dark ones however; and here, "amid the smoke and stir of this dim spot," are fabricated a large portion of our enjoyments in the ship.   Each mess has a cook; and besides these, there is a ship's cook, who attends to the men's food, after it has been deposited in the coppers: when he thinks it sufficiently boiled; he carries a dish of soup and meat to the officer of the deck, who must taste and pronounce them fit to be served out, before it can be done.   I have often been amused with this part of our quarter deck spectacles.   The galley coppers must be examined daily by one of the surgeon's mates. A little forward of this, and on the right, is the brig, with its rough inmates; and the clank of irons forms a kind of musical accompaniment to the incessant grumbling and bickerings of the cooks.   They have a constant auditor, in a man, with a soldier's dress, and a bayonet or cutlass in hand, who paces back and forward before the brig. The precincts of the brig are fitted up with large pretensions to taste; for, here are seen festoons, and wreaths, and knots, of garlic, onions, celery, and sausages; among which, hang fowls, cabbages, cauliflowers, and perhaps, a pig or two.   They belong to the officers' messes, and are also under the sentry's charge; but they often take wings, and fly away.

'We return on the larboard side; and find all clear, except, half way along, the boys' school, kept by one of the seamen; and kept very well.   He has about a dozen pupils; and you may see, here, all the tricks of such schools ashore; with the gladsome pranks, also, of such schools, when the hour of dismissal comes.   Above us, are heard the heavy sounds of the blacksmith's hammers: his gang have station on the forecastle.

'These things occupy some of our crew.   The remainder are engaged with the numberless duties, connected with the well-being and good order of so complicated a matter as a ship.

'But it is now seven bells, (half past eleven); and we hear the boatswain's mates piping the sweepers: the mechanics all "knock off" work, and put away their tools: the decks are swept; and now we see a small cask ascend through the hatchway, from the cock-pit.   It is slipped to the starboard side of the main deck, and a large tub brought forward, into which its sparkling contents are poured; an equal quantity of water being also added.   We use whiskey, in our navy: rum is the common beverage, in all others.

'Eight bells are now reported to the quarter-master, and by him, to the officer of the deck; who answers, "make it so;" and sends a midshipman, to inform the captain, that it is meridian.   The bell is struck; and two long successive pipes, from the boatswain and his mates, are the signal, that all work is to cease.   The men pass down to the gun deck; the cooks ascend with pans, spoons, and their painted cloths, and hasty preparations are made for dinner: after which, as the drum rolls, all move aft, towards the grog tub.   Around this point of time, concentrate half the meditations of the day: they stow away their tobacco quid; spit; wipe the mouth clean, so as to give every drop its effect;

and at no other time, do they look so happy. I often place myself at the tub, to watch the rolling of the eyes, and the look of supreme gratification, with which they swallow their half pint; for, that is the measure, to each: it is one gill of whiskey, diluted with an equal quantity of water. A rope is drawn athwart-ships, near the tub: each, as his name is called, crosses, and takes his allowance, which must be drunk on the spot. In some ships, they may carry it to their mess; but this often produces drunkenness, and our rule is the best. From this, they pass to dinner. The whole operation is superintended by the officer of this deck, who must watch them closely: he is furnished, by the surgeon, with a sick list; on which are marked those who may be furnished with grog, and the quantity. This list is their great dread; and, to avoid it, they often bear their diseases, in quiet, till they become serious ones. I recollect, in the Brandywine, one day, some men were brought from shore, badly hurt: one had been knocked down, by a Spanish soldier, and much bruised on the breast, with his musket. One of my mess-mates was examining him; and he breathed with difficulty: "But, doctor," he said, "don't put me on the sick list, doctor; this is nothing." Another time, one came down, with a broken finger: the surgeon was examining it; and the fellow was writhing his face into all kinds of curious shapes—when the drum rolled to grog: every muscle took a different twist—"there, now," he cried, "I shall lose my grog." If the surgeon forgets to enter a sick man's name on the list, he will crawl to the tub, if it is in any way possible.

'The ingenuity they shew, also, in procuring grog, is often surprising. I have said, that the bomb-boats are closely watched by the ship's corporal. Well, a man goes over, and barters for a string of sausages: he comes up; his sausages are examined, and turn out to be full of rum, instead of meat. Another buys eggs: something perhaps excites suspicion; they are looked to, and a puncture is found at one end, through which the original matter has been let out, and its place supplied with the more beloved fluid. I saw them caught, one day, at another trick. It is managed as follows. Some of our boats, I may have told you perhaps, are generally kept moored to the ship's stern; and float some ten or twelve feet back of her. No shore boat is suffered to come nearer than twelve yards or so, without permission from the deck. One of these, is gliding along behind us, at the proper distance; when, just as it comes in a line with the ship, something gets out of order in their sails: they stop a moment, to set them right; and then pass on again. You would not suspect what has been done. From our boats, passes out a line of sufficient length, with some small corks at its end, just enough to keep that part on the surface. Among these, is a piece of money: the shore boat has stopped by these corks; whipped off the money; attached a bottle of rum, in its stead, with something to make it sink; and this was their errand. The men now take to fishing: the bottle is secretly drawn up, and carefully stowed away. You will say this is fishing, with a silver hook, with a vengeance.

'I return to the ship. The midshipmen dine at twelve; the cock-pit mess soon after; and the lieutenants, at one:

the last are called to dinner by the bugle. The decks are swept again; and, at one o'clock, all are again called to work. So they continue, till seven bells; when the morning scene, of cleaning up, and grog is repeated; the same quantity of liquor being served out, as before. It makes two gills of whiskey, per day: in some ships, it is served out differently; half a gill, raw, in the morning, and evening; and a gill, diluted, at noon. At eight bells, they have supper, which is the same as breakfast: the sweepers are then called: all cleared up; and the remainder of the day is their own. They disperse around the ship; "spin yarns" joke; play chequers; read; have music on the forecastle, or plait sennitt, for their hats. The boys have their gladsome plays; and a general cheerfulness prevails. We have quarters, in the evening. From these, there is a general moving towards the upper deck; to which the music is now ordered. The drummers and fifers are paraded by the main-mast: "beat the call," is ordered; and some tapping on the drum, calls the quarter-master to the halliards: the sun sets; and immediately, the drums roll: at the third roll, the colours are hauled down, and the night pendant substituted for the long one; marines, in undress, take place of those in uniform; and the band strikes up, "Hail Columbia." How many kind and warm feelings are associated with these sounds! We have music for half an hour; at the expiration of which, its harmony is exchanged for the boatswain's whistle, and their hoarse cry, "all hands stand by your hammocks, ahoy." Our promenade is now spoiled: the men come aft: the tackle of the stern and quarter boats is adjusted; and, at the order, all are drawn up to their places. The petty officers now mount the hammock cloths, and uncover them; and, when ordered, toss out the hammocks: each man swings his hammock at his number, and most of them turn in immediately. A few collect in groups, about the decks; and I have often been an interested listener to their "long yarns," about witches and hobgoblins, battles and shipwrecks. I have heard some, who would compare well with the fair narrator of the Arabian Nights; for many of their stories, like hers, are made as they go along. By eight bells, all are asleep. Just before this hour, in Winter, and nine in Summer, the drums are ordered up again: they beat; roll off, as the bell is struck; and are succeeded by the bugles, with an admirable effect in a calm night. At the second roll, the sentries fire their day muskets; and these are succeeded by loaded ones, for the night.

'A hoarse voice is now heard at the galley, "Put out all fires, lights, pipes, and segars, and every thing that can make a light; except the sentry's light, and the match at the galley—d'you hear there, cooks?" "All out, sir," is the reply; and the master-at-arms, (for it is he,) ascends to make his report to the quarter deck. The forward officers, steerage, and cock-pit, have lights till three bells in Summer, and one in Winter: the same officer sees these out, and reports them also: to the ward room a midshipman is sent, an hour later, to see all fires extinguished. By ten o'clock, the tread of the officers of the watch, is the only sound heard; except the occasional hail of a boat, or, at every half hour, the striking of the ship's time, answered by sentries above, with "all's—well," "all's—well." '

CHAPTER III

HAND TO HAND ON THE SPANISH MAIN

A TEMPORARY patching of relations with the Barbary
Powers had very nearly ended the career of the *Constitution* before she was even launched. The bill authorizing
her construction had contained a proviso: all work on her
was to be suspended should a treaty end (?!) the need
for a navy to operate against the Pirate States. And
work *was* suspended. It was the increasing tension with
France that inspired the appropriation of funds to complete the *Constitution, Constellation,* and *United States*.
A Navy Department, separate from the Army, was organized in April, 1798. On July 2 the *Constitution* first spread
her sails and moved upon the waters of Massachusetts
Bay.

Finally the United States Government took steps to
end French interference with American sea trade. Thus
began our "informal naval war with France." Our ships
were ordered to operate against any French privateers or
ships of war that they might encounter in western Atlantic
waters. For two years the *Constitution* cruised off our
coasts but saw little action. She was then ordered to the
West Indies. Here she figured prominently in a most
stirring episode which is little known, probably for the

reasons which will become evident in the telling of the tale:[1]

'The sun was slowly descending behind the blue peaks of San Domingo, when an American frigate came in sight of the village of Port Platte, situated at the head of a small harbor on the north side of the island, and, furling her courses, hove to, for the purpose of reconnoitering. After scanning narrowly the little anchorage, the frigate put about, and, setting her courses, was soon lost amid the shades of night. The inhabitants of the village had felt great alarm at the near approach of the armed ship, and had reinforced their fort, beside sending a number of soldiers on board of the letter of marque, Sandwich, formerly a British packet, but now in the service of the French, which lay close under the guns of the fort, where she was receiving a cargo of coffee, previous to her making a run for France.

'It was in the year 1800, just after the action between the Constellation and La Vengeance, and the name of the conqueror, Truxton, passed from lip to lip with instinctive consternation. Night came on; the moon had not appeared, and scudding clouds obscured the stars. The *reveillé* had been beaten at the garrison, and the inhabitants of Port Platte had retired to dream of the daring cruizers of the American squadron. The frigate, when she had lost sight of the island, came about, and under easy sail stood in for the shore. She was the Constitution,

[1] "Sketches from the Log of Old Ironsides," by Jesse Erskine Dow; *Burton's Gentleman's Magazine,* July, 1839; edited by Wm. E. Burton and Edgar Allan Poe.

Commodore Talbot, and from the silence that reigned throughout the ship, and the total absence of light from the battle lanterns, the most careless observer would have supposed that she was about to do something for the glory of the old thirteen.

'As she drew nigh the port, two officers might have been seen at the gangway, watching narrowly the lights that twinkled ahead. At this moment, the heavy roar of a cannon came echoing along the waters, and then one after another, the lights disappeared, until none were seen but those which seemed to be designed to burn throughout the night.

' "Now is your time," said the elder of the persons to the younger; "have the second cutter manned, sir, and come to me for farther orders." Thus saying, the commodore, for it was he, looked at the compass and entered the cabin. In a few minutes, a knock at the cabin door, announced the arrival of some officer to make a report.

' "Enter," said the bluff old commodore, and immediately lieutenant Hull, the first of the Constitution, stood before him.

' "Are you ready?" said the commodore.

' "All ready, sir," replied the lieutenant.

' "Then, sir," said the commodore, "you will enter the harbor of Port Platte without being discovered, ascertain whether the craft that lies under the guns of the fort is the Sandwich, and when you shall have done so, return and make a report to me."

' "How shall I ascertain that fact without boarding her?" said the lieutenant.

"SHALL KNOW THE CONQUERED KNEE."

Isaac Hull, the competent and dependable; 25 years of age at Port Platte, 37 in his greatest triumph.

' "You will know her to be the Sandwich," replied the commodore, "by the black stripes around her white masts, and by the shortness of her bowsprit. Make haste, sir, for I long to give you a job."

'The lieutenant smiled as he bade the commodore good night, and, immediately ascending, gave such orders to the officer of the deck as he deemed necessary under the circumstances of the case. The night was pretty well advanced as Mr. Hull wrapped himself in his boat cloak, and seated himself in the stern sheets of the second cutter.

' "Shove off—let fall—pull cheerily, my boys," were the orders he gave, in a low voice, in quick succession; then passing swiftly around the frigate's stern, he pulled for the harbor, and was soon lost sight of.

'For two hours, nothing was heard of the adventurous officer or his boat, and the old commodore began to grow quite anxious about them. Already a pale streak stretched itself along the eastern waters, and the clouds grew thinner and fewer, while here and there a star peeped out, and was reflected back by the waves below.

' "Boat ahoy!" challenged the sentinel at the gangway of the Constitution, as the dash of oars at this moment fell upon his ear.

' "Aye! aye!" replied the officer of the boat, and soon lieutenant Hull crossed the gangway of the ship.

' "It is the Sandwich, sir," said the lieutenant, after reporting his return, and paying the customary salute.

' "Are you certain?" said commodore Talbot.

' "I am, sir," replied the officer, "for I lay directly under her stern, and heard through the cabin windows, which were open, her officers congratulating themselves upon the departure of the Constellation, for such they deem this ship to be. Beside, I noticed her masts and bowsprit, as I swept along under the guns of the fort—they are as you described them to be."

' "I'll have her, by ——," said commodore Talbot, as he looked again at the harbor, which began to show itself amid the haze of dawn. "About ship, sir—set all the studding sails," and, bidding the lieutenant good night, the commander in chief bounced into his cabin.

'The frigate swiftly came about, and took her departure from the land. Soon the studding sails on both sides were spread out to the wind, and, like a mountain of snow, she danced along upon the bosom of the deep until her morning watch looked out in vain for the blue outline of the island of San Domingo.

' "Sail O!" cried the look-out.

' "Where away?" said the officer of the deck.

' "On the lee bow, sir," replied the seaman.

' "Can you make her out?" hailed the officer.

' "She is a sloop, sir, and shows American colors."

' "Hoist our ensign," said the lieutenant.

' "Aye, there comes the Sally in the nick of time," said the commodore, who had left the cabin at the first hail. "Mr. Hull, make a signal for her to run down and speak us; we will soon proceed to business."

'In a short time, the sail, which proved to be the American sloop Sally, came alongside of the Constitution. After a conference with her captain, he and his crew came on board the frigate, while lieutenant Hull, with a party of seamen and marines, the latter led by the brave captain Carmick, immediately repaired on board of the sloop. Having received orders from the commodore, the sloop now put her helm up, and ran for the island.

' "In the course of the night, while running down for her port under easy sail, a shot suddenly flew over the Sally, and soon after an English frigate ranged up alongside.   Mr. Hull hove to, and when the boarding lieutenant gained the sloop's deck, where he found so large a party of men and officers in naval uniforms, he was much surprised.   He was told the object of the expedition, however, and expressed his disappointment, as his own ship was only waiting to let the Sandwich complete her cargo, in order to cut her out also." *

'It was about noon of the following day when the sloop stood in to the harbor of Port Platte.   Before her lay the Sandwich, with her broadside bearing on the approach; and in the rear of her, at no great distance, a battery showed its long row of black teeth for her protection.

'Lieutenant Hull had sent nearly all the men below, before he entered the harbor, and now, having a stern anchor ready, he bore down, like a short-handed lubberly sloop, for the bows of the Sandwich.   As he drew nigh the ship, he said, in a low voice, "Stand by to board," and soon a large number of men crouched under the bulwarks, ready for action.

' "You will be afoul of me," said the lieutenant of the Sandwich, who was leaning carelessly over the bulwark as the sloop came down.

* Cooper's Naval History.

' "I think I shall," was the laconic reply.   In a moment, the sloop struck the bows of the enemy.

' "Let go the kedge!" thundered the lieutenant—it was done like magic.

' "Boarders, away!" cried he; and, seizing his cutlass, he crossed the gangway of the Sandwich, at the head of his men, and carried her without a struggle.

'Captain Carmick, in the ship's boats, now landed, carried the battery, spiked the guns, and retired without the loss of a man.

'A great commotion was now perceptible on shore; but the commander and his crew went swiftly to work to secure their prize, and, though she was dismantled above her deck, and her guns stowed in the hold, before sunset she had her royal yards crossed, her guns scaled, and her crew quartered.

'She now got under way, with the American flag at her ensign-peak, and stood out of the harbor in company with the sloop.

'Evening was slowly fading into night as a ship, followed at some distance by a sloop, bore down for the Constitution.

' "Hail the stranger," said commodore Talbot.

' "What ship is that?" thundered the officer of the deck, through his trumpet.

' "The United States ship Talbot, I. Hull, commander," replied the victorious officer, as he drew near enough to be distinguished by the officers of the frigate.

' "It *is* Hull, by heavens!" said the commodore.   In a few minutes lieutenant Hull came on board and made his official report.   After a short time, the Sally's captain and crew were returned to their vessel, with many thanks, and lieutenant Hull, having received orders to that effect, repaired on board the prize as her commander, and, crowding on all sail, followed the commodore to Jamaica.'

We shall hear much about this Isaac Hull before we are done.

The capture described above was made in a neutral port and was therefore illegal under international law. The act was fully disavowed by the American Government, the ship was restored, and an indemnity was paid. Commodore Talbot's orders had been ill-advised.   In no respect, however, should anything be allowed to dim in the slightest degree the perfection of judgement, skill, and courage exhibited by the "Constitutions" in their consummation of this deed.

CHAPTER IV

A Midnight Encounter

THE trouble with France was finally smoothed out and the *Constitution* was laid up from 1801 to 1803. During this period a desultory naval campaign was waged against the Barbary States. More vigorous measures were now undertaken. Our frigate was placed in commission under Commodore Preble and sent to the Mediterranean to serve as flagship of the squadron assembling there.

Charles Morris, who was a midshipman aboard at the time, tells in his autobiography of an incident which occurred on the way over:

'We had nothing of interest on the passage until near the entrance of the straits of Gibraltar, when, upon a very dark evening, with very light winds, we suddenly found ourselves near a vessel which was evidently a ship of war. The crew were immediately but silently brought to quarters, after which the commodore gave the usual hail, "What ship is that?" The same question was returned; in reply to which the name of our ship was given, and the question repeated. Again the question was returned instead of an answer, and again our ship's name given and the question repeated, without other reply than its repetition. The commodore's patience seemed now exhausted, and, taking the trumpet, he hailed and said, "I am now going to hail you for the last time. If a proper answer is not returned, I will fire a shot into you." A prompt answer came back, "If you fire a shot, I will return a broadside." Preble then hailed, "What ship is that?" The reply was, "This is His Britannic Majesty's ship Donnegal, eighty-four guns, Sir Richard Strahan, an English Commodore. Send your boat on board." Under the excitement of the moment, Preble leaped on the hammocks, and returned for answer, "This is the United States ship Constitution, forty-four guns, Edward Preble, an American Commodore, who will be damned before he sends his boat on board of any vessel!" And, turning to the crew, he said, "Blow your matches, boys!"[1] The conversation here ceased, and soon after a boat was heard coming from the stranger, and arrived with a lieutenant from the frigate Maidstone. The object of this officer was to apologize for the apparent rudeness which had been displayed. He stated that our ship had not been seen until we had hailed them; that it was, of course, very important to gain time to bring their men to quarters, especially as it was apparent we were not English, and they had no expectation of meeting an American ship of war there; and that this object had induced their delay and misrepresentation in giving the ship's name. These excuses were deemed satisfactory, and the ships separated.

'This was the first occasion that had offered to show us what we might expect from our commander, and the spirit

---

[1] i.e., blow *on* the "slow matches" in order to quicken the glowing spark at their ends.

and decision which he displayed were hailed with pleasure by all, and at once mitigated greatly the unfriendly feelings which the ebullitions of his temper had produced.'

It has been a long, long time since the peoples of the United States and Great Britain have felt enmity toward each other. It is trusted that nothing in this volume will serve to destroy any of the long and lasting harmony. It is necessary, however, to realize the feeling that was so often engendered in the breasts of the rival mariners as they met in port and at sea in the early 19th century; otherwise one is unable to appreciate the conditions under which our vessels operated. The attitude of that mighty Sea Power, England, made its effects felt far and wide, in peace as well as in war. An incident which befell Midshipman Morris shortly after the one just recounted presents a good picture of the ways and times. It occurred after the *Constitution* had arrived at Gibraltar. Morris continues in his autobiography:

'While we were thus lying in the harbor a circumstance occurred which furnished an opportunity for the display of the insulting arrogance of a British captain, a quality which had become almost proverbial, in their intercourse with the vessels of other nations. Three men who had been sent from the Philadelphia to the prize' (*Mirboka*) 'managed to desert from her. McDonough and myself were sent into Gibraltar to search for them. They were at last discovered together not far from the mole, which sheltered the English naval establishment; but they discovered us also and immediately separated and fled. Two

LIEUTENANT CHARLES MORRIS.
One of "Preble's schoolboys"; born July 26, 1784.

were soon secured by us, and we learned that the other had entered the dockyard. We requested a sentry who was near to take charge of our prisoners, to which he assented, probably mistaking us for English officers. We then went into the dockyard, where we found the other deserter in a ship's boat, from whose officer he had claimed protection as a British subject. To our request for his delivery, the officer stated the necessity of his referring the decision to his commander, but at the same time he politely offered to take us on board with him, that we might obtain it. He belonged to the frigate Medusa, Captain Sir John Gore. When we arrived on board, we remained on the quarter-deck while the English lieutenant went to make his report to the captain. We were thus detained nearly half an hour, during which time no one entered into conversation with us or offered any civility. On the contrary, when Mr. McDonough asked for some water to allay his thirst, he was directed to the scuttle-butt by the mainmast. The captain came on deck while McDonough was thus absent, which left me to commence the conversation. When the claim for the man was made, on the ground of his being a deserter from our service, the captain replied that he had avowed himself to be a British subject and as such had claimed protection. It was urged in answer that if such was really the fact, he must have practised a deception on our officers, as we did not enter English subjects if we knew them to be such; and that his word ought to have as much weight in one instance as in the other, in the absence of all proof. The captain said he should retain him, and remarked that the man had stated that there were many other English in the Constitution.   Feeling excited by the manner of Captain Gore, I replied that it was possibly true, but I thought not.   He remarked, "We shall take steps to make you give them up," and I replied that I did not think they would.   "We have done such things before as taking men from your ships of war," was his next remark; and I answered that they would not do it again.   A formal demand was then made for the man, to which as formal a denial was given.   A request was then made for a boat to land us, as we had come on board by the invitation of his officer, and this was granted. During our absence, our national character had been ascertained by the officer of the guard, and the men we had left in charge of the sentry had been released.   The commander of the prize, and subsequently the commander of the Siren, repeated the demand for this deserter, but without success.

'. . . The difficulty respecting the deserter having been reported to the commodore, I was sent for to relate the circumstances to him.   The repetition of the conversation roused all the violence of his passion, which, in the absence of the real object, fell upon me.   As I could not believe myself deserving of this severe censure, I made some remarks which only served to increase his anger, and I left the cabin with the assurance of an immediate arrest.   As a precautionary measure I prepared a statement of the conversation with Captain Gore, with McDonough's sanction to its correctness, as he had joined us in time to hear all but the very commencement.

'No arrest was made, however, and my anxieties were

relieved soon after by an assignment to a special and very responsible service, with instructions from the commodore himself. The Medusa had left Gibraltar before the commodore's return, and they did not afterwards meet, which probably prevented some serious difficulties. The other vessels of war at Gibraltar, however, were open in their arrangements for encouraging and facilitating desertions from our vessels, and to this cause it was probably owing that Syracuse was selected by the commodore as our rendezvous, in preference to Malta, where our vessels had previously resorted for supplies.'

CHAPTER V

A PEEP AT MOROCCO

THE Barbary States—the objectives of the American squadron—were four in number, all lining the north coast of Africa. From the Straits of Gibraltar eastward the countries were Morocco, Algiers, Tunis, and Tripoli. Preble, desiring first to make his line of communications secure, turned his attention immediately to Morocco. It was well to have his mind at ease regarding the nation located on the narrow Straits. This was a doubly fitting occasion to settle matters with the Sultan; for, just about this time:[1]

'October 6th, 1803, the frigate Philadelphia, captain Bainbridge, captured off Cape de Gatta a cruizer belonging to the emperor of Morocco, called the Meshboha, of twenty-two guns, Ibrahim Lubarez, commander, with a crew of one hundred and twenty men. This vessel having piratically seized the brig Celia, of Boston, commodore Preble, in the Constitution, accompanied by the Nautilus, and the return squadron of commodore Rodgers, sailed for Tangier Bay, for the purpose of convincing the brother of the sun and moon that a war with the United States would inevitably result in the destruction of his piratical navy.

[1] J. E. Dow, *Gentleman's Magazine,* July, 1839.

42

'Tangier is situated on the northern coast of Africa, but a short distance from Cape Spartel. It is a walled city of Morocco, and is rarely if ever visited excepting by market boats and vessels of war, on account of the long quarantine which is imposed by ports higher up the Mediterranean, upon all vessels who may have touched there. It lies thirty miles west of Gibraltar, is strongly fortified, has fourteen thousand inhabitants, and is the principal seaport of the Moors.

'Its appearance from the sea is beautiful. Castles and forts of white stone, with the blood red flag floating over each bastion; numerous white buildings, with the flags of every commercial nation waving in the breeze above them. Groves of orange and cypress trees towering above the walls, mark the foreground; while far in the blue distance, the mountains of Mauritania towering in grandeur, and to the left, and nigh at hand, the wild and broken summits of Mount Abyla—or in common parlance, Apes Hill—rising high above the straits, complete a picture which, for variety and beauty, is rarely equalled in the Mediterranean. If you turn to the opposite shore, you behold, peeping out from its beautiful olive groves, the little town of Tarifa, in Andalusia, celebrated as the spot where the Moors first landed, under Taric el Tuerto, and commenced the conquest of Spain; and farther out from the main land, you see its light-house, pointing the wandering mariner to the passage between the pillars of Hercules; and, farther up the straits, behold "Dark Calpe's frowning steep," rising like a watchful lion to guard the sunny sea.

'In an inexhaustible stone quarry near the city, which

has been worked from time immemorial, to supply the Moors with mill stones, there stood a pillar, with an inscription upon its base, which informed the reader that it was raised by the wandering Canaanites, who had been driven out of their land, "flowing with milk and honey," by Joshua, the son of Nun; and from the solid blocks of stone that lie about the entrance, and the great extent of the excavation—which reaches out to the sea—it requires but a little stretch of the human mind to believe that the children of Anak once labored there.

'It was sunrise at the straits of Gibraltar, when an American squadron stood by Tarifa point, and hove to in the bay of Tangier. The shores were sleeping in misty splendor, as the commodore furled his topsails and made a signal for the squadron to anchor. Having secured the ships, a salute of twenty-one guns was fired, with the flag of Morocco floating at the fore, which was speedily answered by the battery on shore. Freedom and slavery now lay side by side; the stars and the stripes, and the bloody ensigns of the corsairs, waved together in the breeze, while the rattling of the Constitution's drums mingled with the clashing of the Mussulman's cymbals. It was a stirring hour—the emperor's household had heard the roar of artillery, and wonder sate upon every countenance.

'It was yet early in the morning when the most sublime and mighty prince of Mauritania, aroused from his quiet sleep in his drowsy harem by the report of the Constitution's cannon, repaired to the divan, and held high court. There was a scowl upon his brow as he twisted his magnifi-

EDWARD PREBLE, THE PEPPERY COMMODORE.

A real "old timer" for his day—he was 42 at Tangier!

cent mustachios, and his thin lip curled in scorn, while his dark eye flashed with unusual brilliancy. Before him, were the abject subjects of his will, and myriads of heads bent down in homage as he seated himself, while his body guards, in jewelled robes and spotted turbans, with pomp and pride, took their stations behind his ottoman. At length, beckoning to the bey, he said—"What dogs are these which disturb our royal sleep before the hour of morning prayer? Hasten, Hassan, and bring us information."

'The bey informed him that a large squadron of American vessels of war had anchored in the harbor.

' "Mishalla!" said the emperor, with a look of apprehension, "let them be attended to."

'A white flag now streamed from the nearest bastion, which was answered by a similar display from every ship in the squadron; and then a boat shot from the side of the Constitution, with a noble-looking officer in her stern-sheets, whose uniform showed him to be a captain in the navy of the United States. He was commodore Preble. In a short half hour, the emperor gave the gallant commodore an audience, and Mr. Simpson, the American consul, was placed upon a footing with the consuls of the most favored nations. The emperor, through his interpreter, expressed his regret that any difference had arisen between the two nations, disavowed having given any hostile orders, and declared that he would punish any of his governors who had. He then gave an order, under his seal, for the release of the American brig Hannah, her cargo and crew, detained at Mogadore; and the commodore gave up the Meshboha, the vessel taken by captain Bainbridge, and the Mishouda, the vessel taken by commodore Rodgers, at an earlier period of the war.   Having smoked a pipe and drunk the coffee of the most illustrious Moor, the commander of the squadron was about to retire from the presence chamber, when the emperor suddenly clapped his hands.   Hassen Bey stepped forward.   "Bring me the pen of my father, and the treaty made between him and the new world," said he, "that I may sign my name, and affix my seal to it."

'The pen and the parchment scroll were then brought in, and Hassan Bey, having unrolled the latter on his bended knees, the emperor, in the presence of his divan, made his mark and affixed his seal below the ratification of his father; and it is just to state, that ever afterwards he observed its stipulations with the strictness of an honest Mussulman.   Three years ago, this treaty, which was to continue fifty years from its date, expired, and a new one was entered into, which is now in force.   It is not a little singular that the frigate Constitution, at the request of the consul of Tangier, made her second appearance off that port in 1836, to hasten a treaty with the emperor of Morocco.   Will she, fifty years hence, be ready to do the same thing?   God grant it.

'After the usual ceremonies of leave-taking, the divan broke up; the commodore then repaired on board his ship, and fired a salute; the consul hoisted his flag again over his consulate, and the squadron getting under way, the Constitution stood up the straits followed by the Nautilus, while commodore Rodgers and the return squadron proceeded to the United States.'

Preble next directed his eyes toward Tripoli and prepared to undertake a vigorous naval campaign against this easternmost one of the four Barbary Powers.

It is difficult for us today to realize the conditions under which operations were carried on by the comparatively small sailing vessels of a hundred or more years ago. In order to appreciate their heavy task it is necessary for the reader, quite early in the story, to learn the immensity of the obstacles provided by the wind and sea alone. Possibly their force would in many cases seem to us to be not great. Very often, however, it was entirely sufficient to endanger the ship gravely. Furthermore, in certain seasons along the north African coast, the prevailing winds made a bad "lee shore," that greatest dread of all mariners.

Jesse Erskine Dow describes one of the perilous gales encountered by the *Constitution*. His picture is based, no doubt, on a storm experienced in the same waters thirty years later when he himself was on the ship: [2]

'Who has passed through the Straits of Gibraltar and has not become perfectly familiar with the wind that sweeps down the Mediterranean for days and weeks together, with unmitigated fury? A wind that acts as a prohibition to every vessel bound up the straits during its continuance, and whose cold and cheerless whistle I can imagine I hear around me at this moment.

[2] *Gentleman's Magazine,* August, 1839.

'The Levanter is a perfect tyrant; day after day, it sweeps down the long narrow sea, and ever and anon slants from the rock of Gibraltar with a resistless force, bowing to the water's edge the crank merchantmen that obstruct its path, and scattering the xebecs of the Moors to the cliffs and nooks of the Mauritanian shore.   It is supposed to proceed from the Black Sea; but whether it does, or does not, those who endeavor to beat against it look *black* enough in all conscience.

'It was just before the hour of midnight in the Mediterranean, when a tall frigate, under close reefed topsails, came swiftly down before the breath of a Levanter.   Her dead-lights were in, her ports closed, and as she came bounding along athe waves in gloomy silence, she seemed to be looking out for a harbor.

' "A dirty night, sir," said the first lieutenant to the commodore, as he came from the look-out at the forecastle.

' "It is," replied the latter, as he gave a scrutinizing glance at the binnacle compass.

'At this moment, the sails aloft began to shiver and flap against the masts.

' "We are headed off," said the commodore; "call all hands!"

' "All hands!" piped the boatswain's mate, and soon every man was at his post.

' "About ship," bellowed the commodore.

' "Station for stays," said the first lieutenant, and away flew the willing crew to execute the orders of their officers. Soon the ship answered her helm like a thing of life, and coming on the other tack, dashed onward for the space of an hour without any diminution of speed.

‘ “Are we not near the land?” said the officer of the deck to the old master, as he came growling out of the cabin, like a bear with a sore head.

‘ “Very near, sir,” said the master; “it lies under that fog bank to the southward and eastward, and should the wind increase any, or haul to the northward, we shall be on the rocks before eight bells.”

‘ “That is a great consolation, truly,” said the lieutenant, as he turned to look in the direction pointed out by the master.

‘ “Breakers ahead—close aboard!” cried the look-out man from the lee cathead.

‘ “We must wear ship, sir,” said the commodore, in a stern voice, as he came out of the cabin.

‘ “All hands wear ship!” thundered the deck trumpet.

‘ “Put your helm up!” said the commodore.

‘ “Ay, ay, sir!” answered the old cunner at the wheel.

‘ “Shiver the after yards!”

‘ “Brace the head yards square!”

‘ “Pull cheerily, you lubbers—belay!” were the orders given in quick succession by the commodore.

‘ “She comes up to the wind, sir,” said the cunner, touching the tip of his tarpaulin, while he held it on to his head with his other hand.

‘ “Brace the after yards, and haul everything aft!” roared the commodore, as the frigate hung for a moment between two mighty waves, and then plunged up the black side of the hill of waters.

'As she wore round, she passed within a short distance of the rocks, over which the heavy billows dashed in sheets of quivering foam, while thunder, hoarser than that of the lightning-rent heavens, answered in awful murmurs from the rocky caves, and mingled with the shriller notes of the increasing gale.

'The shore was hid in the dark wings of the storm, and naught was seen but the dreadful breakers, whose spray fell like a shower of winter rain upon the trembling deck of the gallant ship. It was a fearful moment; a fathom nearer in, and the shrieks of five hundred drowning victims would have gone up amid the roar of the gale to the God of nature, while ten thousand fragments of the wreck would have strewn that benighted and bloody coast.

'Firm as a rock, stood the gallant Preble and his noble crew, and as the frigate rode by on the top of the crested wave, he saw she headed off from the shore.

' "She has cleared them!" said he, in a thrilling voice. "Pipe down, sir!" and immediately left the deck.

'Commodores must never show their feelings before their crews; they must be firm amid the dangers of the contending elements, as well as amid the iron rain of battle; but when they have reached their cabins, they may return thanks to the God of battles and the king of storms, without interfering with the rules and regulations of the sea service. Commodore Preble was one of the bravest, and, at the same time, strictest officers in the service, and his character is now held up as a model to the aspirant for naval glory.

' "Eight bells!" cried the orderly stationed at the cabin

door, as he popped his head over the railing of the companion-way.

'"Eight bells!" echoed the quarter master at the binnacle, and eight bells were struck by the messenger boy
at the galley. The master looked at the first lieutenant
with a grin of satisfaction, and soon the two took a pull
of half-and-half, in honor of the skill of their commander.

'"I say, Jack, ain't you dry?" said a jolly tar, to his messmate, as he rolled a quid of old Nipcheese poison, of the
size of a young tree toad, from the larboard to the starboard side of his face.

'"My eyes, I *are!*" said the party addressed; "I feel as
though I had swallowed the cook, galley, coals, and all!"

'"Splice the main brace, sir!" said the commodore, to
the lieutenant of the watch, as he mounted the horse-block,
and gave a last look towards the breakers, whose dying
thunder and awful hissing fell upon his ear.

'The ruffle of a drum was now heard amid the howling
of the gale, and soon busy feet were seen moving towards
the red bull, near the scuttle butt. Tin pots of old Jamaica were now turned bottom side up, and Jack was ready
to take another graze by the breakers; "though," as one
of them said, while he hitched up his lee waistband, "if
he could have his own way, he would prefer a couple of
fathoms more of sea room, and not quite so much wind."

'The storm now began to abate, a light stripe extended
along the eastern horizon, and when the day dawned, the
blooming shores of Sicily were seen about ten miles off,
bathed in the purple tints of an eastern morning.

'The commodore, finding the ship had stretched her rigging by her heavy plunges, and that several spars had been sprung by the force of the gale, put his helm up, and ran for Syracuse.   At nine o'clock, he came to an anchor beneath the snow-clad summit of Etna, and saluted the Neopolitan flag with twenty-one guns.   The Levanter was now at an end; countless merchantmen came up, upon the breath of the balmy west wind, and stretched along the Italian coast, while the flags of every nation waved in the breeze, and glittered in the sunbeam.'

CHAPTER VI

"The Most Bold and Daring Act of the Age" [1]

BEFORE Preble had had time to commence very active operations against the corsairs his squadron suffered a most severe loss. On October 31, 1803, the frigate *Philadelphia* ran on a shoal while maintaining the blockade of Tripoli. A sorry page of our naval history was then written when the ship was surrendered to the enemy before a man was lost. At the same time, however, the stage was set for one of our most glorious deeds. The vessel was quickly pulled off, manned, and refitted by the Tripolitans. This great increase in the Bashaw's sea power, coincident with the American loss, put another and much more serious aspect on the whole naval campaign.

As a result the first mission came to be that of recapturing or destroying the frigate. The *Philadelphia* was moored inside the harbor of Tripoli, under the guns of the castle, fully manned, guns loaded. The risk entailed in an attempt to "cut her out" was deemed prohibitive. There would be sufficient danger even in destroying her. Permission, however, was given to attempt her destruction by burning. None of our warships was suitable for the task. Accordingly, another vessel was manned by

[1] The pronouncement of Admiral Lord Nelson.

the regular ships.   It was a captive slave ketch of sixty tons.   Lieutenant Decatur was placed in command, there being ten other officers, a pilot, and fifty-two men aboard. The *Constitution* was in the forefront with a contribution of five officers.   One of these, fortunately, was Midshipman Charles Morris; so we have available in his autobiography an excellent first-hand account of the operation:

'The brig Siren, Lieutenant Stewart, was to accompany us, to assist with her boats and to receive the crew of the ketch (which had been named the Intrepid), in case of her destruction, which was considered probable.   The officers were told to take only a single change of linen, and no time was allowed to prepare stores, as we embarked within an hour after receiving notice, and sailed immediately, on the evening of the 3rd of February, 1804.[2]   Combustibles had been previously prepared and placed in the vessel, with ship's provisions for two or three weeks' supply.   A Maltese had also been obtained to accompany us as a pilot into the harbor, with which he was well acquainted.   We arrived in sight of Tripoli about the 10th, but the wind was fresh from the westward, with strong indications of an approaching gale.   After some consultation between the commanders, the vessels anchored under cover of the night near the entrance, and a boat was sent with the pilot to determine by observation if the entrance was practicable and safe, of which he had expressed strong doubts.   To my surprise I was ordered to go with him.   We went quite close to the entrance, where

[2] From Syracuse.

STEPHEN DECATUR.

When only 24 he burned the *Philadelphia* in Tripoli harbor.
After that he commanded the *Constitution*, a captain at 25.

we found the surf breaking entirely across it; and my own opinion concurred with that of the pilot that no attempt ought to be made.   It was, however, a severe trial to make such a report.   I had heard many of the officers treat the doubts of the pilot as the offspring of apprehension, and the weather was not yet so decidedly boisterous as to render it certain that an attempt might not be made, notwithstanding our report.   Should such be the case and should it succeed, the imputations upon the pilot might be repeated upon me, and, unknown as I was, might be the cause of my ruin in the estimation of my brother officers.   My sense of duty and propriety, however, prevailed over these apprehensions, and my report was decidedly against any attempt to enter the harbor at that time, and sustained all the objections of the pilot.   These opinions were evidently received with much dissatisfaction by a majority, and with some murmurs, but the attempt was abandoned for the time, and the vessels weighed again to get beyond the view from the town before daylight.   This was not done without some difficulty, as the gale increased rapidly.   It continued for four or five days with great violence, and drove us considerably to the eastward, and at one time nearer the coast than was agreeable.

'Our situation on board was far from comfortable. The commander, three lieutenants, and the surgeon occupied the very small cabin.   Six midshipmen and the pilot had a platform laid on the water casks, whose surface they covered when they lay down for sleep, and at so small a distance below the deck that their heads would reach it when seated on the platform. The marines had corresponding accomodations on the opposite side, and the sailors had only the surface of the casks in the hold. To these inconveniences were added the want of any room on the deck for exercise, and the attacks of innumerable vermin, which our predecessors the slaves had left behind them. The provisions proved to be decayed and offensive. Fortunately our confinement did not continue long enough to affect our health or vigor.

'On the morning of the 16th we again obtained sight of Tripoli, with light winds, pleasant weather, and a smooth sea, and stood in for the town. By arrangement the Siren kept far without us during the day, and her appearance had been so changed as to lull all suspicion of her being a vessel of war. The lightness of the wind allowed us to keep up all appearance of an anxious desire to reach the harbor before night, without bringing us too near to require any other change than the use of drags, which could not be seen from the city. All the crew were also kept below, excepting six or eight persons at a time, that suspicion might not be awakened by unusual numbers; and such as were visible were dressed as Maltese.

'As the evening advanced our drags were taken in, so that we were within two miles of the eastern entrance at dark, the Siren being some three miles without us. The concerted arrangements were for the ketch to wait for the boats of the Siren to join us after dark, that they might accompany us to the attack; but as the sun descended the wind grew fainter, and there was good reason to apprehend that any delay in waiting for the boats might render it very difficult for the ketch to reach the ship. Decatur, therefore, determined to proceed without waiting, and accompanied his decision with the remark, "The fewer the number the greater the honor." One boat from the Siren, with six men, had joined us a few days before, and was still with us.

'The final arrangements were now made, and the respective duties of the several officers, which had been previously allotted, were again specified and explained. The presumed number of our enemy was stated, and the necessity for our utmost exertions enjoined upon us. The watchword "Philadelphia" was issued, to be used as a means of recognition; and as we advanced into the harbor strict silence was enjoined and observed. The injunction, however, appeared to be unnecessary. No one seemed disposed to enter into conversation, but to be absorbed by his own reflections. My own thoughts were busy, now reverting to friends at home, now to the perils we were about to meet. Should I be able to justify the expectations of the former by meeting properly the dangers of the latter? How was I prepared for the death which might possibly be my fate? These, with others of a somber character, mixed with calculations to secure a prominent position when boarding, passed rapidly through my mind; and the minds of others were no doubt employed on similar subjects. The officers and crew were directed to conceal themselves as much as possible, excepting some six or eight. Most of the officers could be distinguished by their dress, and they required concealment more than the sailors. Fortunately, owing to the loss of some articles, which had been replaced by loan from the crew, my own dress corresponded to theirs, which enabled me to keep near Decatur, who I supposed would naturally be among the first to leave the ketch.   The wind wafted us slowly into the harbor, the water was smooth, and the young moon gave light enough to distinguish prominent objects.   One battery was passed, the Philadelphia was in view near several smaller vessels, and the white walls of the city and its batteries were before us.   We steered directly for the frigate, and at last the anxious silence was broken by a hail from her, demanding our character and object.   Then might be seen the eager movements of the heads of the officers and crew who were stretched on the deck, ready to leap forward at the word of their commander, but still resting in silence.   A conversation was kept up between the frigate and the ketch through our pilot, acting under the dictation of Decatur.   We alleged the loss of our anchors during the last gale, which was true, as a reason for wishing to make fast to the frigate till morning, and permission was obtained; but just as the ketch was about coming in contact with the frigate the wind shifted, blowing lightly directly from the frigate, and it left us at rest abeam and about twenty yards from her.   This was a moment of great anxiety.   We were directly under her guns, motionless and powerless, except by exertions which might betray our character.   The Siren's boat was, however, in tow, and was leisurely manned, and took a rope to make fast to the ship.   She was met by a boat with another rope, when both were united, and each boat returned to its vessel.   This rope was passed along the deck and hauled upon by the crew as they lay stretched upon it, and the vessels gradually brought nearer each other. When nearly in contact the suspicions of the enemy appeared to be aroused, and the cry of "*Americanos!*" resounded through the ship. In a moment we were near enough, and the order "Board!" was given; . . . My object in keeping near Lieutenant Decatur, when we were approaching the ship, was that by watching his actions, I could be governed by these rather than by his orders when the boarding should take place. It was well that this course was taken, for Decatur had leaped to the main chain plates of the frigate, before the order to board was given. I had leaped with him, and, probably more favored by circumstances, was able to reach the deck by the time he had gained the rail. The enemy were already leaping over the opposite side and made no resistance; but Decatur, under the supposition that he was first on board, was about to strike me, when I accidentally turned and stayed his uplifted arm by the watchward and mutual recognition. . . . Our men were soon on the decks of the frigate. The surprise had been complete; there was no time for any preparation, and the enemy made scarcely a show of resistance. A few were killed, one was made prisoner, and the remainder leaped overboard and probably reached their cruisers which were anchored near the ship. . . .

'The plan of attack prescribed by our commander was for united action to obtain possession of the ship, with the exception of a boat to intercept communication with the shore, and for the surgeon and a few men to secure the ketch to the ship. When possession was secured, each lieutenant, with a midshipman and specified men, was to receive a portion of the prepared combustibles, and distribute them in designated parts of the berth-deck and in the forward store-rooms, and a smaller party under a midshipman to do the same in the cockpit, and there await orders to set fire, that all might be done at the same time and give all a chance for safe retreat. The party for the cockpit was assigned to my charge. . . . On my way to my station, after examining the cabin, and when passing forward, we met again under similar circumstances.[3] Passing through the wardroom, which I found deserted, I awaited in the cockpit the men who had gone for the combustibles. These were so delayed that we had none when the order was given to set fire; but, as they came a moment after, they were distributed, and fire communicated before we left our station. In the mean time the fire on the deck above us had communicated so rapidly that it was with no small difficulty and danger that our party reached the spar-deck by the forward hatchways. All the others had already rejoined the ketch, except Decatur, who remained on the rail till all others were on board; and the bow of the ketch had already swung off from the ship when he joined us by leaping into the rigging of the ketch. . . . In less than twenty minutes the ship had been carried, the combustibles distributed and set on fire, and all our party again on board the ketch. By great exertions, the two vessels were separated before the fire, which was pouring from the ports of the ship, enveloped the ketch also.

'Up to this time the ships and batteries of the enemy

---

[3] i.e., Decatur momentarily mistook Morris for an enemy, as on the earlier occasion.

BURNING of the FRIGATE PHILADELPHIA in the HARBOUR of TRIPOLI 16 Feb. 1804. By Lieutenant Steph. Decatur, a commander by Heat Courtier

"AND THERE SHOULD BE HER GRAVE."

had remained silent, but they now prepared to act: and when the crew of the ketch gave three cheers in exultation of their success, they received the return of a general discharge from the enemy. The confusion of the moment probably prevented much care in their direction, and, though under the fire of nearly a hundred pieces for half an hour, the only shot which struck the ketch was one through the topgallant sail. We were in great danger from the ship, whose broadside commanded the passage by which we were retreating, and whose guns were loaded and were discharged as they became heated. We escaped these also, and while urging the ketch onwards with sweeps, the crew were commenting upon the beauty of the spray thrown up by the shot between us and the brilliant light of the ship, rather than calculating any danger that might be apprehended from the contact. The appearance of the ship was indeed magnificent. The flames in the interior illuminated her ports and, ascending her rigging and masts, formed columns of fire, which, meeting the tops, were reflected into beautiful capitals; whilst the occasional discharge of her guns gave an idea of some directing spirit within her. The walls of the city and its batteries, and the masts and rigging of cruisers at anchor, brilliantly illuminated, and animated by the discharge of artillery, formed worthy adjuncts and an appropriate background to the picture. Favored by a light breeze our exertions soon carried us beyond range of their shot, and at the entrance of the harbor we met the boats of the Siren, which had been intended to co-öperate with us, whose crews rejoiced at our success, whilst they grieved at not having been able to participate in it.'

CHAPTER VII

In the Pirates' Lair.   Tripoli

WITH the destruction of the *Philadelphia* the stage was set for direct action against the fortifications and light vessels of Tripoli.   The U. S. S. *Constitution* was about to go into action just six years after her completion.   On July 26, 1804, she appeared off the harbor leading a force composed of three brigs, three schooners, two bomb vessels, and six gunboats.

[1] 'The destruction of the Philadelphia amid the gloom of night had taught the Tripolitans to fear the navy of the young republic.   The yell of the drowning Mussulmen— the thunder of the Philadelphia's cannon as they were exploded by the wreathing flames—the crackling of the old hull as it belched forth its gathered torrents of fire and smoke, and the hell-like explosion as the magazine ignited and sent the countless masses of that unfortunate wreck high amid the murky heavens, still rang upon their ears, and filled their breasts with terror.

'Tripoli, however, was a city well walled, protected by batteries judiciously constructed, mounting one hundred and fifteen pieces of heavy cannon, and defended by twenty-five thousand Arabs and Turks.   The harbor was

[1] J. E. Dow, *Gentleman's Magazine,* August, 1839.

protected by nineteen gun-boats, two galleys, two schooners of eight guns, and a brig mounting ten guns, which were ranged in order of battle, at secure moorings, inside of a long range of rocks and shoals, extending more than two miles to the eastward of the town. These shoals protected the enemy from the northern gales, and rendered it impossible for a frigate to approach near enough to destroy them. Each gun-boat mounted a heavy eighteen, or twenty-six pounder in the bow, and two brass howitzers on the quarters, and carried from thirty-six to fifty men. The galleys had each one hundred men, and the schooners and brigs were manned by the same number.

'The weather continued unfavorable until the 28th, when the fleet stood in; but just as the Constitution anchored, a sudden change made it necessary for them to retire, and swiftly they dashed along that rocky shore before the breath of a terrific gale. This gale continued until the 31st, when it blew away the Constitution's foresail and close-reefed maintopsail, and had the sea risen in proportion to the wind, the gunboats and bombs would have been carried down to the charnel house of the mariner.

'On the 3d of August, at noon, the commodore, having formed his plan of attack, made signal for the different commanders to come within hail. After communicating his orders to them, he wore ship, and stood in for the batteries. At half-past two, he made the general signal for battle. In an instant, the enemy's shipping and batteries opened a tremendous fire, which was promptly returned within grape shot distance. Several times the Constitution was within two cables' length of the rocks, and within three of their batteries.   Every battery was silenced so long as the frigate's broadside bore upon them, but as often as she passed by, they were reanimated, and a constant heavy fire kept up upon her.   At this time, in sheering and tacking, the gallant commodore felt most sensibly the want of another frigate.

'At half past four, the wind inclining to the northward, signal was made to retire from the batteries, which was done under cover of the Constitution's heavy cannon. For two hours this noble frigate stood the close fire of the batteries, and the only damages received by her were a wound from a twenty-four pound shot in her mainmast, thirty feet from the deck, the loss of her mainroyal sail and yard, which were shot away, and the dismounting of a quarter-deck gun by a thirty-two pound shot, which at the same time shattered a marine's arm.

'Thus came out, under the protecting wing of our favorite, the gallant squadron, at the hour of sunset, from before Tripoli, and, in the words of the brave commander, we must impute their getting off so well to their having kept so near the batteries of the enemy, and to their having annoyed them so excessively with their grape shot.

'On the 5th August, the squadron was at anchor about two leagues north from the city of Tripoli, while the Argus was in chase of a small vessel to the westward, which she soon came up with, and brought within hail. She proved to be a French privateer, of four guns, which put into Tripoli a few days previous for water, and had left it that morning.   Commodore Preble prevailed upon the captain, for a con-sid-er-a-tion, to return to Tripoli,

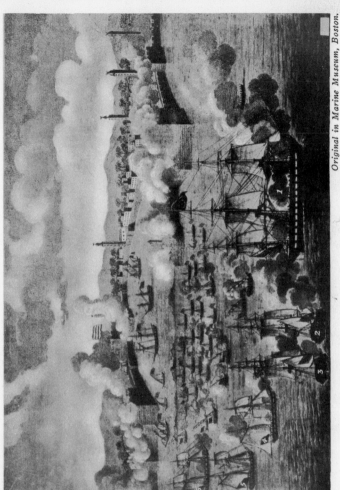

"MILLIONS FOR DEFENSE; NOT ONE CENT FOR TRIBUTE."

"The attack made on Tripoli on the 3d August, 1804, by the American Squadron under Commodore Edward Preble to whom this Plate is respectfully dedicated by his Obedient Servant John B. Guerrazzi. 1. Constitution Frigate. 2. Sirion. 3. Arges. 4. Enterprise. 5. Notlas. 6. Vixon. Sold in Leghorn, 1805."

for the purpose of landing fourteen very badly wounded Tripolitans, whom he put on board his vessel, with a letter to the prime minister, leaving it at the option of the bashaw to reciprocate so generous a mode of conducting the war. On the 7th of August, the Frenchman returned to the Constitution, and brought commodore Preble a letter from the French consul, in which he observed that the attack of the 3d instant had disposed the bashaw to accept of reasonable terms, and invited him to send a boat to the rocks with a flag of truce, which the commodore declined, as the white flag was not hoisted at the bashaw's castle.

'At 9, A. M., with a very light breeze from the eastward, and a strong current, which obliged the Constitution to remain at anchor, the commodore made the signal for the light vessels to weigh, and the gun and bomb-boats to cast off and stand in shore, towards the western batteries, the *prize* boats having been completely fitted for service, and the command of them given to lieutenants Crane, of the Vixen, Thorn, of the Enterprize, and Caldwell, of the Syren. The whole advanced with sails and oars.

'At half past one, with a breeze from north north-east, Old Ironsides (for she received her *sobriquet* in this bombardment)[2] weighed and stood in for the town, but the wind being on shore, made it imprudent to engage the batteries with the ship, as, in case of a mast being shot away, the loss of the vessel would probably ensue, unless a change of wind should favor her retreat.

'On the 28th, the Constitution approached the harbor.

---

[2] An error. It was in the battle with H.M.S. *Guerriere,* in 1812, that the *Constitution* was "rechristened."

Fort English, the bashaw's castle, and the Crown and
Mole batteries, kept up a heavy fire upon her as she
advanced.   At half-past five, she was within two cables'
lengths of the rocks, and commenced a heavy fire of round
and grape on thirteen of the enemy's gunboats and galleys,
which were in pretty close action with the gunboats of
the squadron.   She sank one of the enemy's gunboats;
at the same time, two more, that had been disabled, ran
on shore to avoid sinking; the remainder immediately re-
treated.

'The old ship still continued running in until within
musket shot of the Crown and Mole batteries, when she
brought to, and fired upwards of three hundred round
shot, besides grape and cannister, into the town, the
bashaw's castle and batteries, silencing the castle and two
of the batteries for some time.   In all this unprecedented
exposure to the deadly aim of a land battery, the frigate
was only injured in her sails and rigging—her hull being
but slightly peppered with grape shot.

'On the 3d, the Constitution, to draw off the enemy's
attention from the gunboats, ran within them.   She
brought to within reach of grape, and fired eleven broadsides into the bashaw's castle, town and batteries, in a
situation where more than seventy guns could bear upon
her.

'She did not get out scatheless from this fight; her main-
topsail was totally disabled by a shell from the batteries
which cut away the leach rope, and several cloths of the
sail.   Another shell went through the foretopsail, and
one through the jib.   All her sails were considerably cut

and her running rigging very much injured, but still no shot was received in the hull.'

As was so often the case, the complements of these American gunboats were made up largely of officers and men from the *Constitution* and other large vessels of the squadron. It is therefore fitting to record here the following incident of the campaign. It was told by Decatur to a certain distinguished literary personage who passed it on to the editor of the *Knickerbocker:* [3]

'In one of the actions before Tripoli, while fighting hand to hand with the captain of a gun-boat, Decatur came near being cut down by a Turk, who attacked him from behind. A seaman named Reuben James, who was already wounded in both hands, seeing the risk of his commander, rushed in and received the blow of the uplifted sabre on his own head. Fortunately, the honest fellow survived to receive his reward. Sometime afterward, when he had recovered from his wounds, Decatur sent for him on deck, expressed his gratitude for his self-devotion, in presence of the crew, and told him to ask for some reward. The honest tar pulled up his waist-band, and rolled his quid, but seemed utterly at a loss what recompense to claim. His mess-mates gathered around him, nudging him with their elbows, and whispering in his ear: "He had all the world in a string, and could get what he pleased;" "the 'old man' could deny him nothing," etc. One advised this thing, another that; "double pay," "double allowance," "a boatswain's berth," "a pocket-full

[3] *Knickerbocker Magazine,* March, 1840.

of money, and a full swing on shore," etc.   Jack elbowed
them all aside, and would have none of their counsel.
After mature deliberation, he announced the reward to
which he aspired; it was, *to be excused from rolling up the
hammock cloths!*   The whimsical request was of course
granted; and from that time forward, whenever the sailors
were piped to stow away their hammocks, Jack was to be
seen loitering around, and looking on, with the most
gentlemanlike leisure.   He always continued in the same
ship with Decatur.   "I could always know the state of my
bile by Jack," said the commodore.   "If I was in good
humor, and wore a pleasant aspect, Jack would be sure
to heave in sight, to receive a friendly nod: if I was out of
humor, and wore, as I sometimes did, a foul-weather
physiognomy, Jack kept aloof, and skulked among the
other sailors."   It is proper to add, that Reuben James
received a more solid reward for his gallant devotion, than
the privilege above-mentioned, a pension having been
granted to him by government.'

Then Dow, as he continues his story, quotes from Golds-
borough's Naval Chronicle:
' "During this attack, a thirty-two pound ball from the
Constitution passed through the wall in the apartment of
the prison where captain Bainbridge [4] was sleeping, struck
against the opposite wall, rebounded, and in its fall took
part of the bed-clothes from him, and passed within a few
inches of his body.   In its passage through the first wall
it knocked out a cart-load of stone and mortar, under

[4] The captured commander of the *Philadelphia*.

which captain Bainbridge was buried until the officers relieved him. He was considerably bruised by the rubbish, and received a cut in the right ankle which occasioned a lameness for months."

'What must have been the feelings of Bainbridge, Porter, Jones, etc., as they lay within their gloomy prison-house and heard the thunder of their country's cannon dying amid the fastnesses of Barbary, and felt the rubbish rattling upon their heads, as the iron messengers of vengeance came sweeping through the massive walls with the swiftness of the lightning's flash!

'This series of bombardments caused the haughty bashaw to come to terms, and the next year a treaty was signed on board the frigate—the first instance where a peace was concluded with any of the Barbary states on board a ship of war.'

This was one more story of ships versus forts. The ships could do little actual damage to anything ashore that was of any military value. On the other side the wretched gunnery of the Tripolines brought the ships off virtually unscathed. The attacks showed primarily that the United States had altered its policy from that of paying tribute and ransom for the protection of its commerce and its merchant sailors. It was the blockade of the coast that made the Bashaw ready for peace—this combined with the considerable disorganization of the city caused by the attacks. The treaty would not be hailed by the United States at the present time as a grand achievement of a self-respecting nation. In the negotiations, however, Tripoli held an "ace in the hole" in the persons of the captured officers and men of the *Philadelphia*.   At that period of history, and under all the existing circumstances, the treaty was received with much satisfaction as a notable accomplishment—and no doubt deservedly so.

CHAPTER VIII

BEARDING THE BEY

TUNIS was next on the list:

[1] 'In May, 1805, commodore Barron returned to the United States in ill health, leaving commodore Rodgers in the Mediterranean, in command of the largest American squadron ever known.

'Commodore Rodgers immediately hoisted his flag on board the Constitution, and shortly afterwards, as the echo of the evening gun at the Valetta died along the shores of Malta, the fleet got under weigh, and stood over towards the African coast.   It was on the eighth day after their departure when the squadron made cape Carthage, and on the ninth, at sunrise, anchored in the roads of Goletta.   Before the gallant frigates lay the city of Tunis, the abode of happiness, and the fountain spring of jackasses and orange water.   The signal for the consul to come on board was immediately made, and on the following day he repaired on board the Constitution, and gave the commodore a detailed account of his fruitless conferences with Hamouda Bey.   A council of war was then called, at which Col. Lear, the consul-general, assisted, which resulted in the determination to bombard the town in

---

[1] J. E. Dow, *Gentleman's Magazine,* September, 1839.

the course of thirty-six hours, if a favorable answer was not returned to commodore Rodgers' letter demanding satisfaction.

'Previous to the arrival of the squadron, the Bey had called the American consul to his presence, and, before the assembled divan, demanded the release of a Tunisian Xebec and her two prizes which had been captured by the Constitution for attempting to violate the blockade of Tripoli.   The consul assured him that they would not be released, and the Bey, with a frown, threatened a declaration of war.   He accordingly wrote a letter to commodore Rodgers, and in answer received a visit from his fleet as before stated.   The Bey, up to the very day of the appearance of the squadron, had assumed a lofty tone of menace, and while his guards surrounded the consul with their drawn scimetars and slackened bowstrings, addressed his as follows:

' "Ask any of the christian consuls in this regency if Hamouda Bashaw has ever received such an insult from their government?   The President of the United States must know that my father and grandfather have sat on the throne and ruled a kingdom.   He shall learn from me that Hamouda is not yet dead; and every crowned head in Europe shall approve the eternal continuance of that war which you seem resolved to force me into—for I solemnly pledge myself, that if war is the result, never, while I have a soldier to fire a gun, will I accord peace.   You may form some idea of my character from the difficulty you had to negociate a peace, because you weakly permitted the Dey of Algiers to interfere.   You may also learn my conduct to the Venitians, who rashly forced me into a war; and if

I am doomed to engage in another, it shall be continued to the last hour of my existence. I frankly tell you that the famine in my country has prevented my declaring war against you, in order that I might convince my subjects that their miseries should not be increased, unless I was forced thereto. Without such a motive, you certainly never would have been asked the reason why you captured my vessels; but that just motive to a protraction of our difficulties, must be sacrificed to those considerations which I owe myself and all Europe. You are the first power which has ever captured a Tunisian cruizer in full peace, on any pretext whatever. You are the first that has ever offered unprovoked insults to Hamouda Bashaw, who has ruled a kingdom for twenty-seven years, and been respected by all the world as a sovereign. If I were tamely to submit to such acts of outrage, what should I expect from nations far more powerful than yourselves? You have seen what has been accorded me by Spain, Sweden, and Denmark, whose local situation and maritime force must render them more formidable enemies than the United States. Abstracted from this, the measures pursued are such as do not permit me to enter into any negotiation. Your admirals have done me great and repeated injuries, for the last of which my political existence forces me to insist on a proper reparation."

'At this moment a heavy cannon awoke the echoes of the palace, and, breathless with running, a Janizary entered the presence chamber.

' "Ha, Selim," said the Bey, his curiosity getting the better of his dignity, "comes there a war ship from Stamboul?"

' "Nay, most illustrious and magnificent prince, the christian dogs have entered the abode of happiness."

' "By my grandfather's beard," said the Bey—for he could swear like a christian—"come they with their single frigate to beard Hamouda!—let them retreat in time. Consul! go to your admiral, and bid him not let the morning sun shine upon him by the *'Garden of the World,'* or his head shall answer for his temerity."

'At this moment another Janizary came with the astounding news that the largest fleet ever before Tunis had anchored in the harbor, and that the signal for the "consul Americana" fluttered at the fore of the admiral. Hamouda Bey lost his tone of defiance in a moment. "Consul," said he, "remember me kindly to your admiral" —and, clapping his hands, broke up the divan.

'The next morning captain Decatur was directed by the commodore to proceed to Tunis, and cooperate with the consul in obtaining from the Bey an unequivocal and satisfactory guarantee for the faithful observance of peace. The Bey, still excited, refused to receive captain Decatur in this character; and the captain, in his usual spirited manner, "refused visiting him on any other terms;" and left Tunis to return to the squadron, and report the result of his mission. As soon as the Bey heard of his departure, he manifested great concern. His royal breast appeared to be panic-struck, and he despatched a messenger with a conciliatory letter with such expedition that it "was received on board the Constitution before captain Decatur came alongside."

'The next day a treaty was concluded between the most magnificent prince and the United States; and the Congress, having received on board a Tunisian ambassador, the Constitution, followed by the squadron, got under weigh, and stood out of the harbor.

'As they passed the island of Goletta, the old frigate caught a glimpse of the American flag floating proudly in the breeze, and hoisted an ensign at the fore—then, as if by one simultaneous impulse, the star spangled banner ascended to the fore of every vessel in the squadron, and upwards of two hundred cannon woke their thunder-notes, while two thousand five hundred men raised the loud huzza.

'A faint echo came back upon the dying land-breeze, and "the abode of happiness" was lost from view.'

There now remained Algiers alone of the Barbary Powers. The United States had, in 1795, made a shameful treaty with that country. It was this treaty the signing of which had contributed greatly toward halting the construction of the *Constitution*. The terms of the pact—abstention from piracy in return for tribute—had been lived up to by both sides. Fulfillment of obligations continued in a reasonably satisfactory manner until depredations on American merchantmen were resumed during the War of 1812. Accordingly it was not until 1815 that the whole wretched business was finally ended for all time.

CHAPTER IX

"THE MARINES . . . HAVE THE SITUATION IN HAND" [1]

THERE was undue delay in sending out a ship to relieve the *Constitution* on the Mediterranean station. The term of enlistment then in effect was three years, and many of her crew were held long over time. The months drifted by, and the year 1807 found the ship still cruising in far-off waters. The troubles with the Barbary pirates had ended long since; excusable discontent began to smoulder. Before the atmosphere was cleared an occurrence took place which came as close to resulting in a mutiny as ever was the case in the United States Navy.

In the beginning comparatively small straws showed the direction of the wind. The first incident to be mentioned has significance in the light of later events. Fourth Lieutenant Lewis made the following report to Captain Hugh G. Campbell:

'While in the harbor of Syracuse, on the 30th of may,' (1807) 'being my day of duty, the officer (Mr. Wilmer) who had been with a party of men at the arsenal all day, on returning at sunset — reported two or three of the crew

---

[1] The events of this chapter were recounted, in somewhat different form, in *The Leatherneck* of April, 1928.

for having run away from the arsenal into the town, where,
after a long search he found them drunk.   William Jones
was one of them.   On examination I found him very
drunk and inclined to be insolent which provoked me to
strike him.   He was then exceedingly insolent and as I
thought mutinous, saying repeatedly that "his time was
up" and I had "no right to punish him" and said he was "a
true Englishman" and I think threatened to demand
English protection.   The Endymion (English frigate)
was lying in the harbor.

   'I ordered him to be put in irons, while the Master-at-
Arms was doing this, he continued to use the expressions
I have mentioned and others equally improper and was so
riotous that I was obliged to go down myself and use
force to quiet him.   Messers Wilmer and Shields are
witnesses to the particulars of the above statement.   Mr.
Woolsey also saw a great deal of his riotous conduct after
he was confined.'

   A much more threatening state of affairs arose one
evening nine days later.   The ship was still at Syracuse
and the Captain chanced to be ashore at the time.   Next
morning First Lieutenant Charles Ludlow reported to
him:
   'Yesterday, between 5 and 6 oclock in the evening, I
gave permission for the ship's company to bathe.   Shortly
after, I came on deck and saw two men swimming ahead of
the ship, towards an English frigate.   I immediately informed the officer-of-the-deck (Lt. Burrows) of their
being further from the ship than allowed.   He went

forward and called a number of times before they came back, and as soon as they got on board, took them forward to flog (there being company on the quarter deck at the time)

'A few minutes after I perceived a number of men rushing forward on the forecastle who gave three cheers before I could get forward to know the cause of the noise. At the same time I saw Mr. Burrows on one of the guns surrounded by the men; after clearing them away he gave me the following report, That John Smith, one of the above mentioned men, refused to take his jacket off or stand and receive the rope's end, he intended giving him, for not attending to his orders; and the boatswain's mate (George Prince) had hove his rope's end down and refused to flog him. But previous to the boatswain's mate refusing to flog him, John Hughland, came forward and told John Smith that he was a damned fool if he pulled his jacket off. At the same time he told Mr. Burrows the man should not be flogged.

'It was also reported to me that William Pinkney, boatswain's mate, had taken up a crow bar near Mr. Burrows, while the men were cheering. After this report believing their conduct very mutinous, I had Prince, Pinkney, Smith and Hughland put in irons (the guard during this time was under arms). A few moments after the ship's company gave three cheers again, as if displeased at what had been done. I immediately armed myself and desired the officers to do the same (Mr. Amory [2], Marine officer, with all his detachment under arms). But while arming, the men broke out again with three cheers and a general cry

[2] Probably Second Lieutenant William Armory.

among them "On the forecastle!   On the forecastle!", where they were all rushing as fast as possible.

'I then had the drum beat to quarters, which silenced them and they all went, except James Thompson, who was seen on the forecastle (By Mr. Chauncey and Mr. Willmore) pulling back a man from his quarters and crying out "On the forecastle!", very loudly after the drum had beaten to quarters.   I had Thompson put in irons and all the prisoners brought from their usual places of confinement, aft to the cabin door, with two sentries placed over them, after which I mustered the men at their quarters; beat the retreat; and gave them their hammocks.

'At eight o'clock, had the starboard watch called and the officers put in two watches the officers and the marines of the watch were armed.   The boat that went for you left the ship at the time I desired the officers to arm themselves. All peaceable and answered as usual in the watch until shortly after you came aboard.'

The frigate *Chesapeake* was at last scheduled to relieve the *Constitution;* but she did not put in an appearance and time dragged on.   Finally on June 22 she put out from Hampton Roads.   Her decks were in great disorder, the work on her having been completed over-hastily.   Such unpreparedness in time of peace in that era was nearly as risky as a similar state would be in time of war nowadays. It resulted most disastrously on this occasion.   When the *Chesapeake* was several miles outside of the Capes the British frigate *Leopard* approached.   The American ship hove to upon request and an English officer came aboard. He made the surprising demand that the *Chesapeake's* crew be mustered on deck in order that he might pick out and take back with him some men who were suspected of being deserters from the British navy! Such an outrageous request was of course promptly refused and the *Chesapeake* made ready to resume her journey. Upon the return of the emissary, the *Leopard* opened fire on the *Chesapeake*!—and this in peace time! The American vessel was totally unfit to fight or flee or do anything at all. She hauled down her flag after undergoing a rather long bombardment, virtually without making reply. The Britisher thereupon took four alleged deserters out of her. Thus ended an incident which for different reasons is one of the blackest in the records of each navy.

One of the four men—one who may have been English *born*—was hanged; the others were returned with apologies—*four years afterwards!*

The *Chesapeake* had to return to port to refit once more. This resulted in heavy repercussions across the sea. The *Constitution* had now been away from home for four years. On August 15, the ship being in Malaga Roads, her Captain wrote to the Secretary of the Navy:

'Sir:—I left Syracuse the 12th of June and anchored here on the 2d instant (the Hornet in company) where I intended to fill up our water and proceed immediately to Gibraltar in the expectation of meeting the frigate Chesapeake, which vessel I have frequently been informed was fitting out for this station. But to my great disappointment and surprise, I find, upon perusal of a Boston paper, that she had been attacked by the British fifty-gun ship (Leopard) and obliged to return to port. In con-

"WHERE KNELT THE VANQUISHED FOE."
Spar deck of U. S. S. *Constitution*, 1931.

sequence of which I have determined to wait here for further information by post and shall take the liberty of sending home the Enterprise with every particular respecting the squadron. I am prompted to this measure, in consequence of the term of her crew having expired likewise that of this ship's company, which has occasioned some discontent and disturbance among them.'

This last interpretation was misleadingly mild, to say the least. Word of the *Chesapeake–Leopard* affair had spread quickly through the crew. It became increasingly evident that no relief ship would put in an appearance at any near date. A suppressed hum of excitement was noticeable. On all sides disappointment bordering on despair was seen in the faces of the crew—even of the old tried hands who had grown gray in the service. A veteran quarter-gunner, representing a body of the petty officers, came to the mast and respectfully presented the views of the crew, and inquired as to the prospects of an early release. Lieutenant Ludlow, who was justly popular with the crew, listened patiently and sympathetically to their grievance. He replied to the group with kind and soothing words, and appealed to their patriotism; but to no avail. He repaired to the Captain's cabin and said:

"There is no disguising the fact, Captain Campbell, the men are in an ugly frame of mind; and this affair of the *Chesapeake,* cutting off, as it does, all lingering hopes they have been clinging to, looking for a speedy recall and run on shore, after their long absence from home, has added fuel to the seditious sentiments smouldering in their breasts."

The Commanding Officer listened gravely and then said only a few words to the effect that he would get under way and go to sea the next morning. It was then that the crisis came.

The *Constitution* on that memorable day presented a scene of order, scrupulous neatness, and perfection of detail which ever characterized the famous frigate. At eight bells the drum rolled, the stars and stripes were hoisted and commenced to flutter aloft; a signal was made to the *Hornet:* "Prepare to get under way." This was followed by the call, "All hands unmoor ship!" Not a man of the crew stirred. There was not a move to ship and man the capstan bars. Captain Campbell was standing well aft but took in the situation at once. He directed the officers to assemble on the quarter-deck with all their side arms. Quickly but quietly he ordered Lieutenant Ludlow:

"Inform Mr. Armory that it is my order for him to parade the full marine guard on the quarter-deck and to have them provided with ball and cartridge. Have the two 12-pounders cleared away. Place them in a position to sweep the spar deck to port. Detail midshipmen for both pieces and see that a round or two of grape and canister is placed at hand for each. I believe that is all, sir!"

The order was quickly executed. Soon could be heard the tread of the armed marines nearing their post, Lieutenant Armory at their head. The guard was placed on the starboard side of the quarter-deck facing to port. Two senior midshipmen were put in charge of the 12-pounders. As soon as all were reported "present or accounted for," the order was given: "Pipe all hands aft to muster!"

Four hundred stalwart bronze-visaged seamen tramped aft in column of fours and ranged themselves on the port side of the quarter-deck. What must have been the emotions of Captain Campbell as he looked into the eyes of the crew—brave but misguided, he well knew—as he glanced from one to the other, realizing that a single false move meant an ineradicable stain on the deck of the famed ship.

At a sign from the Commanding Officer the midshipmen, in plain view of the crew, rammed home their charges, removed the leaden aprons, *and lighted their matches*. Swiftly came the order of the Marine Officer, "Load with ball cartridge!" The gravity and menace of the situation were impressed instantly on the mind of every man present —officer, sailor, and marine. Particularly were the crew impressed, observing that they were facing the muzzles of two loaded 12-pounders, burning matches in the hands of the midshipmen—these guns flanked by bristling bayonets fixed on the loaded muskets of the marines. This body of men, they knew, could be relied upon by the officers for loyal support and unswerving obedience to command.

"The boatswains and their mates, step forward" was the next order. This group advanced one step, saluted, and stood with their eyes riveted on the face of the Captain. The latter directed: "Mr. Ludlow, repeat the order to man the bars and get under way. Let the Boatswain and his mates pipe the men to perform that duty in the customary manner."

Then turning to the crew he said: "And now, my lads, for the peace and good will of all here assembled, I earnestly trust that there will be no further mutinous demonstrations coming from among you—no refusal of obedience to lawful commands. For, until you are regularly relieved from service—and I have good reasons for adding you will not be kept here much longer for what is your just due—obedience prompt and implicit, I say, must and will be enforced on the deck of this frigate. Let the sacrifice be what it may, the outcome now rests with you. There will be no further word from the quarter-deck."

Lieutenant Ludlow waved his trumpet and sang out in decided tones "All hands up anchor! To your stations, men!" Without a moment's hesitation the trills and notes from the boatswains' silver pipes pierced the air. Up went the hand of every man in respectful salute to the quarter-deck; away bounded the crew to their respective stations.

And so ended a most sinister situation, saved by a bit of masterly handling.

CHAPTER X

In and Out of the Lion's Mouth

THE *Constitution* was ordered home shortly after the near mutiny, the Mediterranean station being abandoned temporarily. A two-year overhaul in New York was followed by a cruise in home waters from 1809 to 1811. The ship was a member of the Northern Squadron and flew a commodore's flag the greater part of the time. In 1811 she was ordered to convey to France the new American Minister, Joel Barlow. After this duty was completed and before the ship reached home, a number of incidents occurred which were not on the program. Relations between the United States and Great Britain had been getting more and more strained as the years went by. The breaking point was fast approaching.

One of the missions of the *Constitution* during the cruise was that of carrying from France to England Mr. Jonathan Russell, another member of our Diplomatic Corps. The anchor was dropped at Portsmouth. As Dow says:[1]

'Here the spirit of impressment again reared its agitating form. While lying at anchor in the roads, a man jumped overboard, and swam with the tide to the British

[1] *Gentleman's Magazine,* September, 1839.

85

frigate Madagascar,[2] which vessel lay astern of the Constitution. The deserter was too much exhausted when first taken up to state his object, and the Englishman sent a boat to acquaint the commander of the Constitution that one of his men had been picked up by that ship while in a drowning condition. In the morning a cutter was sent from the Constitution to procure the man, but, upon reaching the Madagascar, the officer was informed that the man had claimed protection as an Englishman, and that he had been sent on board the guard ship.

'In the absence of captain Hull, Mr. Morris, the first lieutenant of the Constitution, sought an interview with sir Roger Curtis, the port admiral, and claimed the deserter. The admiral informed Mr. Morris that it was not in his power to give up a *deserter who claimed to be a British subject*. Mr. Morris asked the admiral if he had any evidence except the man's own word to satisfy him that he was an Englishman.

' "None whatever sir," said the swallow-tailed admiral; "but we are obliged to believe him."

'The officer therefore returned on board his ship empty-handed.

'That night, as the evening gun died away over the silent waters, the Constitution's crew were mustered, and after a minute inspection, the watch was set, and extra sentinels posted, with positive orders to fire at any thing that might be seen floating near the ship. About midnight all hands were roused by the hail of the sentinel, and the discharge of three muskets—and on inquiry, it was found

[2] *Madagascar* in error for *Havannah,* throughout.

that there was a man in the water close alongside. A boat was immediately lowered, and, upon its return, brought on board a seaman of the Madagascar's, who had contrived to buoy himself up on some shells of blocks, and profiting by a turn of the tide, to drift down to the Constitution. This man was asked what countryman he was, and he answered in a strong Irish accent, "An American, your honor." He was sent below, with orders to take good care of him.

'The next day the deserter was inquired after by the British commander, and it was intimated that as he had *declared himself an American* he could not be given up. It is believed, however, that no formal demand was made for the Irishman, though it was rumoured on shore that there would be trouble when the Constitution attempted to go to sea, as it was known that she was about to do that night.

'In the course of the day two frigates came and anchored near her; when, disliking his birth, the American commanding officer got under weigh, and dropped out about a mile to seaward. So close were the British ships at the time, that the pilot expressed his apprehension of getting foul of one of them—and he was told to go foul if he could do no better. By careful handling, however, the ship went clear. A frigate followed the Constitution to her new anchorage. About 8 o'clock, captain Hull, who was now on board, ordered the ship cleared for action. The battle-lanterns were lighted fore and aft, and the crew went to their quarters by beat of drum. It is not easy to portray the enthusiasm that existed in this noble ship;

every officer and man on board believing that the affair of
the Chesapeake was about to be repeated—so far, at least,
as the assault was concerned.   The manner in which the
men took hold of the gun-tackles has been described as if
they were about to jerk the guns through the ship's sides.
An officer, who was passing through the batteries, observed to the men that if there was an occasion to fight, it
would be in their quarrel, and that he expected good
service from them.

' "Let the quarter-deck look out for the colors, and we
will look out for the guns," was the answer.

'In short, it was not possible for a ship's company to be
in a better humor to defend the honor of the flag, when
the drum beat the retreat, and the boatswain piped the men
to the capstan bars.   Home came the yielding anchor to
the tune of Yankee Doodle—and the ship, casting to starboard, stood over to the French coast.'

At this point one Moses Smith takes up the story.   He
was a member of the *Constitution's* crew at the time and he
made a record of the events which took place while he was
aboard: [3]

'An English sloop-of-war came following us out of the
harbour.   About midnight she fired upon us.   We were
instantly summoned to quarters, and bore down for her.
Captain Hull hailed:

' "What sloop is that?"

'After receiving an answer, he ordered them to send a

---

[3] *Naval Scenes in the Last War* (War of 1812).   Reprinted in part
in the *Golden Book,* October, 1927, under the title "A Gunner on 'Old
Ironsides.' "

boat, which they did not dare to refuse.   Upon meeting their officer,

' "How dare you fire on us?" shouted Hull.

' "O!—we beg pardon," was the reply; "we mistook you for French."

' "French!   French!" retorted Hull; "you've been in sight all night, and yet can't tell who we are!   I've a good mind to sink you on the spot."

'They found themselves in rather bad hands, and were willing to get off the best way they could.   As soon as we let them off, they squared their yards, and made all sail out of our sight.

'It were such incidents constantly occurring between the navies of the two nations that served to hasten the existing grievances to a crisis, and resulted shortly afterwards in the declaration of war between England and the United States.

'We soon reached the French coast, and entered the harbour of Shireburg.[4]   As we passed up, with an English ship just under our lee, we were fired upon from the fort. The shot struck one of our boats, which were stowed amidships over the hatchway, and then lodged in the hammock nettings.   The Frenchmen soon came to make their apologies, however, saying, they mistook us for English, as we were so close in their company.   So the affair was soon adjusted.   The war then existing between France and England, thus caused us frequent trouble.

'Having duly landed Mr. Barlow, and then accomplished one principal object of our mission, we in a few days

[4] Shireburg for Cherbourg, throughout.

set sail for Holland, to fulfil another commission en-
trusted to us.[5]   That was, to pay to the Dutch a debt of
$28,000, for ammunition furnished us in the Revolution-
ary War.   We reached Texel, and there too the English
were hard by, trying to blockade the port, and to prevent
our landing the money, desirous perhaps of getting hold of
it themselves.   They knew that war was about to be declared with our country, and, it may be, indulged the hope
of soon taking the *Constitution,* money, and all.   But we
were too sharp for them altogether.

'We put the money on shore in the following style:

'When the Dutch boats came off to bring us our water,
we sent along the boats with the specie under cover of
those water-boats.   And since by the law of nations,
boats can never be molested in carrying water and provisions, the English dared not fire at the money craft, for
fear of hitting the others.   By this stratagem, we succeeded in landing all the money in proper shape, although
the creditors themselves, in fear of its being taken, had
advised us not to undertake it, but to wait and pay them at
some future day.

'Before we left, some British braggadocio tried to raise
a fuss with us and get us enraged, by accusing us of false
statements in reference to the draft of our ship.   We had
given it as twenty-four feet, whereas they said there were
but nineteen feet of water upon the bar when we came in.
In this way they hoped to make our craft appear more in-

----

[5] The correct itinerary was briefly: Cherbourg, Texel, Cherbourg,
Portsmouth, Cherbourg, and home. Moses Smith has it: Portsmouth,
Cherbourg, Texel, Cherbourg, and home.

significant than she was, and also create a disturbance between us and the Dutch authorities. But they did not
succeed; we came off with clean papers, and with flying
colours.

'From Texel we returned to Shireburg, and then set sail
for the United States. On our homeward passage, we
fell in with the *Royal Oak,* an English seventy-four. She
had been engaged in capturing and sinking a French
privateer. The captain appeared to feel very consequential after his exploit, and made us a visit in state.
He began to brag of his doings, and said he should serve
all Frenchmen after the same sort. He had run down
the d—n privateer, and sent her, with every soul on
board, to the bottom of the ocean! And he'd do it
again!

'He eyed us and our accoutrements pretty sharp. He
found our guns double-shotted, and every man at his post,
ready for action at a moment's warning. He soon
stopped his bragging, and as he glanced about, his looks
showed that he began to think somebody else *might* be
able to do something as well as he. And I reckon before
the year was out, his mind must have been settled upon
that point. He kept pretty silent, which doubtless was
the best course for him, and after a few salutations, he
returned to his own deck, and we went on our way.

'We arrived back at Annapolis about March, 1812, and
immediately ran up the Potomac as far as the water would
admit. We then took out all the guns and other heavy
articles, in order to lighten ship and so were enabled to
proceed to Washington.'

CHAPTER XI

"Will Live to Fight Another Day"

'June 20.' (1812) 'At 5 P.M. the Commanding Officer, Lieutenant Read, had the crew turned up, and read to them the declaration of war between the United States and the United Kingdoms of Great Britain and Ireland, that had passed the Senate and authorizing the President James Madison to employ the Armies and Navy of the United States against the above written powers. The Crew manifested their Zeal in Support of the Honor of the United States Flagg by requesting of leave to Cheer on the occasion (granted them). Crew returned to their duty, light airs from the Southward and Eastward.'

Thus did the log of the *Constitution* record the start of the War of 1812. The declaration was made on June 18. The ship had been refitting at the Washington Navy Yard for nearly three months. She got away on June 21 and dropped down the Potomac River to the deeper water near its mouth. Here it was possible to fill her up with ammunition and supplies, and to put back all of her guns.

Charles Morris, now a lieutenant, had been ordered to report to the *Constitution* for another tour of duty on board. Let us refer once more to his autobiography, for it describes splendidly the events of the succeeding days. Reaching Washington after his ship had sailed, he

'left the city in the afternoon, in a vessel taking stores
to the ship. I joined her near the mouth of the Potomac
on the 25th of June.

'The equipments of the ship were still very imperfect;
only a part of her guns were mounted, the complement of
men was greatly deficient, those on board were not yet
stationed, and, of course, were totally uninstructed in any
special duties. Captain Hull used all exertions to supply
the deficiency of men and stores, while the other officers
were unceasing in their efforts to complete the equipments,
and exercise and train the men to their various duties, but
more especially with the guns. The ship was taken opposite Annapolis for more convenient intercourse with
Baltimore and ports to the eastward, and on the 5th of
July we began to work down the bay, still continuing to
receive men and stores till we passed out to sea on the
12th of July.[1]

'The ship had been ordered to New York to meet and
join other vessels under the command of Commodore
Rodgers, and our course was directed accordingly. We
had proceded beyond the Delaware, but out of sight of the
land, when, on the afternoon of the 16th, we discovered
four vessels, at a great distance to the NW., and a single
ship to the NE., from which quarter a light wind was then
blowing. The wind changed to the southward about sunset, which brought us to windward, and we stood for the
ship, the wind being very light. The chase was evidently

[1] Cooper states that a hundred men joined her only the night before she
left Annapolis. *(History of the Navy of the United States of America.*
1839).

a frigate, and the first impression was that she might be a part of Commodore Rodgers's squadron.   By 11 P.M., we were within signal distance, and it was soon apparent she was not an American vessel of war.   There being no apprehension that a British frigate would make any attempt to avoid an engagement, Captain Hull felt justified in delaying any nearer approach till daylight of the 17th, when our newly-collected and imperfectly disciplined men would be less likely to be thrown into confusion.   The ship was accordingly brought to the wind with her head to the southward and westward, under easy sail, with a light wind from the NW.   The other ship did the same at about two miles distance.   The watch not on duty were allowed to sleep at their quarters, and the officers slept in the same manner.[2]   As the following morning opened upon us, it disclosed our companion of the night to be a large frigate just without gunshot, on the lee quarter, and a ship-of-the-line and three other frigates, a brig, and schooner, about two miles nearly astern, with all sails set standing for us, with English colors flying.[3]   All our sails were soon set, and the nearest frigate, fortunately for us, but without any apparent reason, tacked and immediately wore round again in chase, a maneuver that occupied some ten minutes, and allowed us to gain a distance, which,

---

[2] The stranger was the *Guerriere*.   It was fortunate that Hull decided to wait; even assuming that he had been victorious in a duel, he could not have escaped the rest of the British squadron.   The *Guerriere*, on her part, mistook her own consorts for Commodore Rodgers' ships.   She had been separated from them and they were then some distance to leeward.   Accordingly, she too kept away from the squadron for a time.

[3] *Guerriere*, 38; *Africa*, 64; *Shannon*, 38; *Belvidera*, 36; *Aeolus*, 32; U. S. Brig, *Nautilus*, a prize; and the schooner, another prize.

though short, proved to be of the utmost importance to our safety. By sunrise our ship was entirely becalmed and unmanageable, while the ships astern retained a light breeze till it brought three of the frigates so near that their shot passed beyond us. The distance was, however, too great for accuracy, and their shot did not strike our ship. Our boats were soon hoisted out, and the ship's head kept from the enemy, and exertions were made to increase our distance from them by towing. This, and occasional catspaws or slight puffs of wind, enabled us to prevent their closing, but as their means were equal to ours, we could gain nothing. A few guns were fired from our sternports, but so much rake had been given to the stern that the guns could not be used with safety, and their further use was relinquished. All means were adopted which seemed to promise any increase of speed. The hammocks were removed from the nettings, and the cloths rolled up to prevent their unfavorable action; several thousand gallons of water were started and pumped overboard, and all the sails kept thoroughly wet to close the texture of the canvas. While making all these exertions, our chances for escape were considered hopeless. For many years the ship had proved a very dull sailer, especially during the late cruise, and it was supposed that the first steady breeze would bring up such a force as would render resistance of no avail; and our situation seemed hopeless. At about 8 A.M., one of the frigates called all the boats of the squadron to her and, having arranged them for towing, furled all sails. This brought her towards us steadily and seemed to decide our fate.

Fortunately for us a light breeze filled our sails and sent us forward a few hundred yards, before her sails could be set to profit by it. With our minds excited to the utmost to devise means for escape, I happened to recollect that, when obliged by the timidity of my old commander, Cox, to warp the President in and out of harbors where others depended on sails, our practice had enabled us to give her a speed of nearly three miles an hour. We had been on soundings the day before, and on trying we now found twenty-six fathoms. This depth was unfavorably great, but it gave me confidence to suggest to Captain Hull the expediency of attempting to warp the ship ahead. He acceded at once, and in a short time (about 7 A.M.) the launch and first cutter were sent ahead with a kedge, and all the hawsers and rigging, from five inches and upward, that could be found, making nearly a mile of length. When the kedge was thrown the men hauled on the connecting hawser, slowly and carefully at first, till the ship was in motion, and gradually increasing until a sufficient velocity was given to continue until the anchor could again be taken ahead, when the same process was repeated. In this way the ship was soon placed out of the range of our enemy's guns, and by continued exertions when the wind failed, and giving every possible advantage to the sails when we had air enough to fill them, we prevented them from again closing very near us. The ship which we had first chased gained a position abeam of us about 9 A.M. and fired several broadsides, but the shot fell just short of us, and only served to enliven our men and excite their jocular comments. The exertions of neither party were

relaxed during this day or the following night. There
was frequent alternation of calms and very light winds
from the SE., which we received with our heads to the
southwestward. When the wind would give us more
speed than with warping and towing, the boats were run
up to their places, or suspended to the spars in the chains
by temporary tackles, with their crews in them, ready to
act again at a moment's notice. At daylight of the second
day, on the 18th, it was found that one frigate had gained
a position on our lee bow, two nearly abeam, and one on
the lee quarter about two miles from us, and the ship-of-
the-line, brig and schooner, three miles from us in the same
direction. The wind had now become tolerably steady,
though still light. The frigate on the lee bow tacked
about 4 A.M., and would evidently reach within gunshot if
we continued our course. This we were anxious to avoid,
as a single shot might cripple some spar and impede our
progress. If we tacked, we might be exposed to the
fire of the other frigate on the lee quarter; but as she was
a smaller vessel the risk appeared to be less, and we also
tacked soon.

'In passing the lee frigate at 5, we expected a broadside
or more, as we should evidently pass within gunshot; but,
from some unexplained cause, Lord James Townsend in
the Aeolus of 32 guns suffered us to pass quietly, and
tacked in our wake, while the others soon took the same
direction. We had now all our pursuers astern and on
the lee quarter, and as the wind was gradually increasing,
our escape must depend on our superiority of sailing, which
we had no reason to hope nor expect. Exertions, how-

ever, were not relaxed. The launch and first cutter, which we dared not lose, were hoisted on board at 6 A.M., under the directions of Captain Hull, with so little loss of time or change of sails that our watching enemies could not conceive what disposition was made of them. This we afterwards learned from Lieutenant Crane, who was a prisoner in their squadron.' [4] (In the course of the morning a ship was sighted some distance to windward. She was supposed to be an American merchantman. The British ships hoisted American colors in order to trap her. The *Constitution* warned her off by displaying the British flag.) 'The sails were kept saturated with water, a set of sky-sails was made and set, and all other sails set and trimmed to the greatest advantage, close by the wind.[5] The ship directly astern gained slowly but gradually till noon; though, as the wind increased, our good ship was going at that time at the unexpected rate of ten knots an hour. At noon we had the wind abeam and as it gradually freshened, we began to leave our fleet pursuer. Our ship had reached a speed of twelve and a half knots by 2 P.M. Our hopes began to overcome apprehension, and cheerfulness was more apparent among us.

'Though encouraged we were by no means assured, as all the ships were still near and ready to avail themselves of any advantage that might offer. About 6 P.M., a squall of wind and rain passed over us, which induced us to take in our light sails before the rain covered us from

[4] The commander of the captured *Nautilus*.
[5] A very valuable contribution to the evidence as to sky-sails on the *Constitution*.

the view of the enemy; but most of them were soon re-placed as the wind moderated. When the rain had passed, we had evidently gained a mile or more during its continuance. Still the pursuit was continued and our own ship pressed forward to her utmost speed. The officers and men again passed the night at quarters. At daylight, on the morning of the 19th, our enemies had been left so far astern that danger from them was con-sidered at an end, and at 8 A.M., they at last relinquished the chase and hauled their wind. Our officers and crew could now indulge in some rest, of which the former had taken little for more than sixty hours.'

Said Captain Hull: "Now we'll take a cruise by our-selves; but if I come across one of those chaps alone, depend on it he shall pay for this."

CHAPTER XII

A GUNNER ON *"Old Ironsides"*

HERE Moses Smith's commentary is of great value. At battle quarters he was the sponger of No. 1 gun. His *Naval Scenes in the Last War* is probably the only extant document written by an enlisted man which covers the capture of the *Guerriere*—an event so vital in the history not only of our navy but of our entire country.

So, after the escape from the British squadron:

'We turned our cruise toward Boston, meeting with merchant vessels occasionally. One of them—bound to New York—we saved by giving notice of the blockade there. The captain presented us with a puncheon of rum for our information; and we presented him our wishes for his safe arrival in return. Rum was then more thought of on board our men-of-war than is now considered profitable.

'In a few days we arrived in Boston, where we met the news that we had been captured by the enemy! It was said we had not ammunition enough. But if those who thought so had remained at our quarters until our ammunition was all gone, they would probably have altered their opinion. We had enough, at least, to tire them "some."

'At Boston we obtained more men, wood and water; and were soon under way on another cruise. We met a number of merchant-men. Those of them that belonged to the enemy we set on fire, taking the crews with us as prisoners of war.

'On the seventh day out from Boston, we met with some of the enemy. It was in the month of August, toward night. The ocean was soon shrouded in darkness. As the night came on, I think I never saw it darker.

'At a late hour a vessel hove in sight, close aboard of us. We thought we saw a light in her cabin; but it proved to be a floating beacon which she had thrown overboard for the purpose of putting us on the wrong track. But we passed this dancing lantern in her wake, and steered directly for the ship. We kept her in view all night; and the next morning she proved to be the *Ranger,* a British sloop-of-war. It was not long before we were in her wake, and steering straight into her stern. On the way, we passed a large Dutch barque, that put new mettle into our speed. She had been taken under English colours by an American privateer, and retaken by the British, being then in charge of the *Ranger*. The American officers and men had not been taken out—so close were we upon them. The *Ranger* had concluded to let go this prize, and make good her own escape; but another large vessel, loaded with hemp and rosin, was set fire to before we could come up, and burnt to the water's edge.

'We soon boarded and took possession of the barque. From her we learned that the *Ranger* had taken another prize, then on the way to Halifax. We ran down toward the *Ranger,* ordering the barque to follow but she refused to do it. We immediately left her to her fate, and stretched away to leeward for the other prize. It took but little time to overhaul her. Captain Hull was on the deck at the time.

' "Load the long Tom," said he, "and give them some."

'No answer.

' "Closer!" cried Hull. "Fire closer!"

'The next shot did the work. Her colours came down, and she rounded to. It was well she did, for a few more shots such as the last would have made it all day with her.

'We took possession in the name of the Stars and Stripes, and soon had the prisoners all out of her, and on board the frigate. She was then manned to send in. Midshipman Madison was put on board as prize-master, with orders to take her to the nearest American port. But she was afterwards taken by the Acasta frigate, carried to England, and the captured thrown into that horrible place, Dartmoor Prison.

'We continued our cruise, taking an occasional vessel from the enemy, and setting her on fire. Many a fine large ship was thus destroyed by the *Constitution.* But we always saved the crews, and living animals. I do not remember that a goat, dog, fowl, or cat was thus burnt up.

'At eleven o'clock on the night of the 18th of August, 1812, a brig hove in sight. It was very foggy, and we were unable to make out what she was. As we came up, Captain Hull hailed her himself:

' "What brig's that?"

' "The *John,* of St. John's."

' "Where are you bound?"

' "Halifax."

' "Come under our lee. We'll send a boat aboard."

'Lieutenant Morris boarded her. A boy of theirs, whom we had brought over from France, was heard to cry out:

' "The old *Constitution!*"

' "Away with your nonsense, lad," said one of the men in reply.

' "You'll find out it is," added the boy. "Don't you see the eagle buttons?"

'Lieutenant Morris had now reached the deck of the *John.* Her captain had ordered his state-room shut, and thrown his guns and cutlasses overboard, supposing us to be enemies. But the room was soon opened again, and our men had what they pleased. This vessel laid by us all night, and proved to be a Baltimore privateer. She had been chased all day by the *Guerrière;* and was afraid of us, on account of the fog.

'The weather had now cleared up; and as we had learned by this adventure something of the whereabouts of the *Guerrière,* we were anxious to be off for her. But our Baltimore-Halifax neighbour had sprung his main-top-mast in trying to get away from us,—we supplied him with a new one, and a quantity of muskets, cutlasses, and ruffles for the enemy's wrists.

'Having learned which way the *Guerrière* was steering when last seen, we crowded all sail in that direction. We steered a northeast course for several hours, until the morning of the 19th of August, 1812. This was the day of the battle.

'We now changed our course, and steered south-east, with a good breeze. At ten o'clock, A. M., the lookout cried:

' "Sail ho!"

' "Where away?" inquired the lieutenant in command.

' "Two points off the larboard bow, sir!" was the reply.

'Hull had now come on deck. His first order was to a midshipman:

' "Mr. German! take the glass and go aloft. See if you can make out what she is."

'German was soon above us, looking intently in the direction named.

' "What do you think?" asked Hull, with animation.

' "She's a great vessel, sir! Tremendous sails."

' "Never mind," coolly added Hull. "You can come down, sir. Mr. Adams," addressing another officer, "call all hands. Make sail for her!"

'But before all hands could be called, there was a general rush on deck. The word had passed like lightning from man to man; and all who could be spared, came flocking up like pigeons from a net bed. From the spar deck to the gun deck, from that to the berth deck, every man was roused and on his feet. All eyes were turned in the direction of the strange sail, and quick as thought studding-sails were out, fore and aft. The noble frigate fairly bounded over the billows, as we gave her a rap full, and spread her broad and tall wings to the gale.

'The stranger hauled his wind, and laid to for us. It

was evident that he was an English man-of-war, of a large class, and all ready for action. In one of her topsails we read these words:

"NOT THE LITTLE BELT"

'We understood this to mean that the ship we were now approaching was not the *Little Belt* which had been previously attacked. But we knew that very well; and subsequent events proved that they might have saved themselves the trouble of telling us of it. We saw it was the vessel we wanted to meet, not the *Little Belt,* but the big *Guerrière,* of thirty-nine guns.

'As we came up she began to fire. They were evidently trying to rake us. But we continued on our course, tacking and half-tacking, taking good care to avoid being raked. We came so near on one tack, that an eighteen-pound shot came through us under the larboard knighthead, striking just abaft the breech of the gun to which I belonged. Splinters flew in all directions; but no one was hurt. We immediately picked up the shot, and put it in the mouth of long Tom, a large gun loose on deck—and sent it home again, with our respects.

'Another stray shot hit our foremast, cutting one of the hoops in two. But the mast was not otherwise injured, and the slight damage was soon repaired.

'Hull was now all animation. He saw that the decisive moment had come. With great energy, yet calmness of manner, he passed around among the officers and men, addressing to them words of confidence and encouragement.

' "Men!" said he, "now do your duty. Your officers

cannot have entire command over you now. Each man must do all in his power for his country."

'At this moment a man was killed on our spar deck. He had run away from us, and was only returned about a fortnight. He fell by the side of long Tom, and never rose again.

'Hull now determined on closing with the enemy.

' "Why don't you fire?" said he.

' "We can't get our guns to bear, as she now lies," was the answer.

' "Never mind, my boys!" said he to the men. "You shall have her as close as you please. Sailing-master! lay her alongside!"

'We came up into the wind in gallant style. As we fell off a little the *Guerrière* ranged by us her whole length.

'The stars and stripes never floated more proudly than they did at that moment. All was silent beneath them, save the occasional order from an officer, or the low sound of the movement of our implements of war. Every man stood firm at his post.

' "No firing at random!" cried Hull in a subdued tone of voice. "Let every man look well to his aim."

'This was the pride of American seamen. Correctness in taking aim did more than anything else in securing the naval victories of the last war.

'A shot from the enemy now struck the spar deck, and word was passed that a man was killed.

'The long Tom had been capsized, and Ike Kingman got a hoist. But jumping up, with a slap of the hand he said to himself, "take that."

' "Now close with them!" cried Hull, raising his voice to its sternest note of command, so that it could be heard on the enemy's decks.

' "Alongside with her, sailing-master!"

'A whole broadside from our guns followed this command. The *Constitution* shook from stem to stern. Every spar and yard in her was on a tremble. But no one was hurt by the recoil of the guns, though several were made deaf by the noise. We instantly followed the thunder of our cannon with three loud cheers, which rang along the ship like the roar of waters, and floated away rapidly to the ears of the enemy.

'This was a Yankee style which the British had not adopted. The English officers often spoke of it to ours, after the war was over. They said they were astonished at the spirit of our men in the toil and heat of the battle. Amid the dying and the dead, the crash of timbers, the flying of splinters and falling of spars, the American heart poured out its patriotism with long and loud cheers. The effect was always electrical, throughout all the struggle for our rights.

'When the smoke cleared away after the first broadside, we saw that we had cut off the mizzen mast of the *Guerrière,* and that her main-yard had been shot from the slings. Her mast and rigging were hanging in great confusion over her sides, and dashing against her on the waves.

'This discovery was followed by cheers from the *Constitution,* and the cry;

' "Huzza, boys! We've made a brig of her! Next time we'll make her a sloop!"

'On board the *Guerrière* was an American, by the name of Ben Hodges. As the battle commenced he appealed to the captain:

' "That is an American frigate," said he; "and I cannot fight against my country."

'How different this from the course of many an Englishman during the war! It was a feeling which the commander of the *Guerrière* respected.

' "Go below, my man," said he. "Go into the cockpit. You may be of assistance there."

'Hodges obeyed the order. As he stood by one of the surgeons, a voice said:

' "I don't see that we've much to do, after all."

' "Hold on a bit, sir," responded Hodges. "The Yankees haven't begun it. I'm thinking, sir, you'll have plenty to do."

'This was just as the action was commencing. In a moment a red glare followed.

' "There!" cried Ben. "They've begun. Now, look out." He had hardly spoken before fifteen or twenty wounded men were tumbled into the cockpit.

' "Your words were true enough, Ben," said one of the surgeons as he took up a knife. "Here's work for us— and plenty of it, too."

'The *Guerrière* returned our fire with spirit—but it passed too high, and spent its force among our light spars, rigging and sails. Our fore-royal truck was shot away, with two pair of halyards; the flag was hanging down tangled on the shivered mast in the presence of the enemy. This sight inspired one of our men, familiarly called Dan

"WE'VE MADE A BRIG OF HER!"

The Constitution smashes the *Guerriere's* mizzenmast.

Hogan, to the daring feat of nailing the standard to the mast. He was a little Irish chap, but brim-full of courage. Without a word from anyone, he sprang into the rigging and was aloft in a moment. He was soon seen, under the fire of the enemy, who saw him too, at the topmast height, clinging on with one hand, and with the other making all fast, so that the flag could never come down unless the mast came with it. The smoke curled around him as he bent to the work; but those who could see him, kept cheering him through the sulphury clouds. He was soon down again, and at his station in the fight.

'Several shot now entered our hull. One of the largest the enemy could command struck us, but the plank was so hard it fell out and sank in the waters. This was afterwards noticed, and the cry arose:

' "Huzza! Her sides are made of iron! See where the shot fell out!"

'From that circumstance the name of the *Constitution* was garnished with the familiar title:

"OLD IRONSIDES"

'By this title she is known around the world.

'Very soon after the battle commenced, Lieutenant Bush fell, mortally wounded. Lieutenant Morris received a wound in his chest; but he bore himself bravely through until we won the day. Lieutenant Wardsworth came nobly forward, and filled the place made vacant by death with great honour to himself and advantage to the ship.

'The braces of both ships were now shot off. The *Guerrière* swung round into our mizzen rigging, so that a part of her laid right over our taffrail. One might see the whites of the eyes, and count the teeth of the enemy. Our stern guns were pouring in upon them, so that we raked the ship fore and aft. Every shot told well. In a few moments the foremast was gone, and our prediction was fulfilled. The great *Guerrière* had become a sloop. Soon after the mainmast followed, rendering her a complete wreck. In the fall of the masts some of our boats were swept off, but the *Constitution* herself was hardly touched, except in some of the yards and sails. Both ships kept firing constantly—our guns continuing to do the most fearful execution.

'One of the lieutenants now asked the captain if he should call the boarders.

' "No!" replied Hull. "No! We can take her without losing so many lives."

'The enemy seemed to have been expecting us to board him. He had placed two carronades on the bowsprit, in such a manner as to sweep off our men as they should attempt to board. These were loaded to the muzzle with musket balls in canvas bags, and would have cut us down like a flock of sheep. . . . I heard the powder-boy nearest me on board the *Guerrière* call to another:

' "Work away, there! Huzza! She'll soon be ours!"

'The women they had with them were engaged in passing powder, and other munitions of war. Amid such activity on the decks of the enemy, courage and prudence demanded that we should be active on our own.

'As an intended insult, the English had hoisted a puncheon of molasses on their main stay, and sent out word:

' "Do give the Yankees some switchel. They will need it, when they are our prisoners."

'But we made a very different use of this molasses from what they intended. Our shooting at hogsheads in the Chesapeake Bay, was now turned to good account. We soon tapped their sweet stuff for them, in a way which they little thought of. The Yankee shot tasted the English molasses, and not the Yankee lips. We made the decks of the *Guerrière* so slippery, that her men could hardly stand! They had more switchel prepared for them than they knew what to do with.

'The action was now nearly at its close. The firing had become less frequent on both sides. All felt the necessity of proceeding at once to repair damages. But we dared not trust the enemy. Notwithstanding his disabled condition, it was evident he would attack us again, the first opportunity. His men were still numerous— his ammunition was but partly spent, and his guns had been cleared away from the lower decks, so as to work to the best advantage. . . .

'We were preparing for an attack in another quarter, when the *Guerrière* suddenly dropped to the leeward, and fired a gun for assistance.'

Meanwhile let us view the battle briefly from the enemy ship. An American merchant skipper, William B. Orne, tells the story in his diary: [1]

'I commanded the American brig Betsey, in the year 1812, and was returning home from Naples, Italy, to

[1] Quoted in Coggeshall's *History of the American Privateers;* 1856.

Boston. When near the western edge of the Grand Bank of Newfoundland, on the 10th of August, 1812, I fell in with the British frigate Guerriere, Captain Dacres, and was captured by him. Myself and a boy were taken on board of the frigate; the remainder of my officers and men were left in the Betsey, and sent into Halifax, N. S., as a prize to the Guerriere. On the 19th of the same month, when in latitude 41° 41′ North, longitude about 55° 40′ West, the wind being fresh from the northward, the Guerriere was under double-reefed topsails during all the forenoon of this day. At two P.M., we discovered a large sail to windward, bearing about North from us. We soon made her out to be a frigate. She was steering off from the wind, with her head to the Southwest, evidently with the intention of cutting us off as soon as possible. Signals were soon made by the Guerriere, but as they were not answered, the conclusion of course was, that she was either a French or an American frigate. Captain Dacres appeared anxious to ascertain her character, and after looking at her for that purpose, handed me his spy-glass, requesting me to give him my opinion of the stranger. I soon saw from the peculiarity of her sails, and from her general appearance, that she was, without doubt, an American frigate, and communicated the same to Captain Dacres. He immediately replied, that he thought she came down too boldly for an American, but soon after added: "The better he behaves, the more honor we shall gain by taking him."

'The two ships were rapidly approaching each other, when the Guerriere backed her main-topsail, and waited for her opponent to come down, and commence the action. He then set an English flag at each mast-head, beat to quarters, and made ready for the fight. When the strange frigate came down to within two or three miles distance, he hauled upon the wind, took in all his light sails, reefed his topsails, and deliberately prepared for action. It was now about five o'clock in the afternoon, when he filled away and ran down for the Guerriere. At this moment, Captain Dacres politely said to me: "Captain Orne, as I suppose you do not wish to fight against your own countrymen, you are at liberty to go below the water-line." It was not long after this before I retired from the quarter-deck to the cock-pit; of course I saw no more of the action until the firing ceased, but I heard and felt much of its effects; for soon after I left the deck, the firing commenced on board the Guerriere, and was kept up almost constantly until about six o'clock, when I heard a tremendous explosion from the opposing frigate.[2] The effect of her shot seemed to make the Guerriere reel, and tremble as though she had received the shock of an earth-quake. Immediately after this, I heard a tremendous crash on deck, and was told that the mizzen-mast was shot away. In a few moments afterward, the cock-pit was filled with wounded men. At about half-past six o'clock in the evening, after the firing had ceased, I went on deck, and there beheld a scene which it would be difficult to describe: all the Guerriere's masts were shot away, and as she had no sails to steady her, she lay rolling like a log in the trough of the sea. Many of the men were employed

[2] The *Constitution's* first full broadside, no doubt.

in throwing the dead overboard. The decks were covered with blood, and had the appearance of a butcher's slaughter-house; the gun tackles were not made fast, and several of the guns got loose, and were surging to and fro from one side to the other.

'Some of the petty officers and seamen, after the action, got liquor, and were intoxicated; and what with the groans of the wounded, the noise and confusion of the enraged survivors of the ill-fated ship, rendered the whole scene a perfect hell.'

And now Moses Smith finishes the tale:

'We sent a boat on board, but could get no satisfaction. His colours were down—but still there was danger of his attacking us unawares. This inspired a determined spirit on board the *Constitution*.

' "Let's sink them!" was the cry that ran along our decks—for we felt that we were deceived.

'At this moment Captain Dacres appeared in one of our boats, and immediately surrendered himself as a prisoner of war. We did not have any switchel prepared for him as he came on board, because we thought he had had enough already. The delivery of his sword to Hull by Dacres was a scene never to be forgotten by those who witnessed it.

'As he placed the hilt in the hand of Hull, his first remark was:

' "Captain Hull! what have you got for men?"

' "O," replied Hull, with a sly smile, "only a parcel of green bush-whackers, Captain Dacres!"

' "Bush-whackers! They are more like tigers than men. I never saw men fight so. They fairly drove us from our quarters."

'We remained by the *Guerrière* all night. The prisoners were taken out and humanely disposed of. We immediately set ourselves at work, repairing damages. Two anchor stocks welded on the foremast, that had been injured by the stray shot, made that as good as new. In one hour's time, we had the gallant frigate as trim as she was when the fight began. But it was not so with the *Guerrière*. The Yankee wounds made in her sides were incurable. She was kept afloat near us, but with six feet of water in her hold. Lieutenant Reed had command. The prisoners were set at the pumps, but they could not all keep her free. She was soon reported to be in a sinking condition, and we hastened to get all the men out of her.

'Some of the captives came on board of us very badly wounded. Their sufferings were greater than can be described, or even imagined. One poor fellow had his under jaw shot off; and while we were watching him, he bled to death. Others, deprived of arms and legs, lingered in the greatest torture, until death put an end to their pains.

'There was one of our men—Dick Dunn—who bore the amputation of his leg with a fortitude I shall always bear in mind. "You are a hard set of butchers," was all he said to the surgeon, as his torn and bleeding limb was severed from his body. Others, whom I could name, bore their amputations equally well. Some of these brave de-

fenders of the nation are among my friends; and I sometimes meet them stumping it through life. In the midst
of all this suffering, Captain Hull was frequently found
tendering the consolations needed in such an hour, and
showing his humanity to the best advantage. He even
looked more truly noble, bending over the hammock of a
wounded tar, than when invading and conquering the
enemy.

'In spite of all the efforts to keep her afloat, we now
saw that the *Guerrière* was rapidly sinking. A council of
war was held on board the *Constitution,* and the decision
was that she should be blown up. It was a moment of
the deepest interest. After removing every thing thought
necessary to be saved, we put a slow match to the magazine, and left her.

'There was something melancholy and grand in the
sight. Although the frigate was a wreck, floating about
a mastless hulk at the sport of the waves, she bore marks
of her former greatness. Much of her ornamental work
had been untouched; and her long, high, black sides rose
in solitary majesty before us, as we bade her farewell.
For years she had been the house of thousands of human
beings; for years she had withstood the shocks of the
winds, the billows and the battle; for years she had borne
the insignia of English valour to different and distant
climes. But her years were now ended; her course was
run; she was about to sink into the deep ocean forever.

'Captain Dacres stood by our taffrail as we squared
away from the *Guerrière*. He seemed to brush away a

tear from his dark eye, as he took the last look of the vessel he had so lately commanded. But whatever may have been his feelings, it must be admitted that he had done his own duty well—and his men had defended their vessel to the last.

'At the distance of about three miles we hove to, and awaited the result. Hundreds of eyes were stretched in that one direction, where the ill-fated *Guerrière* moved heavily on the deep. It was like waiting for the uncapping of a volcano—or the bursting up of a crater. Scarcely a word was spoken on board the *Constitution,* so breathless was the interest felt in the scene.

'The first intimation we had that the fire was at work was the discharge of the guns. One after another, as the flame advanced, they came booming toward us. Roar followed roar, flash followed flash, until the whole mass was enveloped in clouds of smoke. We could see but little of the direct progress of the work, and therefore we looked more earnestly for the explosion—not knowing how soon it might occur. Presently there was a dead silence; then followed a vibratory, shuddering motion, and streams of light, like streaks of lightning running along the sides; and the grand crash came! The quarter deck, which was immediately over the magazine, lifted in a mass, broke into fragments, and flew in every direction. The hull, parted in the center by the shock, and loaded with such masses of iron and spars, reeled, staggered, plunged forward a few feet, and sank out of sight.

'It was a grand and awful scene. Nearly every floating thing around her went down with the *Guerrière*. Scarcely a vestige remained to tell the world that such a frigate had ever swept the seas. We immediately squared away, and were again under a crowd of sail for our native land.' [3]

[3] See Appendix A for ammunition expenditure of the *Constitution*.

CHAPTER XIII

H. B. M. S. *Java* is Smashed

THE *Constitution* sailed into Massachusetts Bay August 29, 1812, ten days after her victory over the *Guerriere;* she dropped anchor off Rainsford Island where quarantine was maintained at that time. All her troubles seemed to be over, at least for the time being. As Captain Hull said: 'Thinking myself safe in port, I told my officers to let the men wash their clothes and get the ship in order to go to Boston; and being excessively fatigued, went to my stateroom. I was sound asleep when a lieutenant rushed down, exclaiming, "Captain Hull, the British are upon us! an armed fleet is entering the harbor!" No agreeable intelligence, certainly, for I was wholly unprepared to engage with a superior force. But determined to sell our lives as dearly as possible, I gave orders to clear the deck for action, weigh anchor, and get ready for immediate action. I confess I was greatly relieved when I saw the American flag and recognized Rodgers.'

It was indeed Commodore Rodgers' squadron, the search for which, more than six weeks before, had led Hull so near to capture. Now these ships were present to join the celebration.

The destruction of the *Guerriere* wrought a most astounding effect on the populace of each nation concerned. Britain received the news with dismay and chagrin which bordered on the ludicrous. Americans were electrified. Hopelessness was dispelled by the realization that Great Britain could be coped with successfully *on the sea!* There was no more thought of giving up the fight—perhaps even of resuming subordination to British sovereignty. There was a further pleasing touch: the *Guerriere* had aroused possibly the greatest amount of hatred of all the ships engaged in the impressment of American seamen and interference with neutral trade.

Captain Hull, already rich in renown, gave up his command in order that another might gain some of the honors which the *Constitution* seemed continually to reap. Captain William Bainbridge took over the ship—now *"Old Ironsides"*—and became Commodore of a small squadron including the frigate *Essex* and the sloop-of-war *Hornet*. He never did come up with the *Essex*. He sailed from Boston, with the *Hornet* in company, on October 26, 1812. On December 13, however, he left her at San Salvador, Brazil, where, for six weeks, he blockaded the British sloop *Bonne Citoyenne*. The *Constitution* went off on a cruise by herself and on December 29 was lucky enough to fall in with His Majesty's Frigate *Java*, bound for the East Indies.

The result of the ensuing engagement was another smashing one-sided victory for the American. As in the duel with the *Guerriere,* the winner was somewhat the stronger ship. The overwhelming margin of each victory was, however, many times greater than can be at-

COMMODORE WILLIAM BAINBRIDGE.

His bad luck changed when he took over the *Constitution* for he captured
the *Java* three months later.

tributed to any physical differences. Let us read the official British report of the fight:

'United States Frigate "Constitution."
'Off San Salvador, December 31, 1812.

'Sir,—It is with deep regret that I write you that His Majesty's ship "Java" is no more, after entertaining an action on the 29th inst., for several hours, with the American frigate "Constitution," which resulted in the capture and ultimate destruction of His Majesty's ship. Captain Lambert being dangerously wounded in the height of the action, the melancholy task of writing the details devolves on me.

'On the 29th inst., at 8 A.M., off San Salvador (coast of Brazil), the wind at northeast, we perceived a strange sail; made all sail in chase, and soon made her out to be a large frigate; at noon prepared for action, the chase not answering our private signals, and tacking towards us under easy sail; when about four miles distant she made a signal, and immediately tacked and made all sail upon the wind. We soon found we had the advantage of her in sailing, and came up with her fast, when she hoisted American colors; she then bore about three points on the lee bow. At fifty minutes past one P.M. the enemy shortened sail, upon which we bore down upon her; at ten minutes past two, when about half a mile distant, she opened her fire by giving us her larboard broadside, which was not returned till we were close on her weather-bow. Both ships now manoeuvred to obtain advantageous positions, our opponent evidently avoiding close action, and firing high to disable our masts, in which she succeeded too well, having shot away the head of our bowsprit, with the jib-boom and our running rigging so much cut as to prevent our reaching the weather-gauge.

'At five minutes past three our gallant captain received a dangerous wound in the breast, and was carried below; from this time we could not fire more than two or three guns, until a quarter-past four, when our mizzen-mast was shot away; then fell off a little, and brought many of our starboard guns to bear; the enemy's rigging was so much cut that he could not avoid shooting ahead, which brought us fairly broadside and broadside. Our mainyard now went in the slings; both ships continued engaged in this manner till thirty-five minutes past four, we frequently on fire in consequence of the wreck lying on the side engaged. Our opponent now made sail ahead out of gun-shot, where he remained an hour repairing his damages, leaving us an unmanageable wreck, with only the mainmast left, and that tottering. Every exertion was made by us during this interval to place the ship in a state to renew the action. We succeeded in clearing the wreck of our masts from the guns, a sail was set on the stump of the foremast and bowsprit, the weather half of the mainyard remaining aloft; the main-tack was got forward in the hope of getting the ship before the wind, our helm being still perfect; the effort unfortunately proved ineffectual, from the mainmast falling over the side, from the heavy rolling of the ship, which nearly covered the whole of our starboard guns. We still waited the attack of the enemy, he now standing towards us for that purpose. On his coming within hail of us, and, from his manoeuvres, perceiving he intended a position ahead, where he could rake us, without a possibility of our returning a shot, I then consulted the officers, who agreed with myself that our having a great part of our crew killed and wounded, our bowsprit and three masts gone, several guns useless, we should not be justified in wasting the lives of more of those remaining, who, I hope their lordships and the country will think, have bravely defended His Majesty's ship. Under these circumstances, however reluctantly, at fifty minutes past five, our colors were lowered from the stump of the mizzen-mast, and we were taken possession of a little after six by the American frigate "Constitution," commanded by Commodore Bainbridge, who immediately after ascertaining the state of the ship resolved upon burning her, which we had the satisfaction of seeing done as soon as the wounded men were removed. . . .

'I cannot conclude this letter without expressing my grateful acknowledgements, thus publicly, for the generous treatment Captain Lambert and his officers have experienced from his gallant enemy, Commodore Bainbridge and his officers.

'I have the honor to be your respectful servant,
'Hy. D. Chads.'

Bainbridge landed his prisoners at San Salvador, the lot including a very heavy number of wounded.

An hour after the *Java* had hauled down her flag the *Constitution* was again in perfect fighting and cruising trim. The Commodore, however, felt that his ship was in great need of a general overhaul so he set sail for Boston. The victors arrived February 27, 1813, and received another tremendous ovation from the multitudes. Although nearly two months had elapsed since the battle, no word of this latest conquest had preceded the frigate to the States any more than in the case of the *Guerriere*.

Captain Horatio Smith, in his story of the ship, tells of the following aftermath of the battle: [1]

'Among the crew who received a generous amount of prize-money was a thrifty seaman, who, in the merchant service, had often commanded coasters and crafts destined for more extensive voyages. His name was Samuel Watson, and Cape Cod was his native place. He had served his country faithfully, and knew every good and bad point in "Old Ironsides" as thoroughly as Bainbridge himself. He had passed through the memorable "chase," had witnessed Dacres surrender the "Guerrière," had trained his favorite thirty-two on the trim, jaunty "Java," and with the striking of *her* flag felt that he could retire with honor in favor of a younger, but certainly not a braver, man.

'From the proceeds of his prize-money he purchased at Kittery a fine little craft adapted for the fishing business, and, shipping a crew, set sail in good time for the Grand Banks. He had scarcely got well to work hauling in the cod when an English corvette, under cover of the fog, came suddenly upon the American craft. There was no time or opportunity to run. The guns of the man-of-war were ready to let fly their contents, while clouds of canvas hung

---

[1] *United Service Magazine,* November, 1891.

"SHALL FEEL THE VICTOR'S TREAD."

The *Java* destroyed by the *Constitution*. *From the painting by Carlton T. Chapman.*

from her heavy yards. Ten minutes later a prize crew and master were on board, while skipper Watson, having nothing to do, gloomily watched the movements of the English sailors, inwardly praying that the "Constitution" might put in an appearance. But she didn't, and the prize schooner was hauled by the wind, her destination being Port Midway Harbor. Fearing that the Yankee tars might find a way of recapturing the vessel, the lieutenant in charge took effective measures to swamp any such hopes that might have been entertained. The schooner was run high and dry on the beach, stripped of sails and rigging, and then the masts unstepped and rolled above high-water-mark.

' "That's a rather neat job, Captain Watson," said the commanding officer, addressing the glum master, who was seated on the taffrail surveying what there was left of his unfortunate investment.

' "Taking into consideration how few men I had, and the disadvantages we labored under, did you ever know of a vessel to be stripped more quickly?" The old man-of-war's man had recognized in the prize-master one of the young officers of the "Java," but through prudential reasons had kept his secret. He now saw an opportunity to get even with his captor, and his sunburnt, weather-beaten countenance brightened up a bit. "Wal, leftenant," said he, "ye have done it purty well for Britishers, but I have a faint recollection of helpin' to do a better job. I helped, not so very long ago, to strip a ship,—a full-rigged ship,—and we beat your time by considerable. Let me see; you've been over two hours. We weren't over *half an hour* [2] on that job; and mind you, we not only took out her three masts, but we ripped away her bowsprit too." "Impossible, Captain Watson; it could not have been done." "But it was." "Then, sir, it must have been one of your well-known Yankee tricks." "Wal," replied Watson, with a grin of satisfaction, "that's what you thought it was at the time, I reckon. *You were thar.* I speak of the time when Commodore Bainbridge, on board the Yankee frigate "Constitution," fell in with the British "Java," Captain Lambert. Perhaps you recollect about how long we were in stripping that ship." '

Another sidelight of the battle: some of the mail taken from the *Java* was first opened (by the U. S. Navy Department) in the spring of 1926!

[2] The duration of the real part of the *Guerriere* battle rather than the *Java* engagement.

CHAPTER XIV

A DOUBLE VICTORY AND ANOTHER ESCAPE

"Old Ironsides" spent ten months of 1813 over-hauling at Boston. On New Year's Day, 1814, she put to sea under Captain Charles Stewart, looking for new laurels. She met with little success, however, for some time. The 14-gun schooner *Pictou* was taken on February 14. On February 23, however, the frigate *Pique* eluded capture. Her commander was one of those ordered to stay away from American ships of the strength of the *Constitution*. He made good his escape during the dark rainy night which terminated the day of pursuit.

On April 3, when nearing home, our ship was spied by two British frigates and had to throw overboard a goodly amount of stores in order to make a clean get-away. The port of Salem could have been made easily without this loss, but no competent pilot was available to negotiate the channel. Marblehead was the harbor finally attained. Divine service was being held in a church nearby. The minister was about to mount the pulpit to deliver his sermon when he received word that the *Constitution* was being chased and was in danger of capture. He rose at once to the occasion by saying: "The congregation is dismissed; let us all hasten to the aid of *'Old Ironsides.'*

Sermons can be heard any day, but the dear old *Constitution* can be saved only once in a lifetime." Whereupon he led his flock to the rescue!

The frigate soon slipped into Boston without difficulty but, this time, the getting out was not so easy. The British no longer had any hopes of secession or of serious defection on the part of the New England states and had started to put real pressure on them. The blockade was stiffened up until it was quite effective. Stewart did not succeed in getting out to sea again until December 18.

This time the *Constitution* sought the enemy on the other side of the Atlantic. Again no worthy antagonist was encountered. It began to appear as if her luck had deserted her. But on February 19 Captain Stewart had a "hunch." He said: "Mark my words, our chance will come, and I assure you before the sun rises and sets to-morrow we shall meet the enemy, and it shall be something more than a single ship." Sure enough, the following afternoon two ship-rigged vessels of war were sighted, the British sloop *Levant* and the light frigate *Cyane*. The latter, by means of camouflage painting, had been made to look like a big two-decker, i.e. a ship with guns on two decks besides the spar deck. There was puzzlement aboard the *Constitution* but Stewart said: "However, let her be greater or smaller, I promised you a fight before the sun went down and, you see, we shall soon have our hands full. We cannot afford to decline the opportunity offered; we may wait long before another presents itself. We must flog them when we catch them, whether she has one gun-deck or two."

"WE MUST FLOG THEM WHEN WE CATCH THEM, WHETHER
SHE HAS ONE GUN–DECK OR TWO."

Captain Charles Stewart; only 36 years of age on his biggest day, he
died at 91.

But let us permit Jesse Dow to tell the tale from its beginning: [1]

'On the 17th of December, 1814, Old Ironsides sailed from Boston, under the command of captain Charles Stewart. She first ran off Bermuda, thence she steered for the Madeiras, and still finding nothing worthy of her thunder, entered the Bay of Biscay.

'Cruizing down the shore of Portugal, she made the rock of Lisbon, and continued in sight of the barren peaks of Ceutra for some days. Here she made two prizes, one of which she destroyed, and the other she sent in.

'While in this vicinity, she made a large ship in the offing, and gave chase, but before she had set her courses, she made a prize, and while securing it, the strange sail disappeared in the distance. This was the Elizabeth, 74, which came out of Lisbon, in quest of the saucy frigate; but captain Stewart stood to the southward and westward, in quest of an enemy, said to be in that direction.—On the morning of the 20th February, the wind blowing a light Levanter, captain Stewart, for the want of something better to do, ordered the helm up, and ran his ship off to the south-west, varying her position nearly two degrees. At 1, P.M., a sail was made on the larboard bow, and the stranger hauled three points to windward, and made sail in chase. In twenty minutes, the stranger was made out to be a ship, and in a short half hour, a consort was seen to leeward, signalizing the ship in chase. At 4. P.M., the ship nearest to the Constitution made a signal to the lee-ward ship, and soon the latter kept away, and ran down

[1] *Gentleman's Magazine,* November, 1839.

towards her, then about three miles under her lee. The Constitution immediately squared her yards, and set her studding-sails above and below. No doubt of the enmity of the strangers now remained. The nearest vessel appeared to be a jackass frigate, and the most distant one, a corvette. The first was carrying studding-sails on both sides, while the last was running off under short canvass, to allow her consort to close.

'Captain Stewart, believing that the enemy was endeavoring to escape, crowded on every thing that would draw, with a view to get the nearest vessel under his guns before night. At half-past four, the Constitution lost her main-royalmast, and the chase gained upon her. A few shots were now fired, but finding that his metal fell short, the attempt to cripple the frigate was abandoned. At half-past five, the drums on board the gallant Constitution beat to quarters, and soon she was cleared for action. In ten minutes, the two vessels of the enemy passed within hail of each other, came by the wind, with their heads to the northward, hauled up their courses, and cleared ship to engage.

'Both of the enemy's vessels, as though animated by a new idea, now suddenly made sail close by the wind, in order to weather upon the American frigate, but perceiving that the latter was closing too fast, they hauled up their courses and formed on the wind, the smallest ship ahead.

'At 6, P.M., Old Ironsides had the enemy completely under her cannon, and yawing gracefully, showed the star-spangled banner beautiful amid the closing shadows

of the ocean night. The strangers answered this proud
defiance by setting English colors, and in five minutes, the
American frigate ranged up abeam of the sternmost
vessel, at one cable's length distance, passing ahead with
her sails lifting, until the three ships formed a triangle,
the Constitution being to windward.

'Now commenced the action, with a vehemence that was
hardly equalled on the sea. At the end of twenty minutes,
the fire of the enemy evidently slackened, and the moon
coming up, captain Stewart ordered the cannonading to
cease. The sea was covered with an immense cloud of
smoke. Beautiful as the silver veil of Mokanna, was the
fleecy screen that rested upon the ocean, and terrible as
the visage of the veiled prophet was the scene that burst
upon the sight of the English three minutes afterwards,
when the rolling vapor passed swiftly to leeward, and
showed the American frigate ready to pour forth her
volleys on either side, from her black row of teeth. The
leading ship of the enemy was now seen under the lee beam
of the Constitution, while the sternmost one was luffing up,
as if she intended to tack and cross her stern. Giving a
broadside to the ship abreast of her, that made a great
many vacant numbers in her mess-book, the Constitution
backed her main and mizzen topsails and topgallant-sails,
shook all forward, let fly her jib-sheet, and backed swiftly,
compelling the enemy to fill away, to avoid being raked.
The leader now attempted to cross the Constitution's fore-
foot, when the latter boarded her fore-tack, shot ahead,
forced her antagonist to ware under a raking broadside,
and to run off to leeward, to escape from her destructive

fire. The Constitution, perceiving that the largest ship
was waring also, wore in her turn, and crossing her stern,
raked her with effect, though the enemy came by the wind
immediately and delivered her larboard broadside; but as
the Constitution ranged up close on her weather quarter,
she struck. Lieutenant Hoffman, the second of the Constitution, was immediately sent on board of her, and in a
few minutes afterwards he returned, with the sword of
Captain Falcon, of H. B. M. ship Cyane, of 34 guns. In
the meantime, the other vessel of the enemy, having
repaired her running rigging, hauled up, and met the Constitution coming down in quest of her. It was nearly nine
o'clock, when the two vessels crossed each other on opposite tacks, and delivered their awful broadsides. The
English ship was satisfied with the first fire and bore up,
while the American followed, raking and boring her with
her broadside and bow-chasers, ripping off the planks, and
mowing down the men, like the fiery thunderbolts of
heaven. The enemy could not stand this riddling long;
the crashing of the planks was heard on board the Constitution at every fire, and the groans of the dying enemy
echoed mournfully over the moonlit wave.

'At 10, P.M., the chase came by the wind, fired a gun to
leeward, and lowered her ensign. Lieutenant Shubrick,
the third of the frigate, was now sent on board of the prize,
and upon his return, the sword of the honorable captain
Douglass, of H. B. M. ship Levant, of 18 guns, was laid
upon the capstan of the Constitution.

'At 1, A.M., the conqueror was ready for another
action. She suffered less in her crew than when she

"HER THUNDERS SHOOK THE MIGHTY DEEP."

Constitution raking the *Cyane* in the course of her moonlight victory over that vessel and the *Levant.*

captured the Java.   Not an officer was hurt; but she was hulled oftener in this engagement than in both her previous battles.   Great credit was deservedly bestowed upon captain Stewart, for the skill and coolness displayed by him on this occasion.   He fought two ships and conquered them without having been once raked; and his backing and filling his single frigate in a cloud of smoke, raking his opponents in turn, and forcing them down to leeward when they were endeavoring to cross his stern or fore-foot, was a piece of manœuvering scarcely paralleled in the annals of any navy.'

This proposition of two ships maneuvering against one brought mutual recrimination from the two British skippers after the fight.   In the wardroom of the *Constitution* the discussion waxed warm, each one blaming the defeat on the other because of various acts of commission and omission.   Said Captain Stewart: "Gentlemen, it is useless to find fault with one another or multiply words.   It would have been all the same whatever you might have done.   If you doubt that, I will put you all on board again, and you can try it over."

On paper the British ships combined were superior to the American vessel, considering weight of broadsides and the mobility of the two ships as compared with one.   Stewart's superb seamanship more than balanced this latter factor, however; and in the light of present day knowledge we are aware of the advantages of the defensive strength and the concentration of fire such as favored the single ship.   Once more, however, the disparity of the results far surpassed any real or imaginary superiority of strength possessed by the American frigate.

There has been much discussion of the ethics of fighting this battle (February 20) after peace had been signed (December 24). The following dates are pertinent, in addition to the fact that the custom of the times led enemies to continue to operate against each other until definitely instructed to cease. Stewart had spoken a passing ship on February 8 and heard that a treaty had been signed though not yet ratified. As he learned months afterwards, the treaty had been ratified on February 17, but a clause provided that hostilities in the eastern Atlantic should be legal until March 19, *i.e.* 30 days later. This latter date legalized, *as to time,* even the capture to be described in the succeeding pages.

On March 10 the *Constitution* and her prizes put in to the neutral (Portuguese) harbor of Porto Praya in the Cape Verdes. Plans were instituted at once for paroling the prisoners and undertaking minor items of refit. Perhaps the most dramatic act of the play still remained, however.

March 12 [2]"was damp and foggy, a heavy bank of mist resting low down upon the water, rendering it impossible to distinguish objects any distance.

'The first and second lieutenants, with a large number of the frigate's men, were absent and busy on board the respective prizes, leaving Lieutenant Shubrick on the

[2] H. D. Smith, "The U. S. Frigate 'Constitution,'" *United Service*, December, 1891.

"Constitution" as executive officer, and right worthily did that gallant gentleman fill the arduous position.

'He was standing on the break of the quarter-deck, superintending some repairs to running rigging, when his ready ear heard an exclamation of wonder from the boyish lips of an English midshipman, followed by a rapid gesture as he directed his captain's attention to the spars of a large vessel towering above the mass of fog. The British commander, who was evidently cognizant of the fact that a heavy stranger was approaching, turned sharply and angrily upon the lad, bidding him in a low, stern tone to hold his peace. But the admonition came too late. Lieutenant Shubrick had heard all and witnessed a portion of the by-play, and glancing towards the entrance of the harbor made out the sails of a large vessel above the fog-bank, hauled by the wind. He immediately reported to Captain Stewart that a suspicious-looking stranger was beating into the harbor, and Stewart, who was shaving, instructed his lieutenant to "call all hands and heave short. Some East Indiaman, possibly. We'll go out and see what he is made of."

'Scarcely had all hands been piped on deck when the top-hamper of two additional heavy ships came slowly pushing through the obscurity. Lieutenant Shubrick descended to the cabin hastily, neglecting the usual knock. There stood Stewart in a light dishabille, before a long plate mirror, completing his toilette. The situation was explained at once; the razor dropped from the commander's hand as he spluttered hastily, his mouth flavored with soap, "Cut!" In a few moments he was on deck, and signaling for the prizes to follow, the "Constitution," in less than ten minutes from the time the order was given, was moving through the water briskly, the wind being moderate from northeast. The prizes followed in gallant style, and with Porto Praya astern, and skirting closely the shore with sails slightly lifting, the three vessels sought to gain the open ocean. It required but a glance to see that the new-comers were far too heavy to risk an engagement, and Captain Stewart felt well assured that the neutrality of so insignificant a place would never be observed while a prospect existed of effecting the capture so well known a cruiser as "Old Ironsides."

'The prisoners on shore had cleared away an old, half-neglected battery belonging to the authorities and commenced an irregular fusilade on their departing foes.

'The frigate, with the "Levant" directly astern, followed by the "Cyane," stood out of the harbor on the port tack, passing close under the east point, and within easy range of the strangers, to windward. Although the hulls of the vessels were enveloped in mist, it was aparent to all that they were men-of-war, and of course English.

'As quietly as possible the "Constitution" crossed top-gallant-yards, boarded fore- and main-tacks, set spanker, flying jib, and top-gallant-sails, braced sharp on a wind. The strangers, still enveloped in fog, tacked together, making all sail in pursuit. All six vessels stood to the southward, with everything set that could draw. The "Constitution" cut adrift the boats towing astern, and at 12.50 P.M. her log indicated her speed as ten and a half knots.'

Let us read James Fenimore Cooper's description of the chase:[3]

'As yet no one had seen the hulls of the enemy, though there could be no mistake as to their character. The mist seemed to settle, however, in the offing, lying nearer to the water, and the air became a little clearer aloft. The vessel that was taken for a frigate weathered on everything, her own consorts as well as on the American vessels. The English officers, prisoners in the "Constitution," could not conceal their delight, and confidently predicted the capture of "Old Ironsides" and the recapture of their own vessels. They announced the chasing ships to be the "Newcastle," 50, Captain Lord George Stewart; "Leander," 50, Captain Sir Ralph Collier, K.C.B., and "Acasta," 40, Captain Robert Kerr. The first two vessels were new ships on one deck, built expressly to overmatch the American 44's. The English prisoners were particularly confident Kerr in the "Acasta" would overtake the "Constitution," which vessel they fancied could not sail, from seeing her jog along at an easy rate in company with her prizes. Stewart kept her traveling on the present occasion, and it was not quite so easy a thing to come up with her, as hope had induced the prisoners to believe. One of the English captains was so sanguine as to get into the quarter-gallery and make signs to the weatherly frigate, inviting her to come on, and exclaiming, in the presence of the American officers, "Captain Kerr, I envy you your glory this day." With Stewart, himself, these gentlemen did not maintain much reserve, pretty plainly intimating that "Old Ironsides" had not the speed

[3] *History of the Navy of the United States of America.*

necessary to get clear of the "British Phœnix," as they termed Kerr in the "Acasta."

'Whatever may have been the fact as regards our own honest old craft, it is certain the prizes were in a bad way. The "Cyane" was a short ship, mounting twenty-two guns on one deck and twelve above, and of course was not very weatherly. Stewart saw that the frigate, or supposed frigate,—for no one had yet seen the hull of the Englishman,—was weathering on her fast, and he made a signal for her to tack. Hoffman went around immediately, and passed his most dangerous adversary, short gunshot to windward, on contrary tacks. The "British Phœnix" stood gallantly on, endeavoring to get into the wake of the "Constitution," and the "Cyane" was soon lost sight of in the haze. Hoffman was a practical, plain sailor, and knew perfectly well what he was about. Instead of running into port again, no sooner had the mist shut in the enemy, than he went about again, and continued making short tacks to windward for twenty-four hours, when, giving the islands a good berth, he squared away for America, bringing his ship successfully into New York.

'At half-past two, one of the English vessels was pretty well up on the lee quarter of "Ironsides." By this time the fog had packed in the water so low that her officers could be seen standing in the hammock cloths, though her ports were not yet visible. She fired by divisions, and conjectures could be made concerning the extent of her batteries, by the flashes of her guns, as seen through the fog. The shot fell within a hundred yards of the "Constitution," but did not rise again. After trying this experiment unsuccessfully, the firing ceased.

'The "Levant" all this time was falling astern, nearer and nearer to the weatherly frigate. Stewart made her a signal to tack. Ballard went around immediately, but could not work off to windward as Hoffman had just done, for seven minutes after he had got about, all three of the Englishmen tacked by signal and were on his heels. This compelled him to run back into the roads and anchor. . . .

'As for "Old Ironsides," she went steadily on her way, and was soon out of sight of her pursuers. Deep was the mortification of the English officers on board her, when they saw their three ships tack together, abandoning such a frigate as the "Constitution," and following a prize into a neutral port.

'The "British Phœnix" was now changed into an Indiaman, and it could never be the squadron they had supposed. It was, however, and Sir George Collier was much condemned for his course. In the end, that officer committed suicide, though whether it was the consequences of morbid feelings in connection with this affair, or some other cause, we do not know. . . .

'The enemy paid no attention to the neutrality of the island, but stood in after the "Levant," and opened a heavy fire on that ship. The prisoners ashore joined them, and added the guns of the battery to the attack.'

'The gunnery of the British fleet under Sir George was fully on a level with his merits as a seaman and tactician.'

(avers H. C. Smith sarcastically.)[4] 'Lieutenant Ballard when pursued by the heavy frigates, succeeded in anchoring his vessel under the guns of a heavy Portuguese battery not over one hundred and twenty-five yards distant. The "Acasta" opened fire deliberately at 4.30 P.M.; the "Newcastle" followed suit as soon as she came up, also the "Leander," while the prisoners on shore fired from the battery they had manned. Ballard watched the shot falling thickly about him, few striking his vessel, which was stationary, and the water comparatively smooth. For fifteen minutes the squadron and fort thundered forth their demands for unconditional surrender in a neutral port, and the unresisting American prize vessel hauled down her flag without having lost a man, but unwilling to sacrifice life by braving longer the chances of sustaining a chance and more effective shot from the enemy.'

[5] 'Of course Ballard submitted, but he had some relief for his mortification in losing his ship, in what passed with the boarding-officer.

' "I presume I have the honor to receive the sword of Captain Biddle, of the United States ship 'Hornet,' " said that gentleman, when Ballard offered his sword.

' "You receive the sword of Lieutenant Ballard, of the 'Constitution,' prize-master of His Brittanic Majesty's late ship 'Levant,' " was the caustic reply.

'The enemy supposed the three ships they had chased to be the "President," Commander Rodgers; "Congress," Captain Smith, and "Hornet," Captain Biddle. Had such

---

[4] *United Service*, December, 1891.
[5] Cooper.

been the case, they would have been much too strong to fight; but the truth rendered their little success bitter, rather than otherwise.'

Not even James, the notorious British naval historian, can account adequately for Collier's maneuver!

CHAPTER XV

Her Turkish Admirers

AFTER the War of 1812 *"Old Ironsides"* enjoyed a well-earned respite from active service. Relieved from combat with Britain, other ships of our navy achieved final and complete relief for the United States from thralldom and molestation at the hands of the Barbary Powers. Meanwhile the *Constitution* laid up at Boston—from 1815 to 1821. In the latter year she started a tour of duty as flagship of the Mediterranean Squadron, returning in 1823.

Next year *"Old Ironsides"* commenced a four-year cruise on the Mediterranean station. In the course of her wanderings she came to anchor between Tenedos and the Troad early in July, 1826. In company were the *North Carolina* and other vessels of the U. S. Mediterranean Squadron.

It will be remembered that George Jones was Schoolmaster of the frigate at this time—and until the end of her cruise two years later. As of July 5, 1826, he writes:[1]

'I was afraid, yesterday, we were going to have our visit spoiled altogether. We had been calculating on having our 4th of July dinner in the palace of Priam; and were waiting for the signal, "communication with the shore;"

[1] *Sketches of Naval Life,* by a "Civilian"; 1829.

142

when, looking Northward, we saw the even horizon broken
by a few objects, small and dim, yet, to a sailor's eye, sufficiently intelligible.   Others succeeded, and then others,
and then the whole horizon was covered with them, the
foremost now coming into full view, and displaying the outlines of large men of war.   It was the Turkish fleet, just
from the Dardanelles, breathing ruin and outrage to the
Greeks; still it was a beautiful sight.   They first ran out
into the sea, and, then changing their course, bore right
down upon us; the foremost, as she approached, shewing
herself a seventy-four, with the Commodore's flag; the
next a large frigate, and the rest sloops and frigates all of
the first class, a few schooners excepted.   A midshipman
now reported that the North Carolina had beaten to
quarters; our drums were ordered up; a short tapping succeeded, in which the words "to quàrters, to quàrters, to
quàrters, to quàrters," could almost be heard; and when
the music, which, at first, was rather slow, had quickened,
until only a roll could be heard, every man was in his
place, and ready for battle.   I except the Purser, A——,
and myself, who risked being sent below, for the sake of the
interest of the scene.   One of bustling alacrity succeeded:
divisions were reported, and then preparations were made
for fight: gun tackle was thrown loose; shot racks filled;
matches placed by the guns; cutlasses and boarding caps
brought on deck;[2] pikes prepared; carronnade slides

[2] Boarding caps were made with two crossed bands of steel hoops,
covered with bearskin, fur side out. They were supplied with ties to go
under the chin in the form of two thongs of bearskin. These caps gave
a particularly ferocious aspect to their wearers. See *A Voice from the
Main Deck,* by Samuel Leech.

greased; cartridge boxes buckled on; grape passed up; and all being in readiness, the bustle was succeeded by an almost painful silence. Not a sound was heard, except the occasional tread of the first lieutenant, or a low order to an officer. Thus we awaited them. On they came, in gallant style: the flag ship still led the van: she had just passed the North Carolina, when a volume of smoke shot from the latter, and the thunder of one of her forty-two's succeeded. Another followed, and another; the firing soon passed through the squadron, and was promptly returned by the Turk.—But do not be frightened: we had no battle, and did not expect one, though it was within the range of possibilities. The preparation was only what is usual, when a large naval force approaches; and is made, in some of our ships, whenever they meet even a merchant-man. The firing was no more than our 4th of July salute, given at noon, our usual time; which the Turk, mistaking for himself, returned, highly tickled, no doubt, to find himself saluted by the whole American squadron. They continued passing us most of the day: one poor fellow ran his frigate on some rocks, in the channel: he crowded sail at first, but that would not do: the ship laid some time, under the action of a heavy sea; and, as soon as she got off, was carried over to Tenedos, and anchored. It appeared to disconcert the rest: signals were exchanged; they hove to, and finally anchored, under the lee of the island. During the afternoon, Commodore Rodgers sent the schooner down, with some of his officers, to communicate with them. They were twenty five in all: two ships of the line, seven or eight frigates, two schooners, the remainder sloops; all good looking vessels.

'While they were passing, the Commodore made signal to us, to "prepare to get under way:" I cast a wishful look to the plains on our starboard; but was soon relieved by another order, to pipe to dinner, and we shall yet have our visit.'

'*Thursday, 6.* . . . .

'The Capudan Pasha had come down from the Dardanelles, to enquire about the injured frigate. We saw him passing in grand cavalcade through the streets, in true Turkish style. First came his guard, consisting of fifteen soldiers, straggling along, without the least order, each carrying a long silver mounted gun on his shoulder, with a brace of pistols, an attaghan, and dirk in his sash: next was an attendant, with a spy-glass; and then came the Pasha, seated on a small horse with rich trappings, an officer on each side, having hold of his saddle. He was dressed in a yellow silk robe, and is a little fat man, with an intelligent and pleasing countenance. A crowd of natives followed. The attaghan is a sword, nearly two feet in length: it is curved inward, like a scythe, and is always kept very sharp: the sheath is of wood, round, and covered with a white metal, like silver, worked into relief, representing houses and trees, with arabesques. The hilt is often enriched with gems.

'The Porpoise has been offered to carry the Pasha to the Dardanelles; and he, on the other hand, proposes to meet us, in his flag ship, at Mitylene.'

A few days later the *Constitution* moved into the Straits of Mitylene. On July 14 Chaplain Jones writes:

'Early this morning, the second division of the Turkish fleet, was discovered beating up the straits, from the South. As they approached, the Commodore ordered our ship to get under way; and we kept under easy sail among them, till they had all anchored, when we returned to our former station. Their force consisted of two ships of the line, and, eight or nine frigates, with sloops, brigs and schooners, making thirty vessels in all. Our ship, as she passed among them, excited much curiosity; and their guns, spars and bulwarks, were covered with gazing crowds. With us, on such occasions, not a man dare show his hat above the hammock cloths, or look through the ports: the captain, the first lieutenant, a few men in the tops, and occasionally the officer of the deck, are the only persons seen; and the sudden changes of sail, to a distant spectator, seem more like a work of magic, than human operation. . . . .

'The Pasha has anchored close on the larboard of the Commodore: he sails in a frigate, a handsome one, but why prefer it to his seventy fours? The answer is a plain one: the larger vessels are always selected by the Greek fire ships; and the very name of brulotte is horrible to a Turkish ear. His ensign is of silk; a pure red, and so long as to reach the water, when the breeze declines: a large red pendant, with a two-bladed sword in the centre, (they call it the sword of justice,) floats from his main. The frigate is of the first class: handsomely ornamented, and clean-looking: in the last particular, it differs from the rest.

He visited the Commodore in the afternoon: when he left the ship, a salute of twenty one guns was fired, the shrouds were manned, and three cheers were given him.

. . . .

'*Saturday,* 15.—Commodore Rodgers, with many of the officers, returned the Pasha's visit this morning: when he left, a salute of twenty-one guns was fired; the pendant at their main was hauled down, and another hoisted, with a red field also like the other, but having a lion and a sentence from the Koran, instead of the two bladed sword. The Commodore was given to understand, that it had never been hoisted to a Christian before.   His frigate is in good order, well finished and clean, in the two upper decks: but his officers excused themselves from shewing the lower one, and its appearance, as seen through the hatches, was not by any means inviting: the men were kept there during the visit.   In the afternoon, their commanders came on board our ships, and presents of shawls were made to our Captains: to the ships, the Pasha sent sheep and oxen, which have been distributed among the officers and men.   The Commodore's band and ours have just been over near his frigate, to give him a serenade.

'*Monday,* 17.—Yesterday   morning,   the   schooner was ordered to sail; the Ontario had gone some days previous; the Erie, I have forgotten to mention, has been engaged all Summer in convoying: so the flag ship and our own were the only ones left: signal was made to us by telegraph, to prepare to weigh anchor, at four in the afternoon.   In the mean time, we had service on board. Towards evening, both ships got under weigh: the wind was from the North; we beat to windward, and then, with all sails set, came down on the Turkish fleet. We ran close by the starboard of the Pasha, and each ship manned her shrouds, and cheered him as she passed. His spars, and guns, and bulwarks, were covered with men and officers: he shewed himself in the quarter gallery, and answered the honours with many bows. Steering sails were then set, and we shot to the Southward; our officers, as they faded in the distance, collecting in groups, to discuss the propriety of shewing such attentions to a Turkish Pasha. It is a question with which I have little concern: I will only state, on the one hand, that the Captain Pasha had requested that our vessels might pass among them, to enable him to see our manner of working ship; and, on the other, that the number of guns in the salute to him was unusual. The most given to an officer in our service, or in any other, is thirteen: seventeen guns are the salute to the Secretary of the Navy; and twenty one to the President of the United States.

'Cheering is a handsome operation, when the men are in clean dress, as they were to-day. The Summer uniform is white canvass shoes; white trowsers, frock (a shirt with blue collar, set off with white fancy work), hat covered with white canvass, and blue belt with white stars. All hands are called on such occasions: at the order, they mount rapidly, and take station in the shrouds, so as to form three pyramids, rising one above another, to each mast; their faces are turned outward, and, at the order, all simultaneously take off their hats, wave them and cheer: the officers usually joining with them.

'We laid to, during the night, just South of the island, and this morning took our former places at the fountain of Vourla.

. . . .

'*Monday, September 4.*—On Friday, the green shores of Sicily came in view; but the breeze was light, and our progress a slow one. On Saturday, it left us altogether, and, when I turned in at night, the sea was smooth and bright as a mirror; the vast firmament seemed to descend below us; the ship appeared to be suspended in the centre of an immense sphere, and if I may say so, one felt in awe and silence the majesty of space. The sails hung idly by the mast, and the officers' tread along the deck was the only sound heard. So I left them. About midnight, I was awakened by a heavy swing of my cot, succeeded by a sudden dash to the other side: the water was pouring into our room, and I could hear its rush across the upper decks, where all was noise and rapid motion. I hurried on my clothes and ran up: the gun deck was clear; hammocks had already been lashed up and stowed; it was lighted up, and the lamps shewed it flooded in its whole extent. I ascended to the next: the rain came down in torrents, but I did not feel it, so deeply absorbing was the scene. I wish I could describe it. The sky was in a constant blaze: the sea was not high, but the waves were broken, confused and foaming, and taking from the lightning an unnatural hue. Above me were the yards covered with human beings, thrown by each flash into strong outline, struggling hard to secure the canvass, and to maintain their precarious footing: the ship rolled tremendously. And now add the wild uproar of elements, the "noise of many waters," the deep and constant roar of winds, the cries of men aloft, the heavy and rapid tread of those below, the reiterated commands of officers, and, rising above all this, the firm and composed orders of the trumpet; and then add to this the heavy rolling of thunder, at times, drowning all these sounds. The first lieutenant had the deck; he had sprung to it at the first alarm, and seizing the trumpet, had called for Black, his favorite helmsman. The ship was soon under snug sail, and now dashed onward at a furious rate, giving to the gale a yet wilder character. All at once, a rocky island seemed to start up from the waters, but the next broad flash shewed a good offing, and we were safe; when suddenly came a loud shout from the forecastle, "a sail on the starboard bow, sir," and then another, "a sail close on the larboard bow, sir." I trembled then; not for ourselves, for we should have gone over them, and have scarcely felt the shock, but for the poor wretches, whom it would have been impossible to save. The helm was put hard down; we shot by, and I again breathed freely, when some one bade me look up to our spars. I did so, and found every upper yard arm and mast head tipped with lightning. Each blaze was twice as large as that of a candle, and thus we flew on with the elements of destruction playing above our heads.

'In about thirty minutes, the wind, which was from the S. W. changed suddenly to the S. E. and became as hot as air from the mouth of an oven: it was the Sirocco, and, I was told afterwards by those most about the deck, brought with it a quantity of fine sand. We were then a

GEORGE JONES, ESQUIRE.

"Old Ironsides'" Schoolmaster, acting Chaplain, and chronicler
extraordinary.

few miles from Maratimo, sixty six from Cape Bon, the
nearest African shore, and three hundred from the nearest
land in the direction of the wind.   It lasted half an hour,
and was a stiff, smacking breeze, but not near so strong as
the one that had preceded it.

. . . .

'Yesterday we had a strong wind and a rough sea all
day: another squall threatened as evening drew round:
the sea was wild and foaming; the waves came rolling on as
if eager to overwhelm us: the clouds rose like dark walls
on the horizon, appearing to shut us up forever to the
treacherous element, while a broad heavy mass rolled on,
over head, "noctem hiememque ferens."   Nothing else
could be seen, except the North Carolina, an indistinct
mass, several miles distant.   She too faded and became a
misty speck, but the usual light was raised at her mizen-
top, to govern our course.   But this suddenly disappeared,
and nothing could be seen; we answered its disappearance
by raising a light to our fore-mast head: all looked in her
direction, when suddenly another light appeared, a mere
point in the distance: it spread, and brightened, and then
shot up, so as to lighten the whole stern and sails.   It sunk,
and was succeeded by another, and this by another similar
one; then was darkness a moment, and next followed three
successive flashes.   We lowered our lantern; her mizen
light again appeared, and all hands were called to execute
the order.   This is the first time I have introduced to you
a night signal: we had two on Saturday night in the midst
of the storm: their effect, in rough or calm weather, is
always very fine.

'The gale came on soon after; it brought one com-plaisánt,[3] and this appeared at our mizen royal-mast head: each of our masts has a chain conductor; the lower part is kept up in calm weather, but let down into the water whenever appearances are suspicious.

'Cum "magno telluris amore." '

And so to Minorca and other storied lands.

---

[3] St. Elmo's fire.   A corruption of "corposant" which is in turn derived from "corpo santo," the Italian and Portuguese for "holy body," or from "corpus sancti," the Latin for "body of a saint."

CHAPTER XVI

ALL ACCOUNTED FOR BUT ONE

THE following July found *"Old Ironsides"* in the waters made famous by the Battle of Salamis fought in 480 B.C. Here the Greeks under Themistocles achieved their notable naval victory over Xerxes' Persian fleet.

A member of the *Constitution's* crew, who calls himself "Oceanus", has left to us an interesting record of the events of July 18–20, 1827. His tale follows.[1]

. . . .

'During an active cruise against the pirates that infested the Archipelago in the summer of 1827, our frigate anchored off the town of Salamis, in Greece, in order to surpress more effectually the fitting out of piratical vessels, and to watch the movements of the Turkish army, then waging a most savage, horrid war of extermination against the Greeks, who were nobly contending, against fearful odds, for that dearest of all prizes—liberty! We hovered around the scenes of this distress, administering to their wants, in all that was consistent with our *neutrality*.

'Ibrahim Pasha commanded the Turkish and Egyptian forces, consisting of forty thousand troops, with a heavy

---

[1] "A Leaf From My 'Log Book,'" reprinted from the *American Monthly Magazine* by the *Army and Navy Chronicle,* August 27, 1835.

park of artillery, a troop of ten thousand well mounted cavalry, and a large body of well armed infantry. After an unsuccessful attempt to dislodge the Greek troops from their position on the Piræus, where they assembled to relieve the troops in the Acropolis, he left Redschid Pacha, with a large force, to besiege that impregnable fortress, and with the remainder of his army took up his line of march for the Morea, which was most nobly disputed by the heroic Greeks—though, unhappily, with but little success.

'The track of the Turkish army was marked by every species of cruel and wanton barbarity. A recital of their enormities would make humanity shudder and blush for its degenerate kind. Towns were burnt—fields and trees destroyed—men, women, and children, massacred indiscriminately. Some were reserved for a life of igniminious slavery—a few escaped to the mountains—where, secreted in the caves, they subsisted on a few muscles, and a scanty supply of stagnant water found in the cavities of the rocks. In such an abode, filled with painful anxiety for the fate of their families, they hid themselves from the savage hunt of their fiendish pursuers, till the Turkish army departed, to visit the next hapless town with its brutal enormities. Then, these half famished creatures would steal down in the night to seek for the broken remnants of their ruined race, by the light of the dying embers of their once peaceful dwellings—and there, amid the dead and dying, might be seen the father, the mother, or the child, bending over the fond object of affection, administering such comforts as their feeble means afforded. Oh! who can imagine or describe the anguish of that heart-breaking scene?

'It was during the period of these unparalleled wants, that four or five emaciated Greeks ventured down to the beach, and made a signal to our ship. They were soon brought on board, and two of them returned to the shore, loaded with provisions for their starving families in the mountains—the others offered to sell a statue of great value that was buried on shore, some distance up the gulf. The captain, regarding the purchase as an act of charity, readily agreed to give the stipulated sum.[2] The ship was forthwith got underway, and anchored within ten miles of the nearest landing. Every thing was got in readiness for the expedition to start next morning at daylight— officers were appointed, men selected, a rude carriage constructed—boats provisioned and armed. Our party consisted of twenty-five men, and in due time shoved off from the ship, and were scudding at a brisk rate with a fair wind. We soon arrived at the landing, and found the statue about three miles from the beach, buried some six or seven feet under ground. It was no easy task to place it on the carriage: it could not have weighed less than five tons; and to transport it down to the boat, was a work of great labor and fatigue; the sun was oppressively hot, and the wheels sunk deep into the sand every roll. We reached the boat about an hour before sunset, wearied, and fatigued beyond imagination; and on mustering the

[2] This statue is no less than the colossal headless figure of Ceres which now stands over the doorway of the Pennsylvania Academy of Fine Arts in Philadelphia. It was presented to that institution by Commodore Daniel F. Patterson of the *Constitution*.

men, were greatly surprised to find one of them missing. Our search in the immediate vicinity proved fruitless, and the many conjectures as to his fate served but to increase our anxiety and perplexity. After many suggestions, W—— and myself resolved to remain and continue the search—the launch in the meantime to return to the ship and despatch a cutter for us. With this arrangement, the boat pushed off from the shore, spread its wings to the evening breeze, and was soon "walking the waters like a thing of life." We watched the boat as it receded from us, with a singular emotion; and with the swing of the hat, and a wave of the handkerchief, they sent us a cheer across the water for the success of our enterprize, that bubbled up its tribute from the heart; and how long we stood gazing on the void created by the absence of our fellows, I know not. The screech of a sorrowing seabird, that was sportingly dipping its wings into the feathery spray, broke our reverie. Then it was, the loneliness of our unprotected situation first dawned upon us; and an involuntary turn toward the direction of our ship, brought the sad reality more forcibly home. After examining the priming of our muskets, we started on our pilgrimage; and with as much singleness of heart as ever animated the bosom of a devotee commencing his most pious march; our object was to find our poor lost sailor; and the consciousness of being engaged in a deed of goodness, buoyed up our drooping spirits, and roused our energies to action. We were determined to solve the mystery of his singular disappearance, and not to return to the ship without some tidings of him. Our feelings were particularly interested, from the circumstance of his being one of the best men in the ship.

'The first object that met our attention was the ruin of an old Venetian castle. It might be, curiosity had attracted him thither, and in the inviting coolness of the place, the recollection of the fatigue, and heat of the noonday sun, would be lost in a sleep of rosy dreams! We entered through the broken archway—traversed the court, where many a saint and hero trod—climbed the massive fragments—explored the subterranean passages, and woke the aged silence with the almost deafening report of our muskets—but all in vain—the beautiful echo alone flung back our summons—and we left that monastic ruin, where taste seemed to have guided the hand of time, full of painful forebodings—nor was our search on the plain attended with better success. We then entered Eleusis. The condition of that poor devoted town was awfully distressing —the imagination cannot picture a more revolting scene. It is enough to say that it had been visited by the Turkish army, and their ruthless, wanton barbarity, led to the indiscriminate massacre of its peaceful inhabitants; their bones were bleaching in the streets; and only the walls of the houses were left standing as monuments of its once happy inmates. We rambled through its deserted streets, clambered up to the vaulted roof of a castellated building, and there discharged our muskets and shouted aloud, with no success. The scene from this elevation would have been a gloomy subject for an artist; the view was bold, various, and picturesque. The town was built on a gentle sloping hill, in the centre of a very extensive plain, bounded on three sides by ranges of sterile mountains; the Aegean sea bathed its southern border, with three or four islands in the perspective—far to the west rose the rocky isthmus of Corinth, with its impregnable castle perched on its summit—the city of the dead was at our feet, and the setting sun threw a light of singular beauty over that melancholy picture—several noble ruins were scattered over the plain, relieved at intervals by beautiful olive groves—and the ground was as rich in classic association, as it was desolate in reality. Satisfied with this scene, which harmonized so well with our feelings, we started for a fountain about a mile inland from the town. It was quite in a ruined state, and the crystal water bubbled from the fount into a large basin, and from it leaped sparkingly into two or three others of smaller size. We sat bathing our feet in one of them, conjecturing the fate of the poor fellow we were in pursuit of, when our attention was suddenly attracted by approaching footsteps and voices; we had barely time to put ourselves in order, before we saw five armed men approaching the fountain. Our first impulse was to meet them—and if Greeks, to ask their assistance—if Turks, to act as the circumstances should call for. In either case it was hazardous. The Greeks might, in the indistinct twilight, take us for Turks; or the Turks imagine us Greeks. Our only alternative, therefore, to avoid the consequences of such an irreparable mistake, was to retreat behind the angle of the wall, and thus escape unnoticed. We knew that one wing of the Turkish army lay encamped only a few miles from us, and that in their night visits to the town, to cut off such Greeks

as ventured from their hiding places, their cymetars would
not be particularly discriminating on points of nationality.
With this prospect before us, we prepared ourselves for
the worst.   Presently they arrived, and leaning their arms
against the wall behind us, commenced their ablutions.
Their language was unintelligible, and a glimpse of them,
whose costume corresponded with the Albanian Turks,
decided our course.   Communicating our plans in a faint
whisper, we resolved to rush on them, secure their arms,
and abide the result.   W—— got down on his knees
and surveyed the party.   They were seated closely together, engaged in an animated conversation—their arms
were close to us—and the time was favorable.   I never
shall forget the sensation of that exciting moment.   A
thousand things, unutterably, rushed through my mind—
the perspiration started from my brow—and my whole
frame quivered with deep emotion.   W—— and myself exchanged glances that spoke volumes of feeling, and
the next moment we darted out from behind the fountain,
and stood before the unwelcome visitors, with bayonets
fixed, and fingers on the triggers.   Had a thunderbolt
fallen from the heavens, it could not have surprised them
more.   They jumped, and stood petrified with astonishment.   We spoke to them kindly, but they did not understand us.   Our language—our costume—and our sudden
appearance, astounded them.   They evidently had never
seen such strange looking beings before.   Their first
rational glance, after the restoration of their senses, was
toward their arms—these they saw so well guarded, as to
forbid the possibility of recovering them—and in utter

despair, they crossed their arms on their breasts, and made every demonstration of submission and friendship. We returned their signs, and when fully convinced they were Greeks, we placed our arms beside theirs, and offered them our hands in token of friendship. I really do not know which party had the best cause to rejoice. What with a little "lingua France," picked up in the Archipelago, and significant signs, we made out tolerably well in communicating our wishes and feelings. They were actually Greeks, once living happily with their families in Eleusis, before the Turks destroyed it. I never saw a more wobegone, forlorn expression, depicted on the human countenance, than theirs evidenced in the recital of their painful misfortunes. Together we entered that devoted town where all was ruin and desolation, and I thought their very hearts would burst, as some familiar object met their view, calling up reminiscences at once joyous and happy—startling and afflicting—such deep, deep feeling, I never before witnessed—and one there was, whose grief was past control. Grief and care had done more to bend his manly form, and furrow his noble brow, than time. I saw him kneel and whisper a prayer over the ashes of his kindred, as a big tear trickled down his cheek. Oh! it was a scene, awful beyond description—it called forth our warmest sympathy, and filled us with the most painful emotion. They picked up a few scattered remnants of clothes, bid us adieu, and started for the mountains. They had no homes —the earth was their resting place—and the canopy of heaven their only covering.

'We lingered about the town, discharging our muskets

four or five times, and returned to the beach about eleven
o'clock; there we seated ourselves and waited patiently the
arrival of the boat; and oh! how long the hours seemed.
Time did indeed move with leaden wings. We had
abundant time to contemplate that beautiful scene—the
moon was flinging its silver light on the ruins of the
Venetian castle—its beams were glistening on the placid
bosom of the Aegean sea, whose mirrored surface imaged
a countless number of bright, beautiful stars, that gemmed
the blue heavens.

"—The wind was hushed;
And to the beach each slowly lifted wave,
Creeping with silver curl, prest, kist the shore,
And slept in peace."

'The pensive solemnity of the hour was at last disturbed
by the joyful approach of our boat; the fire from our
muskets soon brought them to us, and in a few minutes we
embarked, and were on our way to our floating home.
The delay in the arrival of the boat had been caused by
their mistaking the landmark, and pulling one or two miles
beyond it. We reached the ship about two o'clock in the
morning, to the relief of the anxious solicitude of our ship-
mates, and our own fatigue. We could not give any satisfactory account of the boatman, and the disappointment
visible on the weather-beaten faces of our hardy crew, was
painfully distressing. The next day the frigate got under
way, stood down to the landing place, and fired four or
five shot across the plain. The sound reverberated
among the mountains with melancholy effect, and there
being no trace of the sign of the man, we continued on our

cruise, leaving it for time to unfold this singular and mysterious affair. I never knew a circumstance to absorb more interest and feeling, and it was sometime before the wonted cheerfulness, that distinguished our gallant frigate, was restored to the ship's company.'

CHAPTER XVII

ALONE AT SMYRNA

THERE seems to be no situation in which *"Old Ironsides"* has not been placed at one time or another during her long career:

[1] '. . . and on the first of October, 1827, we find her lying in the Gulf of Ismyr or Smyrna, under the command of the late gallant and much lamented Patterson, ready to watch over the commerce of our country during the vicissitudes of the European and Asiatic war—a war which Sir Edward Coddrington so soon brought to an end by the tremendous battle of Navarino. The late William the Fourth, of England, was at that time one of the admirals to excute the duty of the lord high admiral of Great Britain; and upon one of the official documents, dictated by diplomacy, and worded in the cold and formal style of state papers, which issued from the admiralty, he had, in pure deviltry, written "Go it, Ned." The companion of the prince understood the hidden meaning of his royal messmate, and on the 20th of October, 1827, the Dartmouth having returned to the fleet, from Navarino, with an unsatisfactory reply from Ibrahim Pasha, admiral Coddrington made the signal to the combined fleets to get

[1] J. E. Dow, *Gentleman's Magazine,* December, 1839.

under weigh, and immediately the English, French, and Russian squadrons tripped their anchors, and, spreading out their immense clouds of canvas to the breeze, bore up for Navarino bay. The Asia led the van, followed by the fleet in two columns. Abreast of the English admiral dashed the French three-decker, with a large white flag— or, as the American sailors used to term it, the admiral's table-cloth—hanging at her mizen; and next, the Genoa, with the black eagles of the czars floating over her poop. Beautiful was the sight! The shores of Greece were before them—the dark blue mountains of the classic land rose in the distance, and a silver veil hung carelessly over their giant heads. The town and castle smiled amid the foreground of the landscape, and the Turkish tents, like a flock of sheep, rested upon the mountain side. A wreath of smoke hung over a neighboring village, and a body of Turkish horsemen returning slowly to camp, told but too well the cause of that symbol of destruction.

'It is not my intention to describe the battle of Navarino. I shall therefore leave the gallant fleet entering the harbor, in face of the Turkish and Egyptian fleets, drawn up in the form of a crescent to receive it, and return to our solitary frigate, whose stars and stripes waved proudly amid the gorgeous banners of the nations of the eastern world—amid the brightness of a Grecian sky. Morning dawned upon the Asiatic, and the rays of the ascending sun tipped with gold the mountains of Natolia, and flashed in splendor from the mosques and minarets of Smyrna. The Constitution now began to make signals for getting under weigh—already the blue peter floated at the fore, and the heavy thirty-two pounder echoed the captain's order, "Come aboard," in a voice of thunder, to the lagging midshipman on shore, when a steamer, under French colors, entered the gulf, and passed swiftly in towards the anchorage. As she swept by the Constitution, she hailed her, and the astonishing news of the unexpected battle burst upon the ears of the American officers.'

And now acting Chaplain George Jones, U.S.N., furnishes us with a first hand account of the scenes witnessed on the succeeding days: [2]

Monday, 29. . . . .

'. . . The first sensation among us, was surprise, mingled with pleasure; the second, wonder how the Turks would be affected by the news, and particularly those of Smyrna. The Pasha, by some unaccountable means, was the first person here that got intelligence of the event, and took his measures immediately. In the harbour it produced great commotion. The merchantmen, whose usual anchorage is off Turk-town, were ordered by the naval commanders to take station by the Frank district, and be ready to receive the Franks, in case of disturbance: while the men of war dropped to within a cable's length of the shore, to cover them in their flight. We kept our place, and the Pasha has sent to the Consul, to express his pleasure at it: the rest, he says, are only challenging hostilities by their distrust: he sent assurance too, that in all cases the American residents will be safe. We, however, gave day and night signals to our Consul,

[2] *Sketches of Naval Life,* by A "Civilian," 1829.

and an officer is constantly kept on the look-out, towards his house: our boats were taken out and small guns fitted to them, so that we were soon in readiness to act, without manifesting any fears. The Pasha has taken a prudent course: he ordered all the Turks into their own district, and companies of soldiers were sent into Frank-town, where our officers have seen them beating their country-men, and driving them out: the liquor shops were all closed, and the Pasha himself has been constantly in the streets. Night went down, and this morning rose, on Smyrna, a troubled city. The Franks are greatly alarmed: the merchants are packing up their goods, and the citizens their furniture: many have removed to the ships. The Turks themselves are not without apprehen-sion; for should excesses arise, their town, it is threatened, will be laid in ashes, and two sloops have taken positions for doing it: the Pasha is erecting batteries on the shore against these vessels. We fear more from the country Turks, than from those of the city, and it is reported, they are threatening to march upon it, but the Pasha has ordered that no one be suffered to leave the villages. A Greek was caught attempting it, at Bournabat, and our officers saw him bastinadoed till his feet were in rags: the Franks, however, are suffered to come in, and all have done so.

'So things remain. A courier has been dispatched to Constantinople, and the Pasha says he will be guided by the course of events in that city.

'*Tuesday* 30.—Scio is reported to have been retaken by the Greeks: it heightens the alarm: we have been getting ball from the hold, and preparing cartridges, and some provisions which we had put ashore for the other ships, have been brought back. A flag was raised at noon, on one of the minarets, taken down, and raised again several times: we do not know its meaning.

'I went ashore in the afternoon, and walked through the streets. The Turks looked sour and scowling; the Greeks frightened; the Franks serious: all passed rapidly and silently on their way; "neque populi, aut plebis ulla vox: sed attoniti vultus, et conversae ad omnia aures: non tumultus, non quies; quale magni metus et magnae iræ silentium est." * No business was doing, except that in one place I saw a Turk buying flint-stones, and in another, two porters carrying lead into their town: soldiers are still kept marching through the streets.

'*Wednesday* 31.—The Pasha refused to let the English residents bring off their property; and this morning we found their smaller national ships anchored as close to the shore as possible: the threat succeeded and their property has free passage. The residents have been sending their goods off as fast as possible: our consul intended to remove his family on board today, but the Pasha heard of it, and sent to him frequently, to say that the Americans have nothing to fear. The French are getting Austrian protections: he heard of this too, and let them know that they had better keep quiet: we received some property on board today.

'* Tacitus. (Among the whole population, not a voice is heard; astonishment covers the features; and ears are turned to every sound: there is not tumult, nor quiet—but there is the silence of great fear, and of great wrath.)'

'*Thursday, November* 1.—Our officers kept on board: the Courier from Constantinople expected every hour.

'*Friday* 2.—I went ashore, and walked through Turktown: there was a strange and unnatural calm in every street, that almost made my blood run cold.

'*Saturday* 3.—The French Admiral came up from Vourla last evening, and spent most of the day with the Pasha. The delay of the courier excites surprise, and many unpleasant surmises.

'*Tuesday* 6.—Things in the same state. A French national schooner came in from Alexandria, by the way of Navarine, which she entered without knowing any thing of the battle. She reports the harbour in a horrible state; covered with blackened timbers, and mutilated bodies. An Armenian just arrived from Constantinople, states that when he left, the city was in great confusion: an embargo had been laid on all the vessels in port.'

Let us now go back to Dow's story, at the moment when word of the battle was received: [3]

'. . . As might well be expected, as soon as the news got wind on shore, the English, French, and Russian residents departed on board of the vessels of their respective nations, leaving the American frigate almost alone in the port, and the American residents about the only Franks in the city of Smyrna. Captain Patterson immediately repaired to the divan of the bashaw, and while ship after ship of other nations dipped their topsails in the waves, the American

[3] *Gentleman's Magazine,* December, 1839.

frigate furled her loosened sails, hauled down her signal of departure, and rested in majesty alone.

'The Turks had not expected such boldness—exasperated as they were almost to madness, and every hour goaded on to revenge the insult offered to their flag, by the arrival of some shattered bark from the scene of action, black with smoke, and wet with blood. A tumult raged in Smyrna; many an English and French residence was sacked; the flags of foreign nations floated no longer upon the Morena, with the exception of the banner of freedom that waved over the portals of the American consulate. Smyrna seemed to be on the eve of a dreadful massacre—"and women wailed and children shrieked in fear."

'Firm and undaunted, however, the gallant Patterson and his suite presented themselves at the palace of the bashaw, and demanded an audience. It was granted, and the American officers were soon in the presence of the incensed governor.

'Around the entrance, stood the bow-string and the bastinado executioners, and the heavy scymetars that flashed by the side of the black slaves, spoke but too plainly the fate that awaited many an innocent citizen of the Turkish town. Pipes and sherbet were presented to the visiters in due form, and after a few salutations, the American captain demanded to know the intentions of the bashaw in relation to the American residents.

'This was bringing matters to a crisis in a style unusual in Turkish diplomacy; but considering the boldness of the asker, and the faith reposed in the honor of the Turks by the American citizens who remained there, the bashaw relaxed his haughty brow, the scowl of anger left his countenance, and rising to his feet, he reached out his hand to captain Patterson, and exclaimed—"Bona Americana, let the consul hoist his flag over the dwellings of his countrymen, and they shall be protected."

'Noon came, and the excitement began to die away— anger now gave way to sorrow—vessel after vessel of the dead and the dying came into port, and ere the Muezzin called the hour of evening prayer, the weeping of the mourner was heard amid the tombs of the cypress groves, and the tears of woman fell upon the scarred and gory features of her dead husband.

'At midnight, the fears of the residents being quieted, and the captain feeling impelled to ferret out a Greek pirate in the straits of Scio, the Constitution unmoored and got under weigh, and at daylight, she passed the anchorage of Vourla, and stood silently down the Levant.'

CHAPTER XVIII

"AY, TEAR HER ENSIGN DOWN!"

THE long and eventful cruise of the *Constitution* finally came to an end. She reached the city of Boston on the Fourth of July, 1828, and happy was the occasion for those aboard and those ashore. She went out of commission on the 19th. This date very nearly marked the end of her career. She was thirty years old and bore many marks of her long and arduous service. She was surveyed, and it was determined that, from a financial standpoint, it would be best not to repair her. The Secretary of the Navy ruled that she be sold or broken up. This seemed the end.

A very fortunate bit of luck intervened to save her. Oliver Wendell Holmes, who was a law student at the time, read of the proposed disposition of the old frigate. He was inspired thereby to write his now famous poem on "Old Ironsides":

'Ay, tear her tattered ensign down!
    Long has it waved on high,
And many an eye has danced to see
    That banner in the sky;

Beneath it rung the battle shout,
  And burst the cannon's roar;—
The meteor of the ocean air
  Shall sweep the clouds no more.

'Her deck, once red with heroes' blood,
  Where knelt the vanquished foe,
When winds were hurrying o'er the flood,
  And waves were white below,
No more shall feel the victor's tread,
  Or know the conquered knee;—
The harpies of the shore shall pluck
  The eagle of the sea!

'Oh better that her shattered hulk
  Should sink beneath the wave;
Her thunders shook the mighty deep,
  And there should be her grave;
Nail to the mast her holy flag,
  Set every threadbare sail,
And give her to the god of storms,
  The lightning and the gale!'

The verses swept the country. A powerful sentiment
was aroused against the sacrilege which had been proposed. It was decreed that the ship be restored to her
original condition and design.

The next consideration was how best to effect the repairs. On February 24, 1831, Commodore Charles
Morris wrote to the President of the Navy Board: 'This

ship from her age & frequent repairs has become considerably hogged & of course her original lines are all altered & injured, this defect can only be remedied by taking her into Dock where they can be perfectly repaired —' The bottom of a ship is said to be "hogged" when the two ends droop with respect to the middle, the keel thereby becoming curved, with the crown of the arc upwards. This condition on the *Constitution* was a result, no doubt, of the excessive weight of her armament. If the "middle body" of a ship droops with respect to the ends the ship is said to be "sagged."

Commodore Morris wrote further: 'If she is repaired by heaving her down, the defect will be still further increased, & besides the risk which always attends the heaving down of a Ship the repairs cannot be so advantageously or so thoroughly made as in a Dock, & the value of the Ship when repaired will not be so great.' To "heave down" a ship is to pull her well over onto her side. Heaving down, when afloat and lying alongside a wharf, necessitates the use of special preventer stays for the lower masts, the heaving down tackles being attached to the heads of these masts.

So it was decided to put the ship in dry dock. Fortunately Dry Dock No. 1 was under construction at the Boston Navy Yard, its completion two years later increasing the facilities of the station immeasurably. The repairs to the frigate were postponed in order to make use of it. The *Constitution* was the first ship to enter and her name has since attached itself to the dock. Captain Jesse D. Elliott reported as of June 24, 1833: 'I have to inform the Commissioners of the Navy Board that the United States Frigate Constitution was taken into Dry Dock at this yard at ½ past 5 oclock this morning and at 1 oclock P.M. was safely shored and secured.'

The keel of the old ship was found to be not only hogged but also thirty inches out of line. These matters were corrected and many other pieces of work were undertaken. The result was that at the end, *"Old Ironsides"* was her former self in all respects. The money expended was greater than the original cost. The gain from her restoration, however, was more than can be measured in dollars and cents. This overhaul is of further significance in that it was the first of her several major refits; in each case the work warded off her destruction at the hands of "the harpies of the shore." Josiah Barker, a Naval Constructor of note in those days, was in charge of the rebuilding. He was over seventy years of age at the time but was not retired until 1846.

In June, 1834, almost exactly a year after the docking: 'The U. S. Frigate Constitution was undocked on Saturday last: and is now safely moored between the 74 $\frac{s}{=}$ Columbus and Independence.–' And thereby hangs another tale.

CHAPTER XIX

"Old Hickory" Loses His Head

THE Hercules figurehead which was on the *Constitution* when she was launched was shot away in one of the actions before Tripoli. It was replaced by a figure representing Neptune with a trident—the choice of Captain Hull. Before the outbreak of the War of 1812, however, this one had given way to a billet head in the form of a scroll.

In 1833, while the ship was overhauling, President "Andy" Jackson visited Boston and was received with much acclaim. Captain Elliott, who had recently succeeded to the command of the Navy Yard, conceived the idea of substituting for the bow scroll a figure of "Old Hickory" himself. *A Biographical Sketch of Commodore Jesse D. Elliott* [1] outlined his mental processes as follows:

'Captain Elliott, seeing every man striving to be foremost in respectful congratulations; seeing Andrew Jackson received with all the enthusiasm which the greatest favorites can ever hope, with all which they had ever shown to the great and good Lafayette, with all which they had shown, years before, to the revolutionary Monroe; seeing that they would not let him rest from

[1] Published 1835.

their civilities by day or night, and even shod with silver
the horse on which he rode,—justly conceived that he
could not perform an act more gratifying to the people
of Boston than by placing upon the bows of what they
called their favorite ship the image of the very man before
whose living image they were then almost bowing down
to worship.   He communicated his views to the commissioners of the navy, who gave to the act their official
sanction.   Was there no precedent for this?   Has the
image of no public man, of no President of the United
States, ever before appeared upon any of our national
ships?   During the administration of John Adams, his
own image was placed upon the corvette "John Adams."
The same ship has been rebuilt upon an enlarged scale,
and the same image has been placed upon it by the present
administration.   Under the administration of James
Monroe, the image of Washington was placed upon the
"Washington," that of Franklin upon the "Franklin,"
that of Columbus upon the "Columbus," that of Sir
Walter Raleigh upon the "North Carolina," and that of
Commodore Stewart upon the "Cyane."   Under the
administration of John Quincy Adams, the head of De
Witt Clinton, then governor of New York, was executed
for the "New York," built at Norfolk.   Under the same
administration the head of Captain John Smith was placed
upon the bow of the "Potomac," and his coat-of-arms
upon her stern.   For this act, then, there were precedents
in abundance.   At the same time he proposed as orna-
ments for the stern the heads of Hull, Bainbridge, and
Stewart, the commanders of "Old Ironsides" in her three

several victories over the "Guerrière," the "Java," and the "Cyane" and Levant." As before said, the commissioners approved of the whole proceeding, and an artist was employed to execute the work.'

Partisans holding the political faith opposite to that of Jackson received word of the project with anything but equanimity. A veritable hornets' nest was stirred up throughout the local press and public. Such "desecration" of *"Old Ironsides"* herself was too much. There follows here a handbill which typifies the more rabid feeling that existed in some quarters:

'FREEMEN! AWAKE!

'Or the Constitution will sink!

'It is a fact that the "Old Glory President" has issued his special orders for the Colossean Figure of his Royal Self in Roman Costume to be placed as a Figure-Head on "OLD IRONSIDES"!!! Where is the spirit of '76?— where, the brave tars who fought and conquered in the glorious ship,—where, the Mechanics, and where, the Bostonians who have rejoiced in her achievements? Will they consent to placing a figure-head of a Land Lubber at her bows? No! let the cry be "All hands on deck" and save the ship by a timely remonstrance expressing our indignation in a voice of thunder!

'Let us assemble in the "Cradle of Liberty" all hands up for the Constitution—let the figurehead (if mortal man be worthy) be that of brave Hull, the immortal Decatur, or the valiant Porter and not a tyrant. Let us not give up the ship, but nail the flag of the Union to the mast, and let her ride the mountain wave triumphant, with none aboard but the Sons of Liberty all flesh and blood, having the hearts and souls of Freemen.

'North-Enders! Shall this Boston built ship be thus disgraced without remonstrances. Let this Wooden God, this Old Roman, building at the expense of Three Hundred Dollars of the Peoples money be presented to the Office Holders who glory in such workmanship, but for God's sake SAVE THE SHIP from this foul disgrace!

'A NORTH–ENDER'

Here Captain H. D. Smith takes up the story: [2]

'L. S. Beecher, a celebrated and skillful master of his art, a native of Boston, executed the design, which was a representation of President Jackson in the Hermitage scene, holding in his hand a scroll, with the motto, "The Union, it must be preserved."

'About the 21st of March' (1834) 'the artist informed Captain Elliott that three prominent citizens had offered him fifteen hundred dollars for permission to carry the image away in the night; and that he might, if so disposed, realize twenty thousand dollars out of the operation. Beecher had too fine a sense of honor, and valued his personal integrity too highly, for the bribes and inducements to be false to his trust, freely whispered in his ears, to produce any effect. He had promised to carry the work through to completion, and he valued his word above the possession of gold. He fitted up his attic as a

[2] *United Service Magazine,* December, 1891.

The cause of all the excitement. The first Jackson figurehead, placed on the *Constitution* in 1834.

studio, allowing no one but members of his own family to enter that apartment. Threats of mobbing and personal violence fell unheeded around the artist as he plied his tools deftly and rapidly. He was not one to be deterred by intimidation. But Elliott, becoming alarmed at the extent and depth of feeling developed among all classes in the community, resolved, as a matter of safety and prudence, to have the figure-head removed to the navy-yard.'

The unfortunate Elliott experienced some difficulty even in connection with this transfer, as may be seen from his letter to the Secretary of the Navy:

'Navy-Yard, Boston, March 31, 1834.

'Sir,—As the operations of this yard have of late been subjected to the criticisms and unnecessary attention of a few of the citizens of Boston and its environs, and as several of my official acts have been misrepresented through the public prints, I have deemed it my duty to give the department a statement of facts relating to the subject, that, should any call be made upon it for documents, it may be enabled to comply with it by answering the whole subject at once.

'Having understood from the artist who was to carve the figure-head for the Constitution, and from hand-bills extensively distributed outside, that threats had been made against its completion or removal, and wishing to prevent the people of Boston from being eternally disgraced by a few heated political partisans through a midnight removal,

I determined to remove the head to the yard in the usual manner, that is, by boxing it up and bringing it from Boston in the launch.

'I accordingly on the 21st inst. directed Sailing-Master Hixon, upon whose discretion I could rely, with a boat's crew composed of the seamen and ordinary seamen of the yard, to proceed to Boston and receive the head. I also ordered him not to take any arms with him, nor to let any of his party.

'The officer executed his duty at nine o'clock in the morning, and the whole affair was concluded to my entire satisfaction.

'In the evening of the same day, having been informed by anonymous hand-bills and reports of conversations outside that an attempt would be made to take the head from the yard, I sent for Master Commandant Percival, and directed him, confidentially, to receive on board the Columbus certain cutlasses and boarding-pikes that would be sent down to him by Captain Smith, so that in case of any necessity they could be used by the seamen and ordinary seamen belonging to the yard; but of this necessity, I stated to both him and Captain Smith confidentially, I had no expectation; but still I deemed it my duty to take this precautionary measure.

'Captain Percival received this order without raising a question against complying with it, and went on board, as I concluded, to make the necessary preparations for having it executed.

'Captain Smith, the executive officer of the yard, was then ordered to send the arms on board; this he did by giving instructions to the gunner to go with them.

'Upon the gunner's going on board the ship, Captain Percival sent for him, and refused to receive them without a written order from Captain Smith. The gunner then went for Captain Smith, but not finding him, returned and took the arms away.

'The gunner then reported the same to me, when I sent for Captain Percival and demanded an explanation; this he refused to give in any other manner than by saying he would receive no orders from a gunner. I told him it was my order, and he knew it previously; he again replied he would receive no order from a gunner or any other officer of a navy-yard. I then suspended him from duty, and placed the direction of the ship in the hands of Lieutenant Varnum, who received the arms and executed the order with promptness.

'The next day Captain Smith came to me, and said that Captain Percival was wrong, and would probably make an explanation that would be satisfactory.

'Captain Percival did so, and was restored to duty. This, sir, is the true statement of the case, and I should not have deemed it necessary to bring it to the notice of the Department, were it not for the attempt that has been made to produce a wrong impression upon the public mind, without a proper disposition to correct it.

'Respectfully,
'J. D. Elliott.

'Hon. Levi Woodbury,
    'Secretary of the Navy.'

And now the plot thickens: [3]

'The figure-head was placed upon the frigate, and fully confiding in the integrity of all within the navy-yard, and treating with indifference all anonymous threats of violence from without, he took no particular pains to guard it. The frigate was moored with her head to the west, between two ships of the line, or seventy-fours, the "Columbus" and "Independence," both guarded by sentinels, and Elliott supposed that no one could approach by water without detection, and was satisfied that by land it was inaccesible excepting to treachery.

'Captain Samuel Worthington Dewey was a native of Cape Cod, bearing the reputation of an eccentric and erratic character.[4] In the midst of the figure-head excitement, when political rancor was at fever-heat over the subject, Dewey arrived at Boston from the West Indies with a cargo of sugar. His employers, Henry and William Lincoln, disposed of both vessel and cargo, leaving the master with time hanging heavily upon his hands. For lack of better employment he turned his attention to the frigate "Constitution" and her now famous adornment.

'One day, while sitting in the inner office of the firm on Central wharf, the conversation turned upon the all-absorbing question agitating all circles and classes. "It would not take much to induce me to go over there," pointing in the direction of the navy-yard, "and remove

---

[3] H. D. Smith, *United Service Magazine*, December, 1891.
[4] From what follows, it seems that "dare-devil" would be more accurate than "eccentric and erratic."

View of the Constitution, as moored between the U. S. 74's Columbus and Independence, at the Navy Yard, Charlestown, Mass., in June, 1834.

From the American Magazine, October, 1834.   The first Jackson figurehead is seen, before mutilation.

that figure-head some night." The junior member of the firm replied, lightly, "Dewey, if you will carry the job through, I'll give you a check for one hundred dollars." "Done!" was the quick response. "I will take that."

'No importance was placed upon the circumstance, and the conversation was well-nigh forgotten by the younger partner, who was well acquainted with Dewey's foibles.'

The project was not forgotten by Dewey, however. He undertook to perform the deed; then later he recounted his experiences to Samuel Adams Drake who describes them as follows: [5]

'In that immense crowd, which had witnessed the rebaptism[6] of Old Ironsides, stood a young Cape Cod seaman. His father, a brave old captain in the 3d Artillery, had doubtless instilled some strong republican ideas into the youngster's head, for he had accompanied him to Fort Warren' (later Fort Winthrop) 'during the War of 1812, and while there the lad had seen from the rampart the doomed Chesapeake lift her anchor, and go forth to meet the Shannon. He had heard the cannonade off in the bay, had noted the hush of the combat, and had shared in the anguish with which all hearts were penetrated at the fatal result.

'Old Ironsides was moored with her head to the west, between the seventy-fours Columbus and Independence. The former vessel had a large number of men on board, and a sentinel was placed where he could keep the figure-

[5] *Old Landmarks of Middlesex.*
[6] The *Constitution* was undocked in June, 1834.

head in view; another was posted on the wharf near at hand, and a third patrolled the forecastle of the Constitution; from an open port of the Columbus the light fell full upon the graven features all these precautions were designed to protect.

'On the night of the 2d of July occurred a thunderstorm of unusual violence. The lightning played around the masts of the shipping, and only by its lurid flash could any object be distinguished in the blackness. Young Dewey—he was only twenty-eight—unmoored his boat from Billy Gray's Wharf in Boston, and, with his oar muffled in an old woolen comforter, sculled out into the darkness. He had reconnoitered the position of the ships by day, and was prepared at all points. At length he found himself alongside the Independence, the outside ship, and worked his way along her big black side, which served to screen him from observation.

'Dewey climbed up the Constitution's side by the man-ropes and ensconced himself in the bow, protected by the headboards, only placed on the ship the same day. He extended himself on his back, and in this position sawed off the head. While here he saw the sentry on the wharf from time to time looking earnestly towards the spot where he was at work, but the lightning and the storm each time drove the guard back to the shelter of his box.

'Having completed his midnight assassination Dewey regained his boat, to find her full of water. She had swung under the scupper of the ship and had received the torrent that poured from her deck. In this plight, but

THE VILLAIN OF THE PIECE.

Merchant Skipper Samuel Dewey who decapitated "Andy" Jackson. He was a cousin of George Dewey, later to become the hero of Manila Bay.

never forgetting the head he had risked his life to obtain, Dewey reached the shore.'

Carrying the trophy in a gunny sack he went straight to his mother's house on School Street. Her woodshed was the first hiding place of President Jackson's head. The excitement and rage of the Democrats assumed such alarming proportions, however, that Dewey thought it best to find another and more secure place of concealment. Accordingly the head was conveyed to the residence of Henry Lincoln on Gooch Street, West End. There it was packed in a champagne basket and placed under an old-fashioned bedstead with encircling curtain.

Not long afterwards Nicholas Biddle, the president of the United States Bank, visited Boston. (This bank was one of the major political issues of the day.) During his stay forty-four of the most active and prominent Whigs invited him to a dinner at one of the leading coffee houses. After the meal the servants were sent from the room and the doors were locked. The head of the famous figure was laid upon the table and loud were the many cheers with which the exhibit was greeted.

After the excitement caused by the dark deed had subsided somewhat—and it had been no ordinary excitement—

[7] 'Dewey packed up the grim and corrugated features he had decapitated and posted off to Washington. At Philadelphia his secret leaked out, and he was obliged to exhibit his prize to John Tyler and Willie P. Mangum,

[7] *Old Landmarks of Middlesex.*

afterwards President and acting Vice-President, who were then investigating the affairs of the United States Bank. These grave and reverend seigniors shook their sides as they regarded the colossal head, now brought so low, and parted with Captain Dewey with warm and pressing offers of service.

'The Captain's intention to present the head to General Jackson himself was frustrated by the dangerous illness of the President, to whom all access was denied. He however obtained an audience of Mr. Van Buren, the Vice-President, who at once overwhelmed him with civilities after the manner in which that crafty old fox was wont to lay siege to the susceptibilities of all who approached him. Upon Dewey's announcing himself as the person who had taken off the Constitution's figure-head Mr. Van Buren gave a great start and was thrown off his usual balance. Recovering himself, he demanded the particulars of the exploit, which seemed to afford him no small satisfaction. Captain Dewey wished him to receive the head. "Go to Mr. Dickerson," said the Vice-President, "it belongs to his department; say you have come from me." To Mahlon Dickerson, Secretary of the Navy, our hero accordingly went.

'The venerable Secretary was busily engaged with a heap of papers, and requested his visitor to be brief. The hint was not lost on the Captain.

' "Mr. Dickerson, I am the person who removed the figure-head from the Constitution, and I have brought it with me for the purpose of returning it to the Government."

'The Secretary threw himself back in his chair, pushed his gold-bowed spectacles with a sudden movement up on his forehead, and regarded with genuine astonishment the man who, after evading the most diligent search for his discovery, now came forward and made this voluntary avowal. Between amazement and choler the old gentleman could scarce sputter out,—

' "You, sir! you! What, sir, did you have the audacity to disfigure a ship of the United States Navy?"

' "Sir, *I took the responsibility.*"

' "Well, sir, I'll have you arrested immediately"; and the Secretary took up the bell to summon a messenger.

' "Stop, sir," said the Captain, "you cannot inflict any punishment; I can only be sued for a trespass, and in the county where the offense was committed. Say the word, and I will go back to Charlestown and await my trial; but if a Middlesex jury don't give *me* damages, my name's not Dewey." The Captain had explored his ground: there was no statute at that time against defacing ships of war, and he knew it. Mr. Dickerson, an able lawyer, reflected a moment, and then put down his bell. "You are right, sir," said he; "and now tell me all about the affair."

'The Captain remained some time closeted with the Secretary, of whose treatment he had no reason to complain.'

Medical Director Edward Shippen, U. S. N., who was a college mate of Secretary Dickerson's son, leaves to us an epilogue:[8]

[8] "Among Our Contemporaries," *United Service Magazine,* January, 1892.

'Mr. Dickerson came from New Jersey, but his son, a distinguished patent-lawyer, after his death moved to New York, and transported to the house he had built many valuable things, among others General Jackson's head, which, for fear of accident, he carried himself. In the train a person who was passing through, attracted by the head in Mr. Dickerson's lap, stopped and said, "Beg pardon, but is not that the head of General Jackson which was set on the "Constitution's" bows so many years ago?"

' "Yes. How did you know it?"

' "Because I carved it."

'It was Sewall, a celebrated carver, who had long before left Boston and gone into mining and ranching, and was then on his way to pay a visit to his native town.'

CHAPTER XX

A 24-POUNDER ADRIFT IN A GALE

THE bow scroll which was displaced by the Jackson figurehead was mounted on a tall lamp post at the head of the dry dock. After Dewey's "heinous crime" the Navy Department allayed further antagonism, so far as possible, by ordering the decapitated figure to be covered temporarily with canvas. Eight months later the *Constitution* sailed for New York with an American flag painted on the canvas. She was to be there for only a very short period. Accordingly, before she left Boston, Elliott had forwarded to the New York Navy Yard plans and specifications for carving a new head and putting it in place. Incidentally, Dewey had performed his decapitation through the chin, not the neck.

At this point it might be well to list the other figureheads which have adorned the old ship since 1835, for there has existed much confusion on the subject. The first Jackson figure with the new head was replaced by a second complete figure of Jackson, probably during the ship's stay at Portsmouth, N. H., from 1855 to 1860. It is certain from photographs that this second Jackson figurehead was in place in 1858 when the vessel was on the ways for overhaul. It was removed, probably during the

Philadelphia refit (1871–76), and sent to the U. S. Naval Academy. One careful investigator and well informed historian states that a large American eagle with outspread wings followed Jackson on *"Old Ironsides' "* bow. This was replaced by a bow scroll some time before 1897. New billet heads were substituted during the overhauls carried out in 1907 to 1908 and 1926 to 1931.

With "Andy" Jackson patched, with other special repairs completed, and with stores loaded, the good ship was ready for active service again after a lapse of seven years. So:[1]

'In the month of March, 1835, Old Ironsides, under the command of captain Jesse D. Elliott, left the port of New York for Havre, to bear thence Edward Livingston and family, preparatory to a declaration of war—which seemed inevitable—with France.

'The French minister, Mr. Serrurier, had left for Brest three days previous, and it was considered all important for the Constitution to enter the English channel prior to the arrival of the French vessel at her port of destination. Accordingly all speed was made in departing from New York, and on the 10th when the blue summits of the Jersey woodland sank astern amid the freezing glories of a north easter, she took her departure for Land's End, with her gun and berth decks lumbered up with provisions, cordage, plank, etc., while her weary master's-mate nodded in his unquiet sleep over the spirit-room hatch.

---

[1] J. E. Dow, *Gentleman's Magazine,* 1840. The writer of the "Sketches" was by this time actually aboard the *Constitution,* serving as Professor of Mathematics.

'It is a solemn thing to bid one's native land good night, even when the balmy west wind whispers from the shores, bathed in the glories of summer, and when the god-like stars look down in their majesty from the still vistas of heaven; but when the wind roars amid the rigging, and the waves roll like tumbling mountains around you; when the Mother Carey's chicken skips along astern and the white-capped billow curls over the sinking bows; when the winter's lightning, with its blue and hell-like blaze, flashes in uncertain quantities around the horizon; and the splitting mizen topsail makes the boldest and vilest look aloft; then it is not only a solemn, but it is an awful task, a task which wrings the hardest heart, and damps the cheerfulness of the lightest spirit.

'Night came early upon the ocean, and with it an increase of wind. The waves commenced rolling in a very uncertain manner; we had what seamen call a cross sea; and it was cross enough, God knows. The dead lights were now shut in; the top-gallant yards sent down; the guns housed; and the topsails close reefed. The bonnet was taken from the jib, the spanker brailed up, and the foresail reefed. Onward the good ship swept over the raging flood; and when the watch was called, she seemed to plough her way through waves of fire, while the red foam hissed upon her white hammock cloths, and shot up in fiery spray around her bows.

'A cold rain fell sparsely around. The thunder note of the breeze, as it rattled the slackening rigging, seemed fast gaining upon the roar of the agitated deep. The ship's stores were now nearly stowed, and the casks and barrels that could not be put under hatches were lashed to the staunchions. A double allowance of grog was served out; a cold and scanty supper was taken by the weary seamen upon the gun-deck; and then the hammocks were swung fore and aft, and sleep seemed at last about to end the toils of the first day at sea; but the first lieutenant seemed to have his doubts about the propriety of carrying such a quantity of canvas in such a storm, and after several hurried visits to the spar deck, and as many returns to his state-room, he came to the ward-room hatch, and sung out to the midshipman of the watch, "Mr. Moffit, tell the carpenter to have axes placed by the main mast"—then turning into the ward-room he endeavored to eat his supper in quiet. But no; the well-filled cup of cold coffee flew out of his hand, and followed the travelling sugar-bowl from one side of the ship to the other; while a puff of wind, as the mizen topsail shivered, put out his candle and left him to grumble over his ruined supper in darkness.

'That night was a busy one for the mariner; the gale increased with every hour; and the old frigate skipped from wave to wave like a sheer-water dipping her wings in the foam as she past along; while she creaked and groaned like spirits of the damned in torment. Her masts seemed ready to jump out of her; her heavy bowsprit and sprit-sail yard buried her bows in the waves, and the canvas that she carried seemed just ready to start from the bolt ropes. Ten o'clock came and the master at arms had put out all the lights excepting the one in the ward-room. There a solitary candle gleamed from the sailing master's lantern, and lit up the countenances of the idlers of the mess, who had gathered in a knot to talk over the prospect of a swift passage and a speedy war. The tables were lashed to staples driven in the deck, and the chairs capsized, and lashed underneath to their legs. The ship leaked through her rudder casing, and hogshead after hogshead of sparkling water was swabbed up by the ward-room steward, and the jack of the dust, from the purser's state room.

'The purser had a large box of stationery, which he had placed in the mess-room for safe keeping until morning. This box he placed athwart ships, with one end resting against the bulk-head of the state-room, and the other chocked by a cleat nailed upon the deck. Upon this box sate the purser, then myself, and then the veteran and scientific sailing master. Hanging on to the table, with both hands, stood the first lieutenant; while the doctor, as he lay in his cot, grasped the side of it with almost super-natural power, and hinted that the light hurt his eyes, *ergo* it was time to put it out. Some minutes had elapsed since the last puff of wind, and we had all relaxed our hold. Jokes were passing like cents in the steerage; and the dying notes of the old sea-dogs' song by the galley, sounded with uncommon clearness. A heavy roar was now heard—a tumbling crash as though an Alpine avalanche had de-scended upon the poop, immediately followed, and then the order of the lieutenant of the watch—"Look out to windward!"—rung wildly around. Down to her bear-ings, to leeward sank the ship—ten feet strait ahead pitched the old sailing master and landed upon all fours—while forty feet through the middle air flew your humble servant, who brought up, all standing, against the lattice-work of the first lieutenant's state-room. The sailing master kept his singular and unexpected position—the purser, like an old cruizer, hung on to the stationery; and I, poor landsman, greenhorn, and lubber, neglected to watch the weather roll, and, before I could say Jack Robinson, flew with the velocity of a foot-ball, and landed, far more scared than hurt, in the master's bunk, among chronometers, sextants, quadrants, hour-glasses, and tell-tale compasses. A gale of wind destroys etiquette; and a heaving sea brings the sea sick admiral to a level with the cabin boy.

'A cry of distress now rung through the ship. The first lieutenant sprang up the ladder with the agility of an old seaman. "Silence," thundered the trumpet as he reached the deck, and the voice of man died upon the water. A heavy thump started all hands forward; and a succession of jars, at the bows of the ship, soon gave evidence of the matter. A forecastle gun had left its carriage, and turned a somerset out of the port where it hung by its breeching-rope; and, as the old frigate rolled upon the wave, it thumped against her iron-sides like the battering ram of Titus against the walls of Jerusalem.

'Our flying jib-boom now snapped off like a pipe-stem, and flew to leeward like a feather thrown from a gray gull's wing. A tremendous sea again broke over the stern in its majesty, and the red torrent with its crest of lighter foam sparkled as it curled around the carronades, and hissed as it rushed through the lee-gangway. It stove in the commodore's gig, and sent the thin planks like chips

TWENTY-FOUR POUNDER, U. S. S. *CONSTITUTION.*

upon the water. As the wave rolled over us, I saw the black gun-wale of the gig, with the word "Constitution" in white letters upon it, riding triumphantly over the sea of blood, a type of our salvation in after time, and of our preservation amid the carnage of civil war. Another wave followed, and then the old frigate, shaking herself like a water-witch, righted, and sailed along her course, but not without being endangered by the iron plum of four thousand pounds weight, that hung at her starboard bow.

'The captain now made his appearance—a red kilmarnock tipped his head, and streamed out to leeward like the pennant of a bashaw of three tails. In a moment he saw the critical situation of the ship. The trumpet was put in requisition.

' "Stand by to cut away the starboard bow gun!" rang above the full fury of the gale.

' "All ready forward, sir!"—was the scarcely intelligible response of the carpenter's mate, who raised his voice to its utmost pitch; and it was not a small one, either.

' "Cut! cut! d—n you, cut away!" thundered the trumpet—a bright gleam of the axe was seen forward—a grating sound was heard—and then the iron mouth piece of the starboard bow went down to the plains of ocean to sleep in silence for ever.

'The cause of this accident was as follows: The gunner had been on the sick list all the way out; and the raw yeoman that acted for him had neglected to key the gun to the carriage.

'The ship was now hove to. The gale still raged in its fury around her; but the laboring of the masts and timbers was over. She kept her bows to the wind, and, like a thing of life, sprang up to meet the crest of the mountain wave.

'The next day, when the storm had abated, a marine died, and was buried with the rites usual in a ship of war. As the soldier's body went down to its last resting place, an old tar chucked over the rail a full allowance of pig-tail, and exclaimed to his messmates, while a tear skulked in the corner of his eye, "I say, Jack Adams, the soldiers are now right. Fifty-three guns—fifty-three marines— did'nt I tell you we had one more than our compliment, when the old bow chaser got a leave of absence, and went on a cruize to the bottom?"

' "Aye! aye! you're right enough, now," said a boat-swain's mate in reply—"I never knew a gun to go without a small-arm man to watch it." '

CHAPTER XXI

Weathering a Lee Shore

Homeward bound! The *Constitution* sailed from Plymouth, England, on May 16, 1835, for New York. Our old friend Jesse Erskine Dow was an eyewitness to a thrilling experience which befell the ship soon afterwards. He writes: [1]

'It was at the close of a stormy day in the month of May, 1835, when the gallant frigate Constitution, under the command of captain Elliott, having on board the late Edward Livingston, then minister at the court of France, and his family, and manned by nearly five hundred souls, drew near to "the chops" of the English channel. For four days she had been beating down from Plymouth, and on the fifth at evening, she made her last tack from the French coast.

'The watch was set at eight, P.M. The captain came on deck soon after, and, having ascertained the bearing of Scilly, gave orders to keep the ship "full and bye," remarking at the same time, to the officer of the deck, that he might make the light on the lee beam, but he stated he thought it more than probable that he would pass it with-

---

[1] "Old Ironsides on a Lee Shore," from the *Gentleman's Magazine* of March, 1840. This same sketch, in slightly different form, first appeared in the *Democratic Review* of April, 1839.

out seeing it.   He then "turned in," as did most of the idlers, and the starboard watch.

'At a quarter past nine, P.M., the ship headed west by compass, when the cry of "Light O," was heard from the fore-top-sail yard.

' "Where away?" asked the officer of the deck.

' "Three points on the lee bow," replied the look-out man—which the landsman will readily understand to mean very nearly straight ahead.   At this moment the captain appeared, and took the trumpet.

' "Call all hands," was his immediate order.

' "All hands!" whistled the boatswain, with the long shrill summons so familiar to the ear of an able seaman.

' "All hands," screamed the boatswain's mates; and, ere the last echo died away, all but the sick were upon deck.

'The ship was staggering through a heavy swell from the Bay of Biscay.   The gale which had been blowing several days had increased to a severity that was not to be made light of.   The breakers where Sir Cloudesley Shovel and his fleet were destroyed in the days of Queen Anne, sang their song of death before, and the Dead man's Ledge replied in hoarser notes behind.   To go ahead seemed to be death, and to attempt to go about was sure destruction.

'The first thing that caught the eye of the captain was the furled main-sail, which he had ordered to be carried throughout the evening, the hauling up of which (contrary to the last order that he had given to the officer of the previous watch, on leaving the deck) had caused the ship to fall off to leeward two points, and had thus led her into a position on a "lee shore," upon which a strong gale was blowing her with such force as to render her chance of safety almost hopeless. That sole chance consisted in standing on *through* the breakers of Scilly, or in passing them by a close graze along their outer ledge—was this destined to be the end of the gallant old ship, consecrated by so many a prayer and blessing from the heart of a nation?

' "Why is the main-sail up, when I ordered it set?" cried the commander, in a tremendous voice.

' "Finding that she pitched her bows under, sir, I took it in under the general order that the officer of the deck should carry sail according to his discretion," replied the lieutenant in charge.

' "Master's mate, heave the log," was the prompt command.   The log was thrown.

' "How fast does she go?"

' "Five knots and a half, sir."

' "Board the main tack, sir."

' "She will not bear it," said the officer of the deck.

' "Board the main tack," thundered the captain, "keep her full and bye, quarter master!"

' "Aye, aye, sir!"—the tack was manned.

' "Haul aft the main sheet," shouted the captain; and away went the after guard giving the huge sail, like a sea bird's wing, to the gale.

' "Give her the lee helm when she goes into the sea," cried the captain.

' "Aye, aye, sir, she has it," growled the old sea dog at the binnacle.

' "Right your helm! keep her full and bye!"

' "Aye, aye, sir, full and bye she is," was the prompt answer from the helm.

' "How fast does she go?"

' "Eight knots and a half, sir."

' "How bears the light?"

' "Close aboard on the lee beam, sir."

' "Keep her away half a point."

' "How fast does she go?"

' "Nine knots, sir."

' "Steady so," returned the captain.

' "Steady," sung the helmsman; and all men were silent upon that crowded deck for a space of time that seemed to my imagination almost an age.

'It was a trying hour with us. Unless we could carry sail at the rate of nine knots an hour, we must of necessity dash upon Scilly, and who ever, during a storm, touched those rocks and lived? The sea ran very high; the rain fell in sheets; the sky was one black curtain, illumined only by the faint light which was to mark our deliverance, or stand a monument of our destruction. The wind had got above whistling; it came in puffs of thunder, that flattened the waves, and made our old frigate settle to her bearings, while every thing on board seemed cracking into pieces. At this moment the carpenter reported that the after bolt of the weather fore shroud had drawn.

' "Get on the luffs, and set them on all the weather shrouds—keep her at small helm, quarter-master, and ease her in the sea," were the successive orders of the captain.

CAPTAIN JESSE D. ELLIOTT.
A stormy petrel of the Old Navy, though his looks belie it.

'The luffs were soon placed on the weather shrouds, which of course relieved the chains and channels; but many an anxious eye was turned towards the remaining bolts; for upon them depended the masts, and upon the masts depended the safety of the ship. With one foot of canvas less, fifteen minutes would have been the length of her life.

'Onward plunged, in silent majesty, the overladen frigate, and at every surge she seemed bent upon making the deep the sailor's grave, and her live-oak sides his coffin of glory. She had been hurriedly fitted out at Boston, when the thermometer was below zero, and when her shrouds were set up the lanyards were thawed. Her rigging therefore slackened at every strain; and her un-wieldy masts (for she had those designed for the new frigate Cumberland, a much larger ship,) seemed ready to jump out of her, and take the decks with them. And now —while all was apprehension—another bolt drew—and then another—until at last our salvation hung upon a bolt less than a man's wrist in size. Still the good iron clung to the solid wood, and spite of the twisting and creaking of the channels, it bore us along, the thunder-speaking breakers in gallant style. As we bounded on—for I can compare our vessel's motion to nothing else then *bounding* —the rocks seemed within a few feet of us. Dark as was the night, the white foam scowled around their black heads, while the spray fell over us, and the thunder of the dashing surge sounded like the awful knell of ocean, for the victims ready to be engulphed.

'At length the light bore upon our lee-quarter, and the

broad Atlantic rolled its white caps before us. Previous to this moment all, as I have before stated, were silent; each officer and man was at his post; and the bearing and countenance of the captain gave encouragement to all on board. With but a bare possibility of saving the ship and her complement of men, he placed his reliance upon his nautical skill and courage, and by carrying the ponderous mail-sail when under any other circumstances, it would have been a suicidal act, *he weathered the lee shore, and saved the Constitution.* The main-sail was now hauled up by light hearts and strong hands; the flying-jib and spanker were taken in, and from the Light of St. Agnes the gallant vessel, under close reefed topsails and jib, took her departure and danced merrily over the deep, towards her native land.

' "Pipe down, Mr. Montgomery," said the captain, to the first lieutenant, "and splice the main brace."

' "Pipe down," echoed the first lieutenant, to the boatswain.

' "Pipe down," whistled the boatswain, and his sturdy mates, to the crew, and pipe down it was. Soon "Jack o' the Dust" held his levee on the main gun deck; and the weather-beaten tars, as they gathered about the grog tub and luxuriated in a full allowance of old rye, forgot all their perils and fatigue.

' "How near to the rocks did we go?" said I, to the master's assistant the next morning.

'He made no reply, but, taking down a chart of the British Isles, showed me a zig-zag pencil mark *between a rock and the island breakers,* which must have been a

narrow channel for a fisherman to beat through in a head
wind, in pleasant weather, by daylight.   But Old Ironsides was not to be laid up in ordinary on the rocks that
line the coast of England; and her thunder note may again
compel the British Lion to ask for quarter on the deep.

'I went upon deck; the sea was calm; a gentle breeze
was swelling our canvas from water sail to royal; the isles
of Scilly had sank in rosy light on the eastern waters; and
the clouds of the dying storm were rolling off in broken
masses to the northward and westward, like the flying
columns of a beaten army.'

CHAPTER XXII

An Odyssey

No sailor who shipped on the *Constitution* could claim that any recruiting poster was misleading if it advised him to "Join the Navy and See the World." In those days ships *went to sea* and visited many, many ports—usually in foreign lands. After *"Old Ironsides"* had fulfilled her mission of transporting Edward Livingston to New York she was soon off on another long cruise to the Mediterranean—this time for three years. Many were the havens, rich in romance, that were visited; many were the distinguished visitors who trod her decks; many were the unusual events that took place during this period.

First, Tangiers, Gibraltar, and Mahon, the last named serving as a base. Then Athens, where the ship was visited by King Otho of Greece and his staff, and Prince Calacatroni. On to the eastward, to Cira, Vourla Bay, and Smyrna; then back to Malta, Gibraltar, Tangiers, and Lisbon. While the *Constitution* was at Lisbon the Prince of Saxe-Coburg arrived and was married to Queen Dona Maria. From Lisbon to Malaga, to Gibraltar, and back to Mahon. Here we find a note in an old diary: "Thos D. Allen murdered John Nowlan on shore at Mahon." Toulon, Genoa, Leghorn, Civita Vecchia, Naples—then:

"Sentence on Thos D. Allen carried into effect on board the John Adams."

Down around the "boot" of Italy sailed our ship to Palermo, Messina, and Corfu. Here she was visited by the leading officials of the Ionian Islands—that anomalous entity of international law. The party was led by Sir Howard Douglas, the Lord High Commissioner. Next, to the classic waters of Milo, Napoli d'Romani, and Athens again. We learn that here the *United States* arrived and relieved the *Potomac*. Curiously enough, the only ones of the old ships then remaining in the service were the very first three to be launched—the frigates *Constellation, United States,* and *Constitution*. A still more curious fact is that the *Constellation* and *Constitution* are still on the Navy list, even at the present writing.

From Athens the old frigate sailed to Suda Candia and to Sidon. At this point a squabble nearly eventuated when the Turkish governor at first said he would not return gun for gun in the salute which was being proposed. He acceded when informed that his politeness was not being questioned. Then on to Beirut and Tripoli—in Syria. Here lay a large part of the Egyptian fleet under Ibrahim Pasha and Capudan Pasha. The former was at the time Governor of the Coast of Syria. Both of these high officials together with all of their captains visited the ship and inspected the crew at quarters. At the collation served afterwards, Ibrahim Pasha proposed the health of General Andrew Jackson whose portrait hung in the cabin and whose image adorned the bow as figurehead. The sentiment expressed in this toast is said to have been not very palatable to the French surgeon who was acting as interpreter. During the entertainment Capudan Pasha was somewhat free in boasting of the sailing qualities of his ship. Accordingly, Commodore Elliott agreed to sail in company with him as far as Beirut on the *Constitution's* run to Jaffa. At a dinner seven years later at Hagerstown, Md., the Commodore told about the resulting race. In the distance of ninety-odd miles *"Old Ironsides,"* under a stiff breeze, sailed around the Turk twice, crossing his bow and stern each time.

From Jaffa the course was laid to Alexandria. There Mahomet Ali, the Viceroy of Egypt, and his suite visited the ship. After a long run of nearly a thousand miles the *Constitution* anchored on her old battle grounds off Tripoli, Africa. Then Tunis, Mahon, and Cadiz. On this last run she fell in with a dismasted English schooner, bearing the quaint name of *Perseverance,* and towed her in. In such ways did service of every kind fall to the lot of *"Old Ironsides."* At Lisbon a large party paid a visit to the ship. It comprised Ambassadors, Chargés d'Affaires, Consuls, and Admirals of four Powers—England, France, Denmark, and Belgium.

Another swing around a circuit, visited in part before, took the frigate to Gibraltar, Mahon, Marseilles, Genoa, Leghorn, Civita Vecchia, Palermo, Malta, and Athens again. Here the King and Queen of Greece came aboard with their retinue. The next historic ports of call were the Temple of Minerva, Hydra, Corinth, the Doro Passage, the Plains of Marathon, the Dardanelles.

This was indeed a cruise! The Plains of Troy, Gallipoli, Nagara, and Constantinople. Here the British Minister to Turkey visited the ship. It was Lord Ponsonby, a forebear of the recent Governor General of Canada.

Down through the Grecian Archipelago again to the Holy Land: Tenedos, Scio, Cira, Suda, Jaffa, Cesarea, and Mount Carmel. Our chronicler notes in connection with the monastery on Mount Carmel: "from here Elijah was taken up to Heaven." Tyre, Sidon, Beirut, Tripoli (Syria), and Beirut again. All along the line the ship was gathering relics and antiquities to bring back home. Limasol and Larnaca, on the Island of Cyprus; Jaffa, Alexandria, Larnaca, Malta, and once more back to Mahon for a long stay.

The years had been slipping by during the course of these wide wanderings. The end of the long tour of duty was approaching. A short trip to Malta and Syracuse and back to Mahon again, virtually ended her Mediterranean patrol for this decade. On June 15, 1838, *"Old Ironsides"* really set sail for home. After a short stop at Gibraltar, outward bound, she headed for Madeira; and from there she reached Hampton Roads on the last day of July. This ended a prodigious bit of cruising. From the time she left Boston on March 2, 1835, she had covered 46,635 miles. She had been at sea almost exactly one third of her cruise of 1,221 days.

The *Constitution* brought back a most diverse lot of archeological exhibits for presentation to a varied list of institutions. A summary follows.

To Girard College:

A Roman sarcophagus weighing about 3,500 pounds.
A cabinet of gold, silver, and other metallic coins.
Four boxes of antiquities collected in Palestine and Syria.
A limb of one of the cedars of Lebanon.

To Dickinson College:

A cabinet of ancient coins.
Other antiquities from Palestine and Syria, Corinth, Athens, Crete, &c.

To Washington College:

A collection of ancient coins.

To Jefferson College:

A capital of a column obtained in Cesarea.

To Princeton College:

A collection of ancient coins.
A specimen of marble from Alexandria, Troas, and one from Cesarea.

To Cambridge College, Mass:

Specimens of marble from Alexandria, Troas, and from Cesarea.

To Williams College:

A capital of a column from Cesarea.

To Dartmouth College:

A collection of ancient coins.

"HER EYE ON THE BLOODY TURK."

"Old Ironsides" at Constantinople, July, 1837.

To Kenyon College:

A collection of coins from Alexandria, Troas.
A piece of a column from Cesarea.

To the College of Missouri:

A collection of coins.

To Transylvania College:

A collection of ancient coins.

To the Medical College at Baltimore:

A mummy disinterred at Memphis, Egypt.
A curbstone of a well from Cesarea.
A marble sill from the Temple of Minerva on the Plains
of Troy.
A column from Cesarea.

To Charlottesville University:

Two marble balls, about eight feet in circumference, ob-
tained at the Dardanelles.
A marble head of Bacchus from Tyre.
A vase fished up where the Battle of Actium was fought be-
tween Caesar and Pompey.
A large marble column from Alexandria, Troas.
An eagle made from a piece of marble removed from
Minerva Somnes.

To William and Mary College:

An ibis.
A column from the Plains of Troy.

To the Baltimore Cathedral:

A painting representing the Illumination at St. Peter's and
St. Angela's.

To Georgetown College:
Casts of the Popes.

To Prospect Hill, N. C.:
A column from Marathon.

To the Literary and Philosophical Society at
Charleston, S. C.:
A collection of ancient coins.

To the Navy Department or Government:
Two colossal balls from the Dardanelles.[1]
A sarcophagus from Beirut.

To the American Antiquarian Society of
Worcester, Mass.:
A parcel of ancient coins.

To the Legislature of Pennsylvania:
A copy of an original painting of Columbus and Vespucius.
An eagle made from marble removed from Alexandria,
Troas.

Possibly a more interesting list is that of the animals—
no less—which the Constitution brought back with her.
The distribution of these was as follows:
To the Honorable John Forsythe, of Georgia: a jack.
To Mr. Hibbs' plantation, Tennessee: a Maltese jenny.
To Elizabeth City, Va.: a jack.
To Charles Carson and John C. M'Allister, Dauphin
County, Pa.: a jack.

[1] One of these balls formed a part of the Navy exhibit at the Sesquicentennial Exposition at Philadelphia in 1926.

To James A. Gallagher: a Maltese jack and a large Arabian bay horse.

To T. B. Jacobs, Lancaster County, Pa. (for Commodore Elliott) : three Andalusian hogs, two broad-tailed Syrian sheep, some Minorca chickens, some grain, grass, and garden seed, and one Minorca jack.

To Mrs. Jacobs: one superior Arabian mare.

To Mr. John T. Barr, of Missouri (for Commodore Elliott) : four Arabian mares, one Andalusian colt, and three Arabian colts.

This latter list is of special interest in that it involved Commodore Elliott in some of the trouble which he encountered soon after the ship reached home waters. He was suspended from duty for four years on various charges of harshness in discipline and also for cluttering up the berth deck with the above mentioned live stock. Unfortunately, therefore, a courtmartial ended the cruise just about as inauspiciously as the figurehead incident had begun it. On the whole, however, it was no doubt remembered happily by nearly everyone on board.[2]

[2] See Appendix B for J. E. Dow's informal "log" of the cruise.

CHAPTER XXIII

CLEARED FOR ACTION IN 1841

THE *Constitution* did not long remain inactive on this occasion. She went back into commission at Norfolk on March 1, 1839, just seven months after her arrival. She was scheduled for a far voyage to the west coast of South America and an extensive tour of duty on that station. Captain Dan Turner was in command and Commodore Alexander Claxton had hoisted his broad blue pennant on *"Old Ironsides."* Fortunately for us, a certain Henry James Mercier was a member of the ship's company the entire time; he has left us an excellent record of the cruise.[1] The early pages contain intimate descriptions of life aboard ship during some fair and foul weather encountered on the outward voyage. En route from New York to Vera Cruz a sunny day provided a picture which Mercier paints as follows:

'It was on the first of June, we were about four or five days sail from the Islands of Grand Caymans, and with our yards braced up sharp, our ship was moving along with as much speed as any other craft on the wind possibly could: it was one of those delightful afternoons peculiar

---

[1] *Life in a Man-of-War,* or *Scenes in "Old Ironsides,"* by a Fore-topman; 1841. Reprinted by Houghton Mifflin Co.

to the latitude we were now in, scarcely a cloud floated in
the horizon, but the firmament was one uninterrupted tint
of beautiful azure; all on board took advantage of this
lovely weather, and almost the whole of the ship's company were scattered about on the spar-deck, enjoying in
various ways the beautious serenity of the scene.   When
a vessel-of-war is sailing "on the wind," her crew have the
finest times imaginable, almost verifying the old woman's
remark of "sitting down and letting the wind blow them
along"; they have no studding-sails to set, no bracing to
do, (for the yards are expected to be as sharp as they
can well get them) and save once in a while "a slight pull
of this bowline," or "a small haul aft of that sheet," they
scarcely touch a rope for days or perhaps weeks together.

'The hands had just been turned to after dinner, and
the sweepers had but laid by their brooms after skimming
them slightly over the different parts of the deck allotted
to them.   In the gangways you might perceive groups of
industrious ones with their clothes-bags lying near them,
calculating with serious face what quantity of frocks and
trowsers would be sufficient to serve them the three years'
cruise.   That long cadaverous looking customer, with
such a rogueish twinkle in his eye, who you may observe
with a half-worn jacket in his hand, that is a thorough-
bred "down easter" up to every move in a man-of-war, he
is trying to shove that same jacket off to the young fellow
near him for three dollars when grog money is paid.

'Perceive that old quartermaster, whose florid cheeks
and rotund paunch plainly demonstrate that "Uncle
Sam's" beef and pork, which he has eat for the last

eighteen years, are capable of raising as respectable a corporation as your dainty viands ashore; he is surrounded by five or six of our green-horns, and with a small piece of *nine thread* is endeavoring to knock the principle of *stopper-knots* and *Matthew Walker's* into the thick heads of his all-attentive pupils. Under the refreshing shade of the boats a crowd of worthies are stretched out, who despite the noise and outcry on every side, are transporting on the balmy breeze the mellifluous music of their nasal organs, they appear like many of Adam's sons on *terra firma,* to take the course of time just as it comes, never torturing themselves concerning what the future may bring forth, but in the words of the old rhyme

"They eat, and drink, and sleep—what then,
    They sleep, and drink, and eat again!"

Groups of light-hearted apprentice boys, with the roseate tint of health o'er spreading their youthful countenances, their eyes sparkling with jocund delight, and their buoyant hearts unoppressed with care, are pursuing their antic gambols throughout every part of the deck, without one solitary thought of the disquietudes and perplexities that may possibly intervene to mar their pleasures and cloud their brows, ere their term of servitude is expired. Some sons of poetry and romance are imbibing the balmy influence of the weather on the *booms,* taking perhaps a painful glance at the past, or their souls wrapped up in some delightful revery of the future, thinking of bygone scenes with heartfelt regret, and contrasting them in their imagination with those that await them in the rich and luxurious lands of Chili or Peru.

'The lieutenant of the watch, with his well polished speaking trumpet in hand, is walking with measured stride the weather side of the quarter-deck, paying scarcely any attention to the scene around him, appearing to be completely absorbed in his own meditations. Old Bunting, the quartermaster in the boat, is scanning with half-closed eyes the weather leech of the main top-gallant sail, letting the officer of the deck know he is *awake* by occasionally singing out to the man at the wheel "no higher," when the ship is two or three points off the wind, and "luff you may," when the sails are lifting. . . .'

From Vera Cruz the *Constitution* went back to Havana and from there began her run to Rio de Janeiro. On this leg she sailed more then seven thousand miles. Then off for Valparaiso around the Horn:

'Providence favoured us with a delightful breeze for a length of time after our departure from Rio; in fact we carried it so far, that we all began to flatter ourselves with the pleasing hope that we would make our passage to the Pacific in as short a time as any other ship ever accomplished it; and as our good old craft, with a cloud of canvass, urged onward like a greyhound from the slip, pleasure filled every bosom and delight beamed in every eye. On the twenty-seventh of September we made Staten Island, and on the twenty-ninth the dreary and snow-capped summit of Cape Horn broke upon our view. The spar-deck was now literally crowded with the components of every part of the ship, who, with no little bustle, ascended the hammock-nettings and rigging, to feast their eyes upon this celebrated and much-talked-of cape. There it was, quite as cold and comfortless as it ever was represented: there was the goal we had been long striving to reach; there was the cheerless head-land, the thoughts of encountering which had caused many to feel disheartened; and there was the barrier that had yet to be passed ere the pleasing scenes of Chili or Peru would glad our sight.

' "And is that Cape Horn, that we've been making such a fuss about?" remarked one of the galley cooks, popping his wooly head above the forecastle netting, a sneer curling his ebony proboscis. "Hell, I thought 'twas twice the place it is—they talked so much about it, I imagined we'd get a regular *peeling* 'afore we'd round it." "Don't hollo before you're out of the wood, Mr. Snowball," cried an old sheet-anchor man—"I've been as close as this to the Cape, and yet smelled hell before I doubled it. I wouldn't be afraid to bet a small trifle, but what we'll have to take some of the old lady's *muslin* off before supper; believe me, I don't like the looks of it yonder." "What, don't you think this fair wind will carry us round, Sam?" enquired one amongst the crowd. "I do not, indeed," replied the man addressed, "just look off there—the old Cape appears to be preparing to put on his night cap, and that's a sure sign of a *snorter,* take my word for it;" every eye was now cast in the direction pointed out by the forecastleman, and it was perceptible that a change of weather was about to take place—large black masses could be perceived, as if rising from out the horizon, following each other in rapid succession—the heavy mist that at first was scarcely discernable, had now completely enshrouded the snow-topped summit of the Cape; the frighted sea-birds flitted along the surface of the water with ominous scream, and the luminary of day, surrounded by a fierce and blood-red zone as it was about to depart angrily into the western waters, plainly betokened the brewing of a storm.   We were not deceived—the predictions of the forecastleman were realized, for it came on sudden and fierce, scarcely giving us time to make the necessary preparations for its unwelcome visit; and instead of the auspicious breeze of the preceding evening, to which every sail was spread, and under the influence of which we had moved swiftly and gracefully along, our gallant ship was next morning struggling against the tempestuous elements, almost under her bare poles.   The gale continued without intermission for sixteen or eighteen days, buffeting which "Old Ironsides" proved herself the sturdy and efficient sea-boat she was always celebrated for: no ship was ever more comfortably secured against the bitter blasts and drenching billows than was ours on this occasion; the gun-deck ports were tightly shut in and caulked with masterly judgement, and made completely water-tight by the application of several thicknesses of tarred canvass on the outside, rendering our main-deck in this boisterous weather a warm and comfortable shelter to its inmates.   The hammocks were kept below during the continuance of the gale, and were duly occupied by their proprietors in their several watches, for which our Commodore and Captain received the heart-felt thanks and warm panegyrics of a grateful ship's company; in a word, nothing was left undone that could in any measure add to our comfort and security, or serve to dissipate the sadness of the chilling and dreary scene by which we were surrounded.

'Our main-deck was so darkened from the effects of the closely shut ports, and heavy tarpawling which enveloped every hatch, that our lads were obliged to mess on the lower deck; and I assure you that the ludicrous scenes that might be observed almost every mealtime, as the rolling and pitching of the ship brought them in collision with each other, would distort the risible muscles of the most austere. One day in particular, our frigate under close-reefed storm-sails laboured dreadfully, rolling almost her spar-deck guns under—dinner was piped, and our lads were huddled together around their several messes, endeavoring as they best could to transmit the contents of a pan well filled with bean-soup to the inner man.   Each one as he received his *quantum,* placed himself in some solid and secure position to commence his meal, taking advantage of the interval between every roll of the ship to bring a portion of the delicious liquid to his impatient lips; a fellow on the forward part of the deck, sung out lustily, "look out for your beans;" the words were scarcely uttered, than, before any body could make a second preparation, she gave one of the most tremendous rolls I think I ever experienced; I actually thought she would never *right* again; my eyes, what a scene now presented itself—away went simultaneously with one movement—in one confused mass, kettles of hot water—baskets of small biscuit—pans of soup—pots—kettles—frying pans—gridirons—and all the *etceteras* of the galley; here might be seen a poor fellow struggling amidst a heap of clothes-

bags—spit boxes—pots—pans and spoons, endeavoring to
regain his feet, which the well-greased slippery deck almost
rendered an impossibility; further along, you might observe two or three marines well besmeared with soup,
trying with rueful countenances to gain possession of the
paraphernalia of their mess chest, which, as well as themselves had been tumbled into the main-hold at the first
onset, with but little ceremony.   In the midst of the uproar, the *bon-mot* and *repartee* flew around with rapidity,
(for at what time will not Jack enjoy his joke,) and though
many lost their dinners on the occasion, and several got
sore heads and pummeled ribs from the effects of their
falls, yet all with one accord joined in the laughter that
this affair occasioned.

'We encountered the "peltings of the pitiless storm"
for about seventeen days, but without an accident of any
kind taking place;—the spirit of the tumultuous gale
began to tire, and as we dragged our way almost im-
perceptibly to the westward, a bountiful Providence
favoured us once more with fair winds and delightful
weather; the light spars were got aloft—topgallant and
royal yards crossed, the lofty studding-sails again spread
to the inspiring breeze; and as our skimmer of the seas
danced merrily onward towards the Chilian shores, our
lads in their present lightheartedness forgot the rough
reception they met with when doubling the Cape.'

The shadow of death fell heavily upon the officers of
the *Constitution* on this cruise.   Shortly after entering
the Pacific, R. R. Pinkham, the third lieutenant, departed

this life. Let us, through the pen of Mercier, witness a burial at sea a hundred years ago:

'The twenty-ninth [2] was a delightful day; we were moving along with studding-sails set, and our old frigate from the velocity with which she skimmed over the sparkling billows, appeared as if endeavoring to make up for the detention occasioned by the adverse winds and tempestuous weather when off the cape. As the bell's sharp clang proclaimed it noon, sail was shortened, and our ship hove to with the main-topsail to the mast, and the thrilling and doleful cry of "All hands bury the dead," issued from the mouths of the boatswain and his mates. The entire ship's company, neatly and uniformly dressed in white frocks, blue jackets and trowsers, now repaired to the spar-deck, and formed themselves, with order and silence, abaft the mainmast. A death-like stillness prevailed—not a whisper was heard throughout the ship— and now the heavenly and soul-thrilling air of the Dead March in Saul pealed forth from the several instruments of our musicians, and as the sweet sounds were wafted away upon the inspiring breeze, every bosom was filled with awe and solemnity. The corpse was now borne on deck by six captains of guns belonging to the division of which the deceased had the command, and as they laid their melancholy burden upon the platform that was in readiness to receive it, and from which it was to be launched into the boundless deep, the tear of sorrow and affection could be observed dimming the eye of many a gallant officer standing by, as he perceived the remains of

[2] Of October, 1839.

him, who perhaps had braved with him the dangers of the perilous ocean, in youth and manhood about to be engulfed in his watery tomb.

. . . .

'The burial service was now read in an audible and solemn voice by our first lieutenant, and the gloomy and desponding countenances of the assembled crowd plainly told that their feelings were in unison with the melancholy occasion that had drawn them together. At the doleful words, "we commit his body to the deep," the end of the platform was raised—a plunge was heard in the water— the entire marine guard, drawn up in the lee-gangway, discharged three vollies of musketry—and in another moment not a vestige remained to point the spot where the son of Ocean had sunk to his unfathomable resting-place.'

After a stop at Valparaiso *"Old Ironsides"* reached Callao on November 26. This was to be her base and she laid up there for three months at the start. Then began her more active service on the station, lasting more than two years. Serving as flagship she cruised from one port to another on the west coast of the continent—Puna, Ecuador; Payta and Callao, Peru; Valparaiso and Talcahuana, Chile—back and forth showing the flag, up-holding our rights, guarding our interests.

On March 6, 1841, during her last stay at Talcahuana, Commodore Claxton passed away, an officer well beloved by the men. He had been aboard two years to the day when death took him. His body was transported at once to Valparaiso for burial. From *Life in a Man-of-War* it would seem that the setting and the ceremony were most picturesque and impressive:

'On the eleventh—sad and disconsolate was the appearance the gallant and far-famed frigate Constitution presented, with her flags hanging listlessly at half-mast, as she dropped anchor in the harbour of Valparaiso; a boat had been sent in the previous evening, mentioning the melancholy object of our present visit; and as we drew up to our berth, we had the pleasing gratification of beholding every man-of-war and merchantman, of five or six different nations, with their banners suspended at half-mast, as a tribute of respect. The news of Commodore Claxton's death, at Valparaiso, was as an electric shock; they could not for one moment believe, that the roseate, healthy individual, who but a few short days before was participating in their festivities, the gayest of the gay, and whose affability and courteousness had the effect of winning upon the hearts of all those with whom he chanced to commingle, was now lying a cold, stiffened corpse, a lump of inanimate clay; his once vigorous limbs palsied by the cruel hand of Death;—but such is the mutability of everything human; for life is but

"A tale told by an idiot,
Full of sound and fury, signifying nothing."

In accordance with the customary regulation of the place, at once superstitious and ungenerous, which prohibits the dead body of any person, how exalted soever his rank, from being paraded through the streets after sunrise, we were constrained to send the remains of Commodore Claxton on shore to the dead-house at day-break, on the morning of the twelfth; but still this observance of their frivolous custom did not debar us from paying him, ere he was consigned to his mother earth, all the respect his high station and exemplary virtue so well entitled him to. At eleven o'clock, our boats, containing the officers, musicians, the entire marine-guard, and about two hundred and fifty of our hardy tars and apprentice boys, neatly and uniformly dressed in blue jackets, tarpaulin hats, and snow-white frocks and trowsers, left the ship's side; and following each other in graceful rotation, they pursued their solemn and almost noiseless course towards the shore, impelled by the slow and measured minute-stroke. Upon the mole they were met by a numerous assemblage of the *élite* of Valparaiso, together with the officers from the British frigate President, the French frigate Thetis, the Danish frigate Bellona, the Chilian frigate Chilia, and the French sloop-of-war Camille, as well as the masters, supercargoes, &c., of every vessel in port, and a detachment of royal marines; and as the first minute-gun from our ponderous thirty-two pounders boomed over the waters and reverberated amongst the distant hills, the soul-thrilling anthem of the Dead March in Saul, from the instruments of our musicians, arose upon the balmy breeze; and the procession began its silent march towards the sanctuary of mortality, in the following order :—First, came out the band dressed in their plain, neat uniform—the sombre drapery of death pendent from each instrument; followed by our marine-guard, whose firm measured tread, erect stature, and glittering appendages, formed a sight truly martial;—the Chaplain of Her Majesty's ship President followed next in order; after whom, eight American Naval Officers as pall-bearers; next, dressed in suits of deep mourning, came the body servants of the deceased—their downcast countenances proclaiming how severely they felt this sudden and unexpected bereavement; foreign Consuls and foreign Naval Captains followed next; after whom, Rear Admiral Ross, accompanied by the French and Chilian Commodores; and now came Captain T——, our respected commander, accompanied by the United States Consul, as chief mourners; and his moistened eye and sorrowful visage, told but too plainly how sincere was his affection, and how deep-rooted was the grief he felt for the individual he was now paying the last tribute of respect to.   Next in order came foreign and United States Naval Officers—two and two—according to rank; followed by some hundreds of merchants, merchant captains, and citizens dressed in deep mourning; immediately after, the most interesting part of the procession, came the United States apprentice boys—two and two—dressed in their neat naval uniform, and moving with the most perfect order and decorum; they were followed by about two hundred of the petty officers and seamen belonging to the Constitution; who, from their quiet, orderly, and solemn deportment during the obsequies, reflected credit upon themselves as well as upon the ship that was manned by such a specimen of the Yankee sailor.   Bringing up the rear, and closing this mournful train, came a detachment of the Royal marines from Her Majesty's ship President, with arms reversed—their bright scarlet coats and glittering accoutrements, forming an elegant contrast to the short blue jacket, lined frock, and flowing trowsers of our tars. In the order I have endeavored, but feebly, to describe, did they bend their slow and melancholy steps up the winding declivity, at the summit of which was located the small but neatly laid-out burial place; wherein many a gallant son of Neptune lay mouldering into dust, far, far, from the shores of happy Columbia or merry England. The narrow path, together with every pinnacle of rock, or dizzy precipice, as well as the windows and verandas of the houses adjacent, were literally swarmed with in- divduals of every age and sex, for their eyes were never before greeted with such an imposing spectacle;—and to view the solemn train wending its way along the circuitous and craggy road, whilst the plaintive and soul-touching strains of the Dead March from the instruments of the musicians, and the death-like sound of the muffled drum, were borne upon the pinions of the breeze, ever and anon accompanied by the booming sound of the minute gun; it was indeed a scene long, long to be remembered. At length we reached the sanctuary of the dead, and the capacious coffin containing all that was now left of the once humane and indulgent officer, sincere and devout Christian, generous and upright man, was borne from the dead-house by ten of our ship's company, and laid upon the brink of the yawning and insatiate cavity that was soon to swallow it from our sight forever. A death-like still- ness prevailed; not a whisper was heard from the sur- rounding crowd;—every eye was bent in the direction of the grave—every ear was inclined to catch each word that fell from the lips of the devout minister; who, in an audible and harmonious voice, read the burial service.—Here was a scene worthy of contemplation; to behold the Naval officers of four different nations, throwing aside every feeling of ancient malignity, religious enthusiasm, or political prejudice, coming forward simultaneously—their bosoms in perfect unison with the mournful occasion—to pay the last sad tribute of respect to a brother-sailor in a far foreign land. The funeral service ended, and the coffin lowered into its dark, narrow resting-place; it was gratifying in the extreme, as our marine-guard discharged the three customary volleys over the grave, to behold the detachment of Royal marines from the British frigate President, form into line and pay our deceased commander-in-chief a like farewell tribute; the circumstance made a deep impression upon the minds of our men; and it spoke loudly for the kind-heartedness and generosity of Real Admiral Ross, and showed plainly that his friendship for the deceased during their short intimacy, had become strongly cemented.

'The mournful train now retraced their steps towards the mole, in the same quiet, orderly manner; and as our tars vacated the burial place and cast a long, last, lingering look upon the silent grave that held in its cold damp embrace their revered commander-in-chief, many an humble prayer was breathed forth from the lips of those hard, reckless sons of Ocean, for his future happiness, as pure and holy in their import as any that ever ascended to the throne of the Most High. As the boats shoved off from the mole to return to our bereaved frigate, the reverberating sound of the minute-guns, fired from every vessel of war in port, added another link to the chain of gratitude that already so closely bound us to our foreign naval friends. . . .'

This unhappy duty completed, the frigate returned to Callao once more—her fifth visit—remaining there for three and a half months prior to the start for home.

Now, the years 1837 to 1841 had witnessed one more grave crisis between the United States and Great Britain. This one was a result of the famous *"Caroline* incident." Matters had been drifting along for some time with little improvement. For ships at Callao, word from home was one of the rarest of commodities. No one could know what might have happened at any time until months had elapsed. At length:

'Whilst preparing for our departure, news was received on board, through a letter, of the death of President Harrison, and the serious turn the case of McLeod and the burning of the Caroline had taken in the United States;— now was the aspect of affairs changed, and "war, grim-visaged war" became the all engrossing topic throughout the ship; our Captain was on the alert in a moment, (remember he had smelled powder before,) and the first move, the entire bulkheads of the cabin and pantry were taken down, to give room to work the guns aft; shot-plugs were got up, and suspended convenient for use; battle lanterns were arranged in their proper places; a large quantity of extra cylinders were filled, and transported to the forward magazine; in a word, twenty-four hours subsequent to the receipt of the news, the far-famed Frigate

Constitution, England's greatest *eye-sore* last war, the staunch old craft that encircled with unfading laurels the brows of Hull, Bainbridge, and Stewart, was once more "armed for the fight;" commanded by a well-tried son of ocean, and surrounded by a crew, though young in years, yet possessing the spirit of true Yankees; who would willingly have made "Old Ironsides" their tomb, ere they would have allowed her to be wrested from them by an enemy, even of superior force.

'Her British Majesty's Ship President lay at anchor near us, and many a joke was cracked, regarding perhaps the no improbable idea of her and ourselves coming in contact; she had at that time the worst of usage on board; desertions were frequent, and her crew were in a state of the greatest dissatisfaction, (to give it the easiest term,) and some of our old fire-eaters gave it as their opinion, that should we come to the *scratch,* her men wouldn't fight with that ardour British tars are celebrated for. The day previous to our departure, we beat to quarters, and passed the word to fill up the shot-racks and shot-boxes with round, grape, and canister; and now was a scene rife with interest, though coupled with confusion, which could have been avoided had things been done *ship-shape.* Whilst so employed, the Frigate President and Sloop-of-War Acteon got under-way, and commenced manoeuvering about the harbor, and our wags let off their sallies of wit on the occasion, although in one sense of the word things *did* look suspicious.'

These sallies of "wit" are too painful to repeat! Moreover, the lack of organization evident during the ammunition passing makes it preferable to gloss over that operation also. Suffice it to say that more than two hours were required before the shot racks and boxes were filled.

' "What a pretty kettle of fish we'd make of it, if the President and Acteon would take us on the ground hop, as the Phoebe and Cherub did the Essex last war in Valparaiso, if it takes us this length of time to get our shot up," spoke up a dry old sea-dog, with a knowing shake of the head. "Oh! we could *pipe belay* or pass the word to them to hold on till we got our racks filled again," rejoined Flukes with a laugh. "There is little danger of such a thing as that taking place, mates," chimed in old Binnacle, the quartermaster, "we are all of a match for the President, big and saucy as she looks, and the little Dale that lies yonder would give the Acteon a dose of Yankee *pills,* that would take her sometime to digest." This remark of the old quartermaster's drew forth a murmur of approbation from the assembled crowd, for however they might condemn the austere and nonsensical theories of the executive officer, which were often of such a nature as to irritate the feelings of the most passive and uncomplaining, yet the gallant time-honoured old frigate that had been our habitation for the last twenty-eight months, was endeared to every bosom as strongly as when she fluttered the pennant of our deceased, though not forgotten commodore. With such remarks as the above did they beguile the time, whilst passing and repassing from the shot-lockers to their several guns, until the drum beating the retreat proclaimed that everything was in readiness with regard to our armament; and an enemy's ship (should one feel inclined to make the experiment) would find that "Old

Ironsides," with her present commander and crew, was now the same staunch, invulnerable structure

> As she was wont to be, in days long past,
> When she withstood the battle and the blast.'

At any rate the *Constitution* got to sea next day without incident. The date of departure was July 11, 1841, and her destination was Rio. In company for a day or two were the U. S. Sloop-of-war *Dale* and the U. S. Schooner *Shark*. However:

'As I mentioned in the foregoing Sketch, we were quite sanguine we would not reach Rio without some hostility, for it was the general opinion on board that war had been declared; and we were well aware if such was the case, plenty of English armed vessels would be cruising between the mouth of the river La Plate and the coast of Brazil; and consequently we'd have to *stand our hand* with them, which thank Heaven we were well prepared for, as far as a good staunch sea-boat, a cool, determined commander, and a crew of young, willing hearts could go in repelling the attack of any craft of the same mettle, or to stretch a point I don't think we'd turn tail to a larger one.

'A few nights after we had bid farewell to our friends of the *Dale,* sometime between eleven and twelve o'clock, when the gun-deck was as still and noiseless as a sick chamber, the watch below to a man being sunk in profound slumber, and the watch on the spar-deck, with the exception of the look-outs and the men at the wheel, &c., stretched at full length busily engaged in what sailors technically term *caulking,* which in the language of folks on shore would

amount to *sound sleeping,* the drum and fife were heard
to break the silence that prevailed, by beating vehemently
to quarters; here was a sudden surprise, every one was in
motion instantly; the occupants of the hammocks below
jumped upon their feet in a moment, and "lash and carry"
was every person's object, for all thought as a matter of
course that a British man-of-war was about to give us a
broadside; but no, Captain T—— took this method of
ascertaining how quick we could get ready for action,
should occasion require us to do so at night; and in this
instance he had the pleasing satisfaction of seeing every
hammock on deck, every man at his quarters, every gun
cast loose and ready to belch forth their deadly contents, in
as short a space of time as could be expected, from the
choicest picked crew that ever manned a Yankee frigate.'

The threat of war was the indirect cause of Captain
Turner shutting down on the crew's tea water. It happened in this wise. The ship was not overabundantly
supplied with firewood—a most necessary item for the tea
water. The skipper had determined to make no stop on
the way home if he should learn from a passing ship that
the United States was at war. Accordingly all hands
maintained continuously the sharpest kind of a lookout for
sails. The tea water assumed an importance second only
to the possibility of war itself. Yet not one sail was
sighted during the entire run south.

'Thus, without falling in with even a single particle of
ice, did we double the Cape that we had so much dreaded to
encounter, and for the fierceness of which every one had

made some preparation;—passed the Falkland Islands, the mouth of the La Plate, still no vessel greeted the eyes of the men at the mast heads, and we began to think in right down earnest something more than common had occurred, for we were now in the very track of ships; but at last, on the twenty-fourth of August, about five o'clock in the evening, "Sail ho!" re-echoed loudly and emphatically. All eyes were turned in the direction pointed out by the men aloft, and a brig was just discernible a long way to the eastward.   To make more sail and tack ship was but the work of a moment; and by half-past twelve o'clock that night we bore down and spoke her.   She proved to be a Brazilian brig but a few days from Rio, and her captain (interrogated in the Portuguese language by a Brazilian Minister taking passage with us) gave us the joyful intelligence that things were as tranquil in the United States as when we left, and that war was *talked* of only.

'During the colloquy, not only the watch on deck, but the greater part of the watch below, who left their hammocks at the first hail, crowded upon the poop; for they all felt interested, and though scarcely one of them understood a single word of the conversation, it was construed fifty different ways ere they reached the gangways; but this much they harped on, they had spoken a vessel, and "tea-water" was the cry from the break of the poop to the confines of the forecastle;—they were not deceived—the captain was as good as his word—for the next evening they had the gratification of beholding the galley pipe sending up its accustomed clouds of smoke to be dispersed by the cheering breeze.

'About eleven o'clock in the forenoon on the twenty-eighth, we discovered a large sail on our starboard bow, standing to the westward; it proved to be the Marion, one of our small class sloops-of-war, who, as soon as she made out our number, ran down for us, and corroborated the intelligence we had already received from the Brazilian brig, viz. that the aspect of affairs at home was as yet quiet. We now made sail, the Marion accompanying us some distance in shore, and at nine o'clock dropped anchor in the truly beautiful harbor of Rio de Janeiro; returning thanks to the Supreme Ruler for having brought us through our difficulties thus far on our passage homeward-bound.'

Many of the features of this voyage lend to it the most amazing similarity to the U. S. Battleship *Oregon's* run around South America in 1898.

The long cruise ended at Hampton Roads on October 31, 1841. The old ship had been away more than two and a half years. During her absence she had been at sea 392 days and had sailed 45,751 miles.[3]

[3] See Appendix C for Mercier's itinerary of this cruise.

CHAPTER XXIV

Around the World With
"Mad Jack" Percival

"Old Ironsides" was in Norfolk for the greater part of the years 1841 to 1844.   She was flagship of the Home Squadron, however, from 1842 to 1843.   Some of this time her commodore was none other than Charles Stewart, now sixty-four years of age.   Nearly thirty years had passed since his capture of the *Cyane* and *Levant*.   He lived to the ripe old age of ninety-one.

The question arose as to the amount of money necessary to put the *Constitution* in first class shape.   Captain John Percival said that for $10,000 he could fix her up so that she would be able to sail around the world.   *And he did.* We have already met "Mad Jack" Percival once in these pages—in one of the mix-ups with Elliott over the Jackson figurehead.   His career had been a wild and varied one. Born in 1779 he had served in his youth as master's mate and midshipman in the Navy until laid off in 1801 when everything was cut down.   Later, while in the merchant service, he was impressed into the British Navy by a Portuguese press gang.   He served on Nelson's *Victory*. Percival was put in command of a Spanish prize which he took to Madeira.   There he and other impressed American seamen escaped to a U. S. man-of-war. In 1809 he was back in the American Navy again. On the Fourth of July, 1813, he borrowed a fishing smack and with thirty-six armed volunteers surprised and captured H. M. S. *Eagle*. The following year he won distinction and promotion and a sword from Congress for gallantry during the *Peacock's* victory over the *Epervier*. Captain Percival at sixty-six years of age, however, seems to have been no longer the "Mad Jack" of "the last war." On the *Constitution's* cruise around the world he appeared the calm, able, and considerate commander, loved and respected by shipmates and foreign dignitaries alike.

This was a gorgeous cruise which commenced at the Norfolk Navy Yard on April 11, 1844. The real start, however, was on May 29 from New York where the ship had gone to take aboard Mr. Henry A. Wise, our new Minister to Brazil. His family totalled thirteen, and Captain Percival turned over the entire cabin to them. The course was not laid direct to Rio de Janeiro by any means. *"Old Ironsides"* headed east to Horta in the Azores for her first stop; then to Funchal, Madeira, and Santa Cruz, on Teneriffe, before recrossing the ocean to Rio. These four places were splendid "liberty ports," and the many days in their harbors were spent pleasantly and profitably.

It is of interest to note the make-up of the crew of the ship during this cruise. On one occasion a poll of the sailors was taken and it was ascertained that nearly half were foreign born. The source of our information divides the men between "foreigners" and "native born

Americans," taking no account of citizenship. There were 200 Americans as against 175 foreigners composed of 95 British, 23 Germans, 23 Scandinavians, and 34 miscellaneous. These 34 included "1 Swiss," and each reader may formulate his own joke about this circumstance. Those in the ship's company who were not counted consisted of 32 officers (all of them Americans), 40 marines, and 10 blue-jackets, making a grand total of 457 persons aboard. The large percentage of foreign born sailors continued to exist for a long time afterwards in the U. S. Navy. It involved no diminution in the loyalty or effectiveness of the crews, however,—as the Spaniards discovered in 1898 contrary to their expectations.[1]

The actual "cruise around the world" started from Rio on September 8, 1844, then the *Constitution* sailed eastward for the Cape of Good Hope. She hove to off Tristan d' Acunha, doubled the Cape, and dropped anchor in St. Augustine's Bay, Madagascar, on October 15. Benjamin Stevens was Captain's Clerk during the cruise and he gives us an interesting description of some of the queer residents of this port:[2]

'Canoes put off from the shore, and we soon had the pleasure of shaking some Malagary by the hand.[3] Prince Green, who owns Tent Rock; John Green, his purser; John Stouts, his toady, and other hangers-on came on board; also Captain Amber, Captain Martin, and others.

[1] See Appendix D for make-up of the crew (December, 1844).
[2] "A Cruise on the Constitution," *United Service,* 1904. The author was still living when his story was published.
[3] Probably meant to be "Malagasy"—inhabitants of Madagascar.

CAPTAIN JOHN ("MAD JACK") PERCIVAL
IN MELLOWED AGE.

He was 67 years old before the completion of his cruise around the world
with *"Old Ironsides."*

Prince Green, who appeared to be the greatest man among them, was dressed in a faded pair of tight white pants, an old "pepper and salt" colored coat, given him by an officer of the Concord, and a navy cap with an old faded gold band.   He was a man about fifty years of age.

'John Green, his purser, as he styled himself, was dressed in the most original manner possible.   An old tattered navy waistcoat, one epaulet, a sailor's hat, and pieces of cotton composed his wardrobe.   To crown the whole he had an American eagle (brass) fastened onto his vest behind.   He had only one eye, and on the whole was the most original looking officer I have ever seen. Most of the other men had nothing but strips of cotton crossing from the shoulder to the hips and fastened round their loins.   They soon found their way into the steerage amongst the reefers, and quickly made a good use of the clothes given them.   One fellow had a shirt given him, and a pair of drawers, which set tight to his legs, and, with the aid of an old straw hat, was soon transformed into an apology of a well dressed man.   With this (certainly to him, at least) finery he was walking the quarter-deck, as proud as any Turkish Bashaw with three tails.   Another fellow was honored with the crown of Neptune (used in crossing the line).

'Nearly all brought letters of recommendation from different whale ships, which were not very favorable to their honesty.   One of them brought a letter signed by "Sam Slick," stating the bearer to be a rascal and not trustworthy.   Not being able to read, he had been gulled into taking it, and it would have done a person's heart

238 On the Decks of "Old Ironsides"

good to see the look of approbation with which he received
the letter again and carefully stowed it away, presuming, I
suppose, that it bore testimony to his honesty, etc.'

There followed next a number of stops in strange and
primitive ports: Mozambique; Majunga Bay, Madagascar; Nos Bey Island, at the mouth of Passandava Bay,
Madagascar; Zanzibar; and Latham's Island.[4] Then
off to the eastward again on November 28, across the
Indian Ocean. At Rio the Captain had had the hull
painted a light gray for the sake of coolness. The crew
appreciated greatly this practical application of the new-
fangled "natural philosophy" that made their home so
livable in the tropic heat. It was a 36-day run to Quallah
Battoo, a notorious pirate nest on Sumatra. Calms and
brisk winds alternated in those Far Eastern waters. One
day the crack frigate "made good" 240 miles "over the
ground," logging 198 miles through the water and being
set ahead 42 more by a favoring current.

Thanks to the light paint and other effective means of
caring for the crew's health, there had been a marked
absence of sickness on board. Before the first death
occurred, almost seven months had elapsed since leaving
New York and there had not been a single serious illness.
This was a great record in those days for a large ship's
company. Moreover, those seven months included four
in the tropics of which two were spent along the coasts of
Africa and Madagascar. The splendid quality of the
crew's food was, no doubt, a contributing factor. Soon

[4] The geographical names in this chapter follow Stevens' record.

after the start the sailors unanimously considered the rations so plentiful that they obtained permission to mess each group of twelve men on nine rations and to receive in cash the difference in the allowance.

Just about the time of the first death, however, an epidemic of dysentery and other ailments struck the ship. After stops at Wylah, Sumatra, and at Malacca, the *Constitution* reached Singapore on February 2, 1845, where the sixth and seventh deaths occurred. The sick list was long. Let us read Captain H. D. Smith's description of the first hours in this port. The particulars are believed to have been given in a letter written by our Consul at Singapore, Mr. Ballestier, whose wife was the daughter of Paul Revere: [5]

'Early in 1845, "Old Ironsides" sailed proudly to her anchorage in the magnificent harbor of Singapore, and, with a precision reflecting the highest credit on the discipline and capacity of the crew, took in sail, rounding to and letting go anchor in a style challenging the admiration of the numerous foreign men-of-war, who were close observers of everything connected with Columbia's famous frigate.

'The vertical rays of a tropic sun and the deadly breezes of the African coast, freighted with the insidious seeds of disease in every respiration, had made sad havoc among the rank and file of the ship's company. Many a stalwart, bronze-faced seaman, who alike had "braved the battle and the breeze" in all quarters of the globe, laughing

[5] *United Service,* January, 1892. The same anecdote in different form appears in *Old Landmarks of Middlesex.*

with impunity at dangers and climatic influences, now suc-
cumbed, seeking the "sick bay" for the first time. The
frigate was in all but name a hospital, the starboard side
of the large, airy gun-deck being thickly slung with cots
and hammocks for the enervated invalids. Mad Jack,
with characteristic kindness of heart, disguised perhaps by
an assumed austereness of manner, had given up his cool,
spacious cabin for the accomodation of the sick.[6]

'There was an indescribable "something" in the appearance of the frigate indicating the sad state of affairs existing within her stanch and massive walls. At Rio the hull
had been painted a light lead color, a graceful ribbon of
crimson marking the water-line, adding a pleasant relief
to the somewhat odd color adopted for the dress of a man-
of-war.[7] The effect, on the whole, was pleasing, but the
chafe, wear and tear of a long passage, with the action of
salt water and buffeting of heavy seas off the Cape, had
destroyed all this. Aided in part by the long sunny days
met with in the Indian Ocean, the new tint adopted by
Mad Jack had faded, disappeared in spots, allowing the
old, grimy, sombre coating to again assert itself, creating
anything but a pleasing effect, while long, ragged, irregular
blotches of iron-rust disfigured the shapely hull, rendering
her absolutely hideous in appearance. But while the old
craft suffered in point of beauty below, aloft all was taut
and trim. The tapering spars were stayed to a nicety, the
ponderous yards squared with mathematical precision,
sails furled with the pride and care bestowed upon such

---

[6] Actually it was the forward cabin that was turned into a sick bay.
[7] It was the gun-deck stripe that was painted red, not the water-line.

duties by all faithful, true-hearted seamen who love and
cherish a pride in the appearance of their ship; rigging
taut and black as ebony, ratlines square, and running-gear
hauled taut,—not an "Irish pennant" visible or a slovenly
passed gasket on yard or boom; with canvas white, and
bright-work reflecting back the sun's rays, while the broad
deck, white and spotless, with battery smooth and shining
like satin, spoke volumes for the attention and capacity
of the officers, the dispositions and quality of the men.

'The "Constitution" had swung to her anchor, the gangway ladder had been adjusted just in time for the accomodation of a magnificently-appointed barge, which
dashed alongside in charge of a midshipman.   Skipping
lightly over the side, the youngster doffed his cap, present-
ing the compliments of Commodore Chads, whose broad
pennant was displayed on board Her British Majesty's
frigate "Cambrian."

'But a short time elapsed before the commodore called
in person.   He was a fine-appearing man, of distinguished
presence, about fifty years of age, standing six feet in
height, and erect as a life-guardsman.[8]   His smile was
pleasant and genial as he returned, with an easy gesture,
the salutes of the officers drawn up to receive him.   He
halted a moment at the cabin companion-way, surveying
the ship fore and aft, alow and aloft, a curious expression
apparent in his bright blue eyes.   He then descended to
the private apartment of Captain Percival, who rose from
his seat, receiving his distinguished guest leaning on
crutches, he being a martyr to inflammatory rheumatism.

[8] About *sixty* years old at this time.

242 of Old Ironsides

' "I have hastened on board your ship," said the commodore, after the first salutations were over, "to offer my services, having heard you were suffering from illness, as well as many of your people. My surgeon, whom I have brought with me, who has been long on the station and is familiar with the diseases prevailing here, is at your disposal. Anything I can do for you shall receive my personal attention, for you must know I owe a debt of gratitude to your country."

'He then inquired if he was on board of the identical frigate called the "Constitution" in 1813. He was assured that she was the same in model, battery, and internal arrangements, although rebuilt. The commodore, smiling, replied he was glad to meet her *again;* that she was an old acquaintance of his, and that in the action with the "Java," after Captain Lambert had received his fatal death-shot, he had by virtue of rank assumed command, fighting the vessel until compelled to strike. "Although we were defeated," continued the commodore, "there are no reminiscences connected with my career more fragrant with pleasing remembrances than those bearing upon the skill, gallantry, and bravery of the large-hearted Bainbridge. I remember in particular one episode,—I shall never forget it. We were all on board the 'Constitution' and rapidly nearing San Salvador. Poor Lambert was dying, and I was by his side on the quarter-deck above, when Bainbridge approached, pale and weak from his wounds, and tenderly as a woman whispered a few words of comfort to the poor fellow, at the same time placing in his wan hands the sword he had been compelled to render up. It cheered Lambert's last moments on earth, sir, and the act I can never forget. The 'Constitution' was manoeuvered in a masterly manner, and it made me regret she was not British. It was Greek meet Greek, for we were of the same blood after all."

'He inquired particularly after Bainbridge, and was told that he had died in 1833 from pneumonia. An hour or two previously to his death his mind wandered. At the last moment he painfully raised what was left of his once noble frame, demanded his arms, and ordered all hands called to board the enemy.

'The commodore was conducted throughout the frigate, and viewed with interest each part of the ship. His emotion was apparent as he paused for a moment in the shadow cast by the mizzen-mast. A vivid tableau, the principal actors of which had passed away forever, was brought painfully back to him; but few on board had the least suspicion of the true causes disturbing the usual quiet self-possession of the English commodore.'

Not many weeks later the sick list was down to normal and below normal. Only twenty-seven deaths *from all causes* took place during the entire cruise of considerably more than two years. This was an excellent record in that era for any large group of people, as it constituted an annual death rate of less than twenty-five per thousand.

After more than a month at Singapore, *"Old Ironsides"* sailed to the island of Borneo and anchored off the Sambas River. A boat expedition was sent forty miles up the stream to the town of Sambas to acquire information on trade, politics, botany, etc. Such studies, in fact, were made at nearly every stop. Leaving the anchorage on March 22 the ship took until May 10 to reach Tourin Bay, Indo China. Only four days of this seven-week period were spent "in port"—lying off the mouth of the Borneo River for a trip up to the City of Borneo in the boats. The winds in those seas were fitful and unfavorable, the waters narrow and uncertain. It was quite a common occurrence to make but a few miles in a day, then anchor at night as a matter of precaution.

Let us read Stevens' tale of the *Constitution's* activities in Cochin China: [9]

'This afternoon we anchored in Touron Bay, having been four days within twenty miles of it. Just one month since we left Borneo. This beautiful harbor is almost entirely closed from the sea. The entrance is not seen in particular parts of it. The scenery around it is remarkably grand, and resembles that around Rio de Janeiro. The hills appear to have been thrown together without any regard to order. The town of Touron is situated on the river of the same name and on the left side of the bay. It is completely concealed from view while entering the harbor. Touron river divides the town into two parts, communication being cut off except by boats. The left division of the town contains one fort, as well as the right, and there are other fortifications on islands near the shore. The town is thickly settled as are also the numerous villages around it. One great source of employment to the people is fishing, and the many little boats gliding in and out the harbor seem to cast a cheerful shade over the

[9] *United Service,* 1904.

scene. On the 11th an officer was sent to town to call upon the authorities of the place stating our object in visiting the port, and the probable length of our stay. On reaching the shore he was received by a person apparently of some distinction. They passed through a file of soldiers to a large house or rather store fronting the water. Here the party were treated to tea, that being the common beverage of the Chinese. By means of a Chinaman proper (of whom we had five on board) communication was held in writing between the mandarins and our party. It would be well to remark that the Cochin Chinese use the same characters in writing as the Chinese proper, though one cannot understand the language of the other. To our inquiries for water, provisions, etc., the mandarins gave the most trivial replies, being evidently suspicious of us. They wished to know "Why we came?" "Why we did not go?" "How long we should stay at Macao?" and perhaps twenty other questions, one of which was "What are we going to do at Canton?" to which Lieutenant Chaplin very properly replied, "None of your business." This answer put an end to further inquiries and they said we could have chickens, fish, water, etc. After again drinking tea the party returned on board. The next day, having found an excellent stream of water near the outer fort, we commenced watering ship. No boats ventured to come alongside, and the whole conduct of these people, thus far, evinced a suspicious character, little comporting with what we had been led to expect. Boats were sent to the neighboring villages to procure refreshments, but were not allowed to land.

'On the morning of the 13th I set out at sunrise for the

town in the gig to procure live stock. The market was held directly upon the beach, and women appeared to be the sellers. Soldiers were stationed along the shore, with rattans to keep the crowd in order, occasionally giving some unlucky girl a few lashes, who had strayed out of the path. We found refreshments very reasonable, though the manner of selling did not suit very well. For every lot of things, whether potatoes, ducks, chickens, or pumpkins, they expected a dollar, and often would mix the lots together, so that to obtain three chickens, one would have to buy ten or fifteen pumpkins. Occasionally they would give for change a kind of zinc coin strung by the thousand upon sticks measuring them by the yard, though they would rarely receive them back, the "almighty dollar" being all they cared for. The women, many of them, were good looking, but of small stature. Their complexions are dark and but for the manner of wearing the hair would not, many of them, be distinguished from the men. The children most of them were entirely naked, and ran hither and thither without any attempt being made by their parents to render their appearance a little more acceptable to our modest eyes.

'On the morning of the 14th a boat was seen approaching the ship manned by twenty or thirty rowers, and containing several mandarins, with a body guard. They were received in the cabin and every attention was paid to them that was possible. They were accompanied by an interpreter, who had but little title to the distinction, as he could speak but a little broken Portuguese and Spanish. After an interview of about an hour, they were invited to examine the ship, which they did. Their inquiries seemed to be directed more especially towards our flag, having asked at least twenty times whether we were English or American, and the same suspicion was attached to their movements on board the ship that had characterized our first visit on shore.

'Shortly before leaving the interpreter came back into the cabin and handed the captain an open letter, stating by signs and broken Portuguese, that if he were discovered by the mandarins he would have his head cut off. At 11.30 A.M. they had left the ship. The letter was translated by Dr. McLeod, and found to be from "Dominique Lefevre, Bishop of Isamapolis, and apostolic vicar of Western Cochin," stating that he was imprisoned and calling upon the French admiral (for whom we were taken) to make certain demands upon the king of Cochin China, thereby procuring his release and peace and quiet for the French missionaries. Its date was the 10th of May, but did not state the place of his confinement. A postscript was attached dated 11th in these words: "I am condemned to death without delay; hasten or all is finished." Here was a predicament. A Frenchman was at the mercy of barbarians. He was a Christian and humanity called for our assistance. No French ships were in the harbor, and America and France were upon the most friendly terms. Before assistance could be obtained from Canton he would probably be executed, as the postscript in his letter implied. The instructions of our government to the captain ordered him to afford every aid in his power to citizens of other nations that he might meet during the cruise, and this *I think* was a case in point.   Should we set aside the claims of humanity?   These people respect no civilized powers, will make no treaties and are destitute of all faith in keeping even the slightest promises.   Their conduct to us though not actually uncivil implied a direct and groundless suspicion of our character, though the authorities of Touron had been repeatedly assured that we were a national vessel, only requiring water and refreshments, and willing and ready to pay for what we received.

'At 1 P.M. four boats were well manned and armed, and set out for Touron under command of the captain.   Our force consisted of about eighty men, of which number thirty were marines.   Upon landing at the town the officers followed by a guard of marines and soldiers [10] proceeded to the house in which the former meeting was held. In case of danger, the men were posted from the house to the beach, that everything should terminate as safely as possible.   Though we passed through at least three times the number of soldiers (armed with spears and muskets) as our force consisted of, and were within pistol shot of a fort, and within musket shot of another, all these preparations met with no resistance.   In a few minutes the same party appeared that had visited the ship in the morning and requested to know our business.   The captain (by means of a Chinese scribe) demanded to see the governor of Touron, and was referred to one of the party present as being that personage.   This was doubted and the same question asked and the same reply obtained.   At last the person referred to said that we must first tell our

[10] sailors?

business to him before we could see the governor.   Captain Percival then told him that he had a letter for the French missionary confined at or near this place which he wished to be forwarded to him; that he would wait fifteen minutes for the governor to appear and if at the end of that period he did not come he should take the mandarins present on board of his ship as hostages for the safety of the bishop's life.   The letter for the missionary was left and directed in French and Chinese.   At the termination of the time allotted, no governor having appeared, the mandarins were marched to the beach and from thence taken to the ship.   They expressed a willingness to go and no resistance was offered by any of the people.   A letter to the king had been prepared and was left on shore with a promise from an officer that it should be immediately sent.   For fear of any suspicion, the interpreter who had brought the letter was taken on board, and the three were ushered into the cabin, where they were made as comfortable as possible.   The afternoon of the 15th a force was sent under command of Lieutenant Alden to bring alongside three junks (war) belonging to the king. This was also effected without resistance.   At 5 P.M. our hostages wrote a letter to the king and dispatched it by an attendant who was to be back in two and one-half days. The next day a communication was received from some person on shore wishing three days to send to the king at Hué, a place forty-five miles in the country.   This was acquiesced in, and our hostages wrote another letter to the king, as did the captain in French and Chinese, the purport of which was that in four days we must see or hear from the Frenchman. The next day (17th) a large letter was received, but it amounted to nothing, only stating that soon the Frenchman should come. A considerable correspondence had already passed between the ship and shore, and the promises made by the mandarins did not appear to be fulfilled. On the 18th a letter was brought on board, directed as usual to the captain, stating that the king had sent a mandarin from Hué to arrange matters and requested him to come on shore the following day and bring the hostages. Accordingly on the 19th, accompanied by a strong force, the captain and hostages landed, but finding no mandarin or any sign of one being in the village the party returned on board.

'On the evening of the 19th the hostages were permitted to return on shore, having promised to exert themselves for the release of the padre by going to Hué and stating the case to the king. The next day (20th) the three junks anchored near us got underway and stood for the river. Nine shot were fired over and around them. These they did not mind but kept on. A force was sent after them, and they were brought from under the guns of a fort mounting twenty-four pounders. No lives were lost in this transaction, though many of the Cochinese jumped overboard and swam ashore. In the afternoon the wind freshening, one of the junks drifted on shore, but after much trouble was got off. On the 21st three Cochin Chinese brigs of war were discovered anchored under the land on left of the entrance of the bay. The next day the captain with a small force went towards the brigs and endeavored to get on board but were repulsed. Upon showing the arms, however, we were allowed to come alongside and the captain went on board. Everything was in confusion and though each of the brigs must have had at least 100 men on board and ten guns, yet I am confident no resistance could have been made to a regularly drilled force of fifty men. From the 23rd until the morning of the 27th we obtained no satisfactory intelligence about the padre. From the action of the native officers on shore we were led to believe that none of our letters had been sent to the king, and we despaired of getting the bishop from them unless something unusual occurred.

'On the morning of the 27th, therefore, we stood out to sea with the land breeze. The morning of the 30th we boarded an English ship from Singapore (May 15) for Hong Kong. On board of her was a French priest who informed us that the French squadron was at Singapore— that M. Lefevre's imprisonment was known, and that the French admiral intended (after receiving orders from home) to proceed to Touron Bay to effect his liberation.

'At noon of the 5th of June we put a letter bag on board the American ship Rainbow for New York, and in the afternoon anchored in the outer roads of Macao.

'At the time that the Constitution was engaged in saving the life of the apostolic vicar of Cochin China, since taken possession of by France, Louis Philippe reigned over that nation with the title of king of the French, and he never thought that he should be driven from his government. But he was, escaping over the walls of the Tuileries gardens and under the name of Mr. Smith he landed safely in England, where he died. Previous to his escape from

Europe he wrote or caused to be written through the French minister that the captain, officers and crew of the Constitution were to be rewarded by the government of France for saving the life of Bishop Lefevre, but Louis Philippe took a hurried journey from his capital and no recognition of their services was ever received by the American tars.'

It would seem probable that the latter part of Captain Percival's negotiations and actions were more astute and effective than described by our chronicler.

From Macao *"Old Ironsides"* worked up to Whampoa, the Canton anchorage. There she lay for ten weeks. Then after three more days at Macao she put to sea once again for the first time in nearly three months.

[11] 'As the Constitution was slowly drifting along towards the port of Manila somewhat before daylight, or rather as the light began to appear, we found ourselves nearly surrounded by a squadron of European men-of-war, say twelve or fifteen, but whether British, French, Spanish or otherwise, could not be ascertained. As we had been a number of months without hearing from home, any guess as to our surroundings was as good as another, but the look about them was in the eyes of the old salts on board unmistakably English. One of the floating vessels [12] bore an Admiral's pennant, afterwards ascertained to be the flag of Sir Thomas Cochrane, in command of the China Squadron. The others were frigates, sloops and brigs.

[11] "A Cruise on the Constitution," Stevens; *United Service,* 1904.
[12] A steamer.

They had evidently paid a visit to Manila and were making their way to some port in the Pacific. As a matter of precaution the Constitution—the favorite ship of our Navy—was got ready for action, or rather put in a state of defense; it would never have done in any event to give up "Old Ironsides" to any other nation than the one which built her and had fought her.

'The officers and crew were at their stations, the wind was a dead calm, match fires were lighted, the magazines opened and every preparation was made to show that we did not mean to give up the ship without a struggle or show of defense. And thus things went on from the discovery of the drifting fleet until the time came round to make ourselves known, when the Star Spangled Banner was hove to the breeze, or what little of it there was, and the flag of Old England became unfurled at the masts of our neighbors.

'After a short delay a boat put off from the Admiral's ship and approached the Constitution, and a young officer climbed the side of our ship and stepped on to the frigate's deck. Captain Percival, who was waiting with the first lieutenant, Amasa Paine, of Providence, R. I., to receive him, said, "Is it peace or war?" "Why, peace to be sure." Then the captain of the Yankee ship and the lieutenant of the English steamer shook hands and left for the cabin, where, I think—in fact I know—that they hobnobbed a bit before getting to business. "Captain," said the English lieutenant, "ever since we left Manila ten days ago we have been drifting our lives away. Admiral Sir Thomas Cochrane has an idea that you are loaded with provisions.

Will you help us to a part, to be repaid to you at Honolulu, as, if we are pressed, we have not enough provisions to last ten days longer, while if you can help us we will shower down blessings on your head?"

'Instead of a fight there was a merrymaking; all hands turned to and helped stow away the provisions from the American frigate to the English ships, at the close of which the English ships saluted us, and we separated, mutually pleased with each other.

'Among the many acquaintances we made that day was the owner of a distinguished name, that of the son of the famous novelist, Captain Maryatt, afterwards lost in the Mediterranean.'

On this round-the-world cruise *"Old Ironsides"* healed an appreciable bit of the breach that had existed between the two English-speaking nations.

Our good ship next set out across the Pacific. After purchasing live stock and taking on water in the Bashu group of the Philippine Islands she commenced a 50-day run to Honolulu. There she heard of the imminence of war with Mexico. She got off with as little delay as possible, looked in at Monterey in search of the American fleet, and then found it at Mazatlan. There Commodore John D. Sloat was in command of thirteen ships headed by the Savannah, 52.

After standing by for several months the *Constitution* was ordered to the east coast. She left Mazatlan early in May, 1846, hostilities having started by that time. After a stop at Valparaiso she rounded the Horn on the

Fourth of July in a driving snowstorm. She arrived at
Rio de Janeiro once more, thus completing the circum-
navigation of the globe. Sixteen coffee vessels were anchored there awaiting safe conduct past the area of
hostilities. *"Old Ironsides"* formed them into a convoy
and escorted them to the Delaware Breakwater where they
scattered, all reaching their destinations in safety. Thus
ended the frigate's Mexican service; for she reached the
Boston Navy Yard on September 28, 1846, where she
stayed till the end of the War two years later. She had
been at sea more than half of the long period away from
home; she had visited twenty-six foreign ports and had
sailed 55,000 miles. Her rest was well earned.

CHAPTER XXV

"SAVE THE CONSTITUTION!"

FROM 1848 to 1851 *"Old Ironsides"* put in another long cruise in foreign waters. This time she was flagship of the Mediterranean and African squadrons. On one occasion, when the ship was in the Bay of Naples, Pope Pius IX paid her a visit. In company with him was the King of Naples at whose hands he was receiving shelter in that troublous period. This is the first and only known instance of a pope setting foot on American "territory."

The *Constitution's* time on the station ended as the year 1850 was drawing to a close. She left Gibraltar on her homeward voyage. One dark cloudy night, soon after her departure, she was bowling along in a smooth sea, making ten knots with port forward stunsails set. All went swimmingly till one bell, when "Light ho!" was called from the port cathead. "Where away?" shouted the officer of the deck. "Two points on the port bow!" was the reply. Then the light disappeared.

Five or ten minutes later the dim outline of a brig was detected close under the bows of *"Old Ironsides."* "Hard a starboard!" was the quick order given and the man at the wheel responded instantly. At the critical moment, however, some unauthorized voice yelled "Hard a port!" On hearing this, the Captain repeated the order to the quartermaster, and "port" it was.   The *Constitution* crashed head on into the brig, dismasting her and causing her to founder shortly afterwards.   The primary cause of the accident, of course, was the failure of the victim to carry proper lights and to show them properly.

The unlucky vessel was the English brig *Conservaty,* of Cowes, bound for Barcelona with a cargo of coal for the Spanish government.   She carried a crew of eight all told; seven of them were accounted for gradually—all except the mate.   Oddly enough he too finally turned up— in the *Constitution's* sick bay, in a dazed condition.   To the surgeon's inquiry as to his ailment he gazed around stupidly and asked "Where am I?   How did I get here?"   Next morning, refreshed by a good night's rest, he gave an intelligent account of the disaster and told of his own experiences following the crash.

It seems that our mariner, by a prodigious leap or by some other means unknown to himself, succeeded in grasping the advanced leg of "Old Hickory."   In his unsettled condition of mind he firmly believed that the limb belonged to a human being instead of to a wooden figurehead.   He dangled above the water for several minutes imploring and cursing, by turns, "the damned unmannerly brute" for not assisting him.   Fortunately a man who happened to go forward overheard the diatribe.   Being astonished at the sound of wholesale blasphemy in such an out-of-the-way place he bestirred himself to look under the bowsprit.   Discovering there the nearly exhausted man he grasped him by the collar and pulled him aboard.

The mate continued to swear furiously at "the damned lubber for not helping him sooner"; and "as for the cussed fool who refused entirely to lend a hand, he would get even with him yet." When informed that the latter individual he so roundly abused was the ship's figure, his discomfiture was complete. Whenever the incident was mentioned thereafter, the mate's silence was most expressive.[1]

After laying up at New York for two years *"Old Ironsides,"* for the last of many times, served as flagship of the Mediterranean Squadron from 1853 to 1855. An incident of this cruise was her capture of the American slaver *N. H. Gambell.* The United States had joined the other Powers in outlawing the slave trade a number of years before slavery was abolished in America.

Upon her return the *Constitution* spent five years in the Navy Yard at Portsmouth, N. H.—her first but not her last stay in that port. Most of this time was passed in idleness. During the latter years, however, she was fitted for use as a school-ship at the Naval Academy. She was ordered to Annapolis in 1860 and thereupon commenced her service in that capacity.

How many people realize that the last time *"Old Ironsides"* was nearly captured or destroyed by the enemy was not in the War of 1812 but in 1861? It was another ticklish situation from which she escaped early in the Civil War. Captain Blake, who was superintendent of the Naval Academy at the time, notified the Navy Department

[1] This tale was brought home by the late Real Admiral Thomas S. Phelps who was one of the Junior Officers aboard.

The second of the two Jackson figureheads that have graced the *Constitution*. This one is now at the U. S. Naval Academy.

of the untenable position in which he found his station with its store of arms and ammunition. Park Benjamin, who graduated at Annapolis in 1867, describes the succession of events: [2]

'Finally, he' (Blake) 'proposed, in event of assault, to destroy the munitions of war in the yard, and after embarking the midshipmen on the *Constitution,* to defend her in the harbor or take her to New York or Philadelphia. He also asked for the practice ship *Plymouth* as a further safeguard.

'The position of the *Constitution* was somewhat critical. The Southerners were freely boasting that she should carry the first rebel flag afloat. She was fast aground at high water, the only channel through which she could be taken was narrow and difficult, and she was in easy range of any battery which might be installed on the neighboring heights.

'The midshipmen were kept constantly under arms. Frequently they were summoned to prepare to resist an assault. On the 20th of April, the Norfolk Navy Yard was evacuated and destroyed. On the same date the Secretary of the Navy telegraphed to Commodore Blake to "defend the *Constitution* at all hazards. If it cannot be done, destroy her." Blake received intelligence which led him to believe that an immediate attack upon the ship was contemplated, and he at once took measures to meet it. To obtain timely warning of its approach, which he expected would be by water from the direction of Baltimore, the little schooner *Rainbow* was sent out as a scout.

[2] *The United States Naval Academy,* G. P. Putnam's Sons.

Early on the morning of April 21st, the *Rainbow* came in with the news that a large steamer was in sight, and it was assumed at once that the threatened attack was now to be made. The drums beat the assembly, and every available gun was trained upon the incoming vessel.

'Meantime, Lieutenant Edmund O. Matthews was sent off in a boat to board her and ascertain, if possible, her character. As he came near he was hailed with,

' "What boat is that?"

' "What steamer is that?" was the reply.

' "None of your business! Come alongside, or I will fire into you."

'Matthews complied, and on reaching the deck was arrested by two soldiers. He announced his name and mission to an officer before whom he was brought, and then to his relief found that he was confronting General Benjamin F. Butler, who had seized the ferryboat *Maryland,* and with the 8th Massachusetts regiment was about to land at Annapolis.

'Shortly afterwards Captain Blake himself came aboard. Butler says, in his description of the ensuing scene, that Blake, on learning of his purpose, burst into tears, exclaiming:

' "Thank God, thank God! Won't you save the *Constitution?*"

' "I did not know," continues Butler, "that he referred to the ship *Constitution,* and I answered,

' " 'Yes, that is what I am here for.'

' " 'Are those your orders? Then the old ship is safe.'

' " 'I have no orders,' said I. 'I am carrying on this

war now on my own hook. I cut loose from my orders when I left Philadelphia. What do you want me to do to save the *Constitution?'*

' " 'I want some sailormen,' he answered, 'for I have no sailors; I want to get her out and get her afloat.'

' " 'Oh, well,' said I, 'I have plenty of sailormen from the town of Marblehead, where their fathers built the *Constitution.'* "

'So Butler detailed his best drilled company—the Salem Zouaves—to guard the ship, sent a lot of Marblehead fishermen to report to Rodgers, the Commandant, and Rodgers, to quote Butler once more, "worked with a will, and I shall not forget my delight at his efficiency."

'The arrival of Butler seems to have been in the very nick of time, for Blake, writing under the date of April 22d, says that the *Constitution,* "but for the presence of General Butler's command, would have been boarded last night."

'Commandant Rodgers, with the aid of Butler's men, transferred all the upper-deck guns from the *Constitution* to the *Maryland,* thus lightening the vessel. Then the *Maryland* made fast to the towing hawsers, and the moorings of the old ship being slipped, she was slowly hauled out of her berth only to go at once into the mud. By dint of much labor she was once more got afloat and proceeded on her journey, but early in the evening she took the bottom again off Greenbury Point Light. As night came on the condition of affairs grew critical. The tide was rapidly falling and the ship settling in the shoal, when a message came that the outside channel was being obstructed, and that there were indications that the threatened attack would be made before morning. Kedge anchors were laid out and an effort made to haul the ship into deep water, which had hardly succeeded before a heavy squall threw her aground again. Vessels began to appear in the offing, and the volunteer crew prepared for resistance.

'But it was a false alarm. The newcomers were friendly, and one of them hauled the *Constitution* into deep water, where she anchored. Then her guns were replaced, so that she was now ready to cover the landing of the troops and stores, which, owing to the burning of the bridges of the Philadelphia and Baltimore Railroad, was to be made at Annapolis.

'Meanwhile the school had been turned into an encampment. The Massachusetts troops were soon joined by the 7th Regiment from New York City, to the officers of which the first class gave up their rooms. The colonel, in recognition of their courtesy, ordered a drill for their benefit. That rather worried the youngsters, who wished to return the compliment in kind, lest the civilians should overwhelm them with their superior military skill, but, as usual, Lockwood [8] was equal to the occasion. He chose artillery drill for exhibition, in which the evolutions were executed at double quick. The 7th Regiment had had no experience in rapid manœuvres of that sort, and the light-footed youngsters were entirely at home in them. Therefore no comparisons could be instituted, and the situation was saved.

[8] Professor Henry H. Lockwood, U. S. N.

"Old Ironsides" hauled out on marine railway at Portsmouth, N. H., in 1858.
Note second Jackson figurehead in place.

'On the 24th of April, Superintendent Blake, finding it impossible to continue academic routine with the grounds and buildings occupied by the troops, directed the transfer of the acting midshipmen to the *Constitution,* which meanwhile had been covering the entrance of the transports to the harbor.

'The time for departure had now come. The boys from the North and the boys from the South were finally to separate, and the grief of parting was keen. Then the class of 1861 met and smoked a pipe of peace and solemnly pledged themselves to care for one another however much they might become enemies. Even the non-smokers indulged in a few whiffs. A watchman reported the whole party for smoking in quarters, but Rodgers ignored the charge. And then followed the saddest gathering which had ever taken place within the Academy walls. The buildings were to be given up to the troops, and the students were ordered to embark in the *Constitution,* and sail with her to New York. The drums beat as usual for formation, and they fell in, Northerners and Southerners alike, with their mess crews. Commandant Rodgers had caused the band to be present, and it played the music of the Union.

'As the strains of "The Star Spangled Banner" and "Hail Columbia" poured forth, the youngsters from the South stood there with pale faces and set teeth. Then Commandant Rodgers spoke to them quietly and pleadingly, and finally, when he had said to them all that could be said, he ordered those who so desired to fall out of the ranks. The boys from the States which had thrown off their allegiance left their places. And then came the farewell, and it was pitiful. The arms of those who were to go to the North and of those who were to go to the South went around one another's necks and the tears flowed, and hands linked in a last fond clasp which later were to be raised in bitter enmity. Then the order to leave was given. The Northerners embarked on the tug which was to take them to the ship. The Southerners made their way homeward as best they could, and the old *Constitution,* with the flag which she had so often carried to victory flying at her peak as of yore, stood down the Chesapeake, and laid her course to the loyal North.'

CHAPTER XXVI

Constitution LUCK

THE United States Naval Academy carried on at Newport for the duration of the Civil War and there the *Constitution* served as school-ship for four years. When the establishment was moved back to Annapolis in 1865 she was towed down from Newport—or rather they started to tow her. *"Old Ironsides"* soon ran away from her tug and made the voyage alone. For several hours she logged 13½ knots! She was school-ship at Annapolis till 1871 when she was placed out of commission at Philadelphia for a refit. About three years later she was hauled out and repaired at the old Navy Yard at the foot of Mifflin St. After the Yard was moved to League Island she served there from 1877 to 1878 as a training ship.

Next year she was ordered to Havre with the American exhibits for the Paris Exposition; there she was to wait and bring back her freight the following year. She had a cargo capacity of approximately 830 tons including a 100-ton deck load. The spar deck was loaded with street cars and a locomotive, among other pieces. All of her guns except two 32-pounders were removed and she went to sea with less than sixty men to work her.

Evidently the repairs during the overhaul had been carried out very badly, for many troubles were encountered, as we shall soon see. Happily, one of her officers wrote up the cruise and we are thus enabled to follow *"Old Ironsides"* through her good and bad luck, her tragedy and comedy: [1]

'On a bright, brisk morning of February, 1878, the dear old frigate took her departure from the Delaware Capes and spread her wings for a flight across the ocean. With a humming breeze abaft the beam, just where in the old days she had used to like it best, she struck a clean twelve-knot gait and reeled it off day and night with scarcely the need to touch a brace, until by noon of the tenth day out she had crossed the meridian of Cape Clear, with a fair prospect of making a record-breaking run to the Lizard. It had been many a long year since Old Ironsides had smelled salt water, and she tossed her head, footed it down her course, and swung her dimity like a pretty girl in a Virginia reel.

'But the way of the wind in these latitudes is past all finding out, and before sunset of this tenth day we were wallowing in a cross sea, trimming the yards hither and yon, the speed of the ship and the mercury in the glass falling steadily together, until by midnight we were headed away off to the southward of our course, with bowlines hauled as stiff as staylaces, the weather leaches of the topgallant sails all a shiver, and muggy weather banking down out of the channel. From then on for eleven consecutive

---

[1] "The Last Cruise of Old Ironsides," by Lieutenant Edward W. Very; *New York Times,* September 8, 1906. (This was her last *foreign* cruise.)

days and nights it was a weary fight with an easterly gale
that brought the old ship down to close reefs; tack and
tack with twelve-hour boards between Scilly and Ushant,
we only raised the lights on either hand to find that she
had not gained an inch to windward. Surely the English
Channel had put up the bars against the Constitution, and
though the good ship thrashed along with a steady, un-
yielding drive, the outlook was bad.

' "Bad, aye bad!" grumbled the lieutenant of the watch,
as he pulled down the weather rim of his sou'wester against
the flying spume, and with one eye on the maintopsail and
the other on the swinging binnacle cord, conned the fresh
helmsman at the beginning of a weary first watch.[2] He
leaned up under the shelter of the bulwarks to get a breath,
and the feel of the straining timbers against his shoulder
stirred his sympathy till he talked to the old ship as to a
loved companion.'

At this point the officer of the watch unburdens himself
in a soliloquy, deploring the misappropriation of funds
which had been contributed for the proper rebuilding of
the ship; deploring the employment of the historic frigate
as a freight vessel—an almost fatal act as it turned out.
Because:

' "in danger of sinking you are, old girl, this living
minute, for it is now two days since we found that the
planks under your stern are springing from the stern post
and since then your pumps have never stopped. Nor is
that all, for slashing back and forth as we have been so

[2] 8 to 12 P.M.

long, there has gathered about us a fleet of more than a hundred sail of every rig and nationality under the sun, all hanging on like ourselves, crowding closer and closer, crossing ahead and astern, with no order, no care, no object but to hold on for a shift of wind. And if in this black night one of them touches us—. It shan't be old girl; they starved you, robbed you, heaped ignominy on you, but, begad, the power don't live than can take your luck.

' "What am I here for? Don't I know that a ship might as well be in irons as under close reefs? Are your old timbers groaning at me because I won't let you go? Haven't I got the pluck to lend you a hand to pull out of this mess? Did I never hear of Constitution luck, or haven't I the nerve to put it to the test?"

'So muttering, with affection for the old ship, with faith in her luck, with confidence in his own skill, the lieutenant took the chance of disgrace for a direct disobedience of orders, just to give the good old ship fair play. The captain was asleep, dead tired from long, anxious watching on deck, and if there was no disturbance he would sleep all night; so the boatswain's mate was sent below to get the other watch quietly on deck; two extra hands were sent to the wheel, and as the binnacle light flashed across the face of the grizzled old quartermaster, it showed up a cheery twinkle in his eye as he caught the idea, shifted his quid, and softly whispered a single word; it was a very profane word, but robbed of all profanity in its positive expression of high approval.

' "Lay aloft and shake out two reefs," so the order

passed, and then followed quiet, steady, back-breaking work, swaying up the heavy yards while the old ship gathered way and the increased strain stopped the complaining of the timbers, and she buckled royally to her work until by four bells she was looking a good two points higher and making a clear eight knots through the water. All was well and even the tired marines at the pumps took fresh heart. So it went till near seven bells when dead to windward showed the dense black wall of a vicious squall. The quartermaster shifted a bit uneasily and gave an apologetic cough of warning, but the lieutenant just nodded his head, and then spoke quietly to the old man:

' "Hartley, when I entered the naval school and swung my hammock on this same old ship's main deck to learn the rudiments of seamanship, they told us as a surprising thing to be noted, that the lines of the Constitution were peculiar in that while she was a fast sailer, at the same time she had the most powerful shoulder of any ship known. The wind never blew that could knock her down, and just for that reason it was always necessary to watch carefully in a blow, for she might carry the spars clean out of her before one was aware of the heft of the strain. Now, Hartley, I'm going to try that shoulder."

'There was silence for some minutes, and even the wind seemed to stop its whistling through the rigging; then, with a wild shriek, the squall was on top of her. The sudden blow stopped her all but dead in the water, and she heeled down slowly, over, over, over, till the gun deck ports were awash, and the four men at the wheel with a full turn of weather helm, hung with aching arms and listened, almost frantic, for the word to let her pay off. Then the lieutenant spoke:

' "Hold her men, hold every inch, if she pulls your arms out of the sockets; not a hair off, even if you see the topmasts go overboard."

'The good ship seemed to give a satisfied chuckle, and lifted against the pressure, gathered way and drove straight through the squall like a racer. It was all over before eight bells; the lieutenant was tired out and sore-eyed from the flying brine, but when it came to the question of his relief a difficulty stared him in the face. On the one hand, to make good and get Lizard Point well to leeward, the ship needed the rest of the night under the same press of sail, but the reefs had been shaken out against orders and it wouldn't be fair to make a shipmate share the blame; so the relief was not called, and the long night wore on, while the ship footed it bravely through the tumble, and at last daylight came, showing up the ragged outlines of land ahead. The navigator was called, and the situation was briefly explained. For another weary hour the watch wore on, while the navigator oscillated between the standard compass and the cabin, taking bearings and laying off on the chart, and at last, with a cheery laugh, he came to the weary watch officer and grabbed his hand.

' "Good for you, my dear fellow; you're a trump. The Lizard is forty miles dead to leeward. Falmouth Harbor is wide open right ahead, and we can be at anchor in smooth water in a couple of hours. The best of it all is that the

skipper knows how it was done, and he feels so good over
the outcome that he is not going to say a word.   Let me
have her and you go below and get your forty winks in
peace."

'The lieutenant smiled wearily, and there was that in his
response whose aptness would be lost on the young genera-
tion.

' "You are sure that the old man is not going to haul me
over the coals?   Gad, Charlie, it's Constitution luck.
Take her; I'm dead tuckered out.   Good night."

'So the old frigate won out, and after a few days at
Falmouth to stop the wretched leak, she stretched away
to Havre, landed her cargo, and was docked for a thorough
refit.   Now, while she waits for the time to start back, let
us recall the real meaning, once so well known, but now
wellnigh forgotten, of the expression that the lieutenant
used—Constitution luck.   There is hardly an American
boy anywhere to-day but has held his breath as he read of
the day at Tripoli when the frigate weaved in and out
among the reefs and shoals of the harbor, without a touch,
driving her broadsides home until the castle walls fairly
tumbled about the ears of the Bashaw; or that other time
off the Delaware Capes when for three days the British
fleet tried its best to overhaul her in the light airs and calms
and failed.   Truly, the Constitution was a lucky ship, but
Constitution luck was never meant in that sense.

'Listen; she has a noble British sister, the Victory—all
honor to her—but mark you well it was Nelson that cast
the halo about her.   There is another in France, the Tri-
omphante, but it was the great Admiral Tourville that

made her revered. Old Ironsides has a child, the Hartford, made sacred by the name of Farragut, and so it goes all around the world. But what of the Constitution? She made the men who trod her quarterdeck. Call the grand roll of her commanders through those first eighteen years of her glorious life: Talbot, Nicholson, Preble, Dale, Decatur, the elder Porter, Hull, Bainbridge, Stewart. Great seamen all, and it was the Constitution that either made them great, or gave them their first step up; all save Dale, who took his start with Paul Jones the day of the fight with Serapis before the Constitution was born. Constitution luck was that invariable circumstance that she brought luck to everybody that had her. Search naval history where you will, no other case can be found of such a list of men, all brought to high honor by their connection with the single ship. So the lieutenant had pinned his faith to Constitution luck, not to pull her out of her own scrape, but to shield him safe from the consequence of a disobedience of orders in her service. And she did it.

'Freighted once more and bound for home, the old frigate stood out close hauled by Cape La Heve for another winter trip across the western ocean. Again was the wind from the east, but while before it had tried to bar her out, now it was fair to hurry her along as it was to be but a few hours braced sharp up to get out into the full strength of the ebb tide, and then square away for home. At midnight our friend the lieutenant took the deck, and received the night orders:

' "Course, north a half west; call the captain, pilot, and

"THE HARPIES OF THE SHORE."

"Old Ironsides" turned into a freighter. Unloading at Havre the American exhibits for the
Paris Exposition of 1878. *From L'Illustration, 1878.*

navigator at four bells, and be ready to change the course down channel."

'The wind was soft, the sea was smooth, and all over head was a bright spangled sky, while all around low down was a mist soft, wavy, and harmless as a bridal veil. At four bells the wheel and lookouts were relieved, and as the navigator came on deck and drifted over to the lee side to take a look past the leach of the mainsail, he was greeted with a cheery "good morning" from the lieutenant, perched up at the standard compass.

' "We are right on the course, old man, and ready for the word to square away as soon as you give it to us."

'As the words left his lips, he cast an eye casually aloft and saw—a miracle. Green grass and trees plumb over the maintopgallant yard!

' "Hard down your helm; let fly the head sheets; jump to the weather braces; jump, everybody."

'But it was too late; the keel found the bottom, and with a long, smooth slide the ship came to a stand, while through that wavy bridal veil could be seen the face of a chalk cliff two hundred feet high and not a hundred yards from the end of the flying jibboom. In time the coast-guard boat came alongside with the information that we were ashore on Bollard Head, to which he sympathetically added:

' "You picked the only spot, sir, on the whole south coast of England that is out of range of a lighthouse. St. Catherine's is too far to the eastward, and Portland Bill is hull down the other way."

'The lieutenant wagged his head at the navigator, and remarked:

' "Charlie, that is not much satisfaction for me and none for you, for we have overrun our reckoning thirty-four good miles in ten small hours. I fear me much, old man, that it is going to put most too much of a strain on Constitution luck to pull our necks out of this halter."

'The weather held good, help came in the shape of powerful towboats, and at high water the good ship came off the rocks and was towed to Portsmouth dockyard for an overhaul. There were uneasy thoughts in more than one head, for though it might be alright to cheat in rebuilding her and to turn her into a freight drogher, to put the Constitution on the rocks would brew a storm at home at any rate, while to do it in pleasant weather, only ten hours out of port and with the whole English Channel to navigate in seemed about as bad as possible. Would anybody try to shirk his share of it? That question was not left long unanswered. The dockyard superintendent came aboard, full of sympathy for the captain, who greeted him on the quarter deck, and his first remark was surely a most natural one:

' "It is most unfortunate my dear sir, and there must have been most inexcusable carelessness on the part of your officers."

'Our captain straightened up, his face flushed, and then spoke the true quarter deck of the Constitution:

' "Sir, there is not a ship afloat that has a more competent set of officers than I have here. The responsibility for this accident, whatever the reason, is mine and mine alone."

"WHEN WINDS WERE HURRYING O'ER THE FLOOD,
AND WAVES WERE WHITE BELOW."

"Old Ironsides" ashore on Bollard Head, England, January 17, 1879. *From Illustrated London
News, 1879.*

'It was true, straight talk to a true British seaman, and he came back at the old man quick as a flash:

' "Sir, if they are like you to face trouble like that I believe you; on my soul I do."

'And through this same superintendent, the puzzle gradually grew clear, for a few hours afterward he came aboard and begged permission for a look at our log book. "For, do you know," he remarked, "we have most extraordinary intelligence. Our troopship Himalaya, coming up from Gibraltar, went ashore on Start Point, mistaking the light for Beachy Head, a hundred miles up; and a Swedish bark, with one of our channel pilots, has gone on the Goodwin Sands when they should have been away over on the French side. Now, you were coming straight across channel, and about midway between the two vessels which were going respectively up channel and down. The comparison of your log books should be of value."

'Sure enough, so it turned out. They proved beyond a doubt that the channel had been vexed that night with one of those erratic currents that are inexplicable, but known to come there at times. The Himalaya's officers, and the coast pilot were cleared by British courts, and months afterward a court of inquiry of our own had certified copies of the three logs, and on their evidence cleared all of blame. More than that, British journals flamed out that the Constitution should have gone ashore where there was no light to show a warning, and at once a lighthouse was built at Bollard Head. It was Constitution luck for everybody.

'Who of us will ever forget the day when we were sent

into the cabin to meet Capt. Chads, R.N., and were presented to the fine old fellow who made us a speech like this:

' "Gentlemen, I have long been out of harness and I cannot last much longer, but this is a most satisfactory moment for me to be here and to give you hearty greeting. The moment I learned that this fine old ship was here I made haste to come and see her, for my father was the first lieutenant of the Java on the day of the fight, and he came back to New York in this ship. Many a time he has told me the story, and he had nothing but praise for the courteous treatment that he received as your guest. And more to the point, none could be a better judge; he always insisted that the Constitution was the finest frigate, the most perfect fighting vessel in every respect, of those days. He fought against her on even terms as long as his ship could float. He saw and fully examined her right after the close of the action, and he sailed in her through all weathers for more than a month. That was his conscientious verdict."

'Once more we started out for home and this time we managed to get a good five hundred miles clear of the channel before we struck bad weather. Then in a hard tussle with a piping gale, the rudder-head was twisted clear off and for hours and hours we worked before we could muzzle that loose rudder that banged about threatening to rip the sternpost out of the ship and send us straight to Davy Jones's locker. Of course, when it was finally secured it was of no further use and so we made the run of seven hundred miles to the Tagus steering her with the sails

alone.   The old ship did it in less than four days and
scampered along as if she had been used to going without
her rudder all her life.   The morning that we came off
the bar of the river the wind was wrong for us to attempt
to go up unaided and in response to a signal a towboat
came down whose skipper, appreciating our dilemma,
promptly demanded five hundred pounds sterling to tow
us up.   There was argumentative and persuasive talk on
one side in Portuguese and plain United States profanity
on the other, but the situation was not good for either side
for neither would budge; and then came that luck.   The
wind shifted.   We sheeted home our royals, waved a fond
farewell to the old sidewheel tub, took the combers over
the bar on the jump and raced straightaway up the river
to a snug anchorage in front of Lisbon.

'For the third time within a year the good ship had to be
docked to cover the sins of the thieves that had stolen her
money, and then once more she started out, this time to
reach home at last, with nothing more than a spell of about
four hours a day at the pumps to keep her clear; but no one
minded a little thing like that.   Nor was it all hard work
and unrelieved monotony.   There were things that happened gay as well as grave worthy of the good old ship and
to bring a smile of satisfied remembrance.   Shall I spin
one true yarn of a happening on that last stretch home?

'Among the midshipmen there were two, who, since
they have now reached years of dignity and honor may be
merely distinguished as Brown and Jones.   The captain
was of full habit and sometimes liable to be afflicted with
nightmares, and as a measure of precaution he issued an

order that whenever at night the midshipman of the watch came to the cabin to take the barometer he should notice if the captain happened to be snoring, and if so, wake him up at once. One nasty wet night Mr. Brown went in and heard the captain snoring badly enough to lift the deck beams; so he knocked on the door and waked him up and a colloquy ensued.

' "What is it?"

' "It is Mr. Brown, sir, you were snoring and I waked you up."

' "Oh! How is the weather?"

' "A bit nasty, sir; squalls and rain."

' "Oh, I am much obliged to you, Mr. Brown, you must be wet and uncomfortable. You will find the decanter on the sideboard."

'Of course Brown helped himself, and as this was a little off from the skipper's usual manner with midshipmen, he told about it at the mess-table the next morning with gusto. The next evening was fine and bright and Jones in his turn had the mid-watch. At the proper time he went in to take the barometer and there he had a brilliant idea which he put in execution with a loud thump on the skipper's door, and another colloquy ensued.

' "What is it?"

' "It is Mr. Jones, sir, you were snoring and I woke you up."

' "Oh, I wasn't asleep Mr. Jones, but the decanter is on the sideboard."

' "And do you know," said the captain, as he told about it with a chuckle next morning, "Jones didn't say thank you, and he never stopped to take a drink." '

CHAPTER XXVII

The Triumphant Resurrection

WITH the end of her last foreign voyage the cruising days of the *Constitution* were not yet over. From 1879 to 1881 she served as a training ship for apprentice boys and made many a long run in western Atlantic waters. These were her last sailing days—possibly for all time. After laying up at New York until 1883 she was taken to Portsmouth, N. H. There at the Navy Yard she lay for years in comparative idleness, serving as receiving ship a great part of the time.

Eventually the year 1897 arrived—the centennial of her launching. She was given a brief refit including a 12-day docking in July. Thus prepared she was towed to Boston, her old home port. On her hundredth anniversary—October 21, 1897—"*Old Ironsides*" formed the focal point of a grand celebration staged in her honor both ashore and afloat. Most of the big ships that our navy then possessed contributed their presence—the battleships *Iowa*, *Massachusetts*, and *Texas*, the armored cruisers *New York* and *Brooklyn*—all of them to see war service against Spain within the coming twelve months.

In Boston the old ship remained until 1931—thirty-

four years.   During this period a long fight was waged
against Father Time—contributions and appropriations,
repairs and replacements battling against decay and dis-
integration.   The first gun in the battle was fired in 1900
when Congress authorized the restoration of the ship
if the funds for the purpose should be obtained from
sources outside of the U. S. Treasury.   The Massachusetts State Society of the United States Daughters of
1812 undertook the gigantic task of raising the money.
Their efforts, unfortunately, met with almost complete
failure.

In 1905 the plan was entertained of using *"Old Ironsides"* as a target and allowing her to be sunk by the guns of
the Atlantic Fleet.   On this occasion no Oliver Wendell
Holmes was required to arouse public opinion sufficiently
to prevent this sacrilege.   The following year there
seemed to be a chance of getting Congress to appropriate
some funds for much needed repairs.   The naval appropriation bill was, at the time, in the final stages of conference.   No time was to be lost.   Estimates for the
work were sought and received by wire in forty-eight
hours.   Based on these rapidly made estimates a round
total figure of $100,000 was added to the act and Congress
passed it.   The pertinent clause in the bill authorized the
Navy Department "to expend $100,000, or such portion
thereof as may be necessary to repair the *Constitution* but
not for active service."   This sum, based upon snap judg-
ments only, proved insufficient—as is almost always the
case.   Repairs were made to the greatest extent per-
missible, the work being performed in 1906 and 1907.

When the accounts were closed, the expenditures charged against her amounted to just about $99,996.00! [1]

The years passed with the ship on exhibition at the Navy Yard. Decay and the deterioration of all parts continued their deadly advance. As to strength *"Old Ironsides"* was becoming a mere shell. The ship was doomed unless assistance arrived, and that right soon. On March 4, 1925, Congress authorized "the Secretary of the Navy to repair, equip, and restore the frigate *Constitution,* so far as may be practicable, to her original condition, but not for active service, and, in addition, authorizes the Secretary of the Navy to accept and use any donations or contributions which might be offered for this purpose." Note that "restoration" was authorized, not merely "repairs" as was the case in 1905. There was a great similarity to the 1900 bill in that no money was appropriated; but this time the Navy Department was designated to do the collecting. A splendid campaign was organized with the eminently proper aim of obtaining primarily an immense number of very small contributions. Thus was the great ship brought before all the people, men, women, and children. Her story was told in the schools, and more than ten million offerings of a penny or more were received from boys and girls alone. The work of rebuilding the ship got under way in 1926. A sum exceeding $600,000 was collected eventually—a magnificent effort. [2]

[1] These repairs were carried out by the then Asst. Naval Constructor Wm. G. Groesbeck, U.S.N., under the direction of Naval Constructor Elliot Snow, one of the authors of this book.

[2] The Chairman of The Save *Old Ironsides* Fund was Rear Admiral Philip Andrews, U.S.N., Commandant of the Navy Yard, Boston.

The inspiring motion picture *"Old Ironsides"* without doubt gave much indirect assistance to the cause, in addition to a notable amount of direct aid. Its premiere was held on December 6, 1926, with much official ceremony. Many patriotic manufacturers gave all sorts of material for the refit. The Wellington Sears Company donated a full suit of sails—and that means about 12,000 square yards of canvas. The *Official Bulletin of the National Hard Wood Lumber Association* made the following appeal to the lumber trade:[3]

'This Association has been requested to call the attention of its members to the proposed restoration of the U.S.S. "Constitution," otherwise known as "Old Ironsides," and ask their assistance in this patriotic project. The "Constitution," said to be the oldest wooden ship now afloat, gained a high place for herself in American naval history during the War of 1812 and her visible presence, surviving as it has down to the present day, is justly one of the most venerated relics of the epochal time which witnessed the beginning of our national existence.

.   .   .   .

'Those having in hand the restoration appeal to the lumber trade of the country in the belief that it can, if it will, be of great help by contributing material, or at least by helping to locate the proper material for the work, thus assuring its being available when needed. The object sought in this case is certainly a very worthy one, and we are confident that all of our members will be disposed to do whatever they possibly can toward its attainment.'

[3] Vol. XIII, No. 7, December, 1925.

This or another rallying cry brought a request from the West Coast Lumbermen's Association that they be given the privilege of donating the masts to be used in rebuilding the historic frigate. "Should the Navy accord us this honor," said they—and of course the offer was accepted with much gratification—"the masts will be furnished in Douglas Fir obtained, if possible, from Bainbridge Island, named in honor of Commodore William Bainbridge who was in command of the *CONSTITUTION* in her memorable engagement with the British frigate *JAVA,* December 29, 1812." (Bainbridge Island is just across Puget Sound from Seattle and is passed close aboard by all ships approaching or leaving the Puget Sound Navy Yard, located at Bremerton, Wash.)

Similarly were other donations made, large and small, from far and near. Perhaps the smallest, but none the less an interesting one, was received in 1925 when the restoration was just starting. The following explanatory letter forwarded the contribution:

'Seeing by the papers that there is a movement on foot to repair and preserve "Old Ironsides," I am moved to confess the following crime in order that by so doing I may be enabled to help in this most laudable work.

'Know then: in my second practice cruise from Annapolis, being that year on the U.S.S. *Jamestown,* I did go aboard the *Constitution* in the Navy Yard, Kittery, Me., and did there maliciously and feloniously and solely because of the devil, who, in my earlier years, did often take up his residence within me, unscrew and pry from her wheel abaft the quarter dack, a brass star; which same star still being in my possession and being moved after 40 years by a spirit of penitence, I am sending you by this mail in a separate box in order that it may be restored to its original position.'

Upon receipt of the star an examination was made on board the ship. Sure enough, it was found that there were five screw-holes in the wheel pedestal which matched exactly with the holes in the star.

As the work progressed the time approached for docking the ship. The question was fully considered and discussed as to how to lay the keel blocks on which she was to rest when the water should be pumped from the dock. The amount of her hog was very carefully ascertained. The first measurements indicated that the keel arched upwards an amount somewhere between 12¼ and 14 inches. The age-weakened hull demanded the installation of considerable internal shoring. Eventually a complete cradle was constructed into which the ship should settle. Its parts were adjustable; with elaborate external shoring made ready in addition, the keel blocks were laid level and the final result was satisfactory in every way.

Few persons realize the advantage from an artistic standpoint that is to be gained by "removing the hog." The droop of the bow and stern of *"Old Ironsides"* has deceived many artists and illustrators. It has caused them to portray the ship with an almost straight weather deck and rail. In reality she has considerable "sheer"— that is, the deck rises forward and aft, giving an effect that is very pleasing to the eye.

Filling Dry Dock No. 1—*Constitution* Dock—Navy Yard, Boston, preparatory to docking the frigate (background). Note special cradle in place.

The big day arrived when the *Constitution* was to enter Dry Dock No. 1, the same dock which she christened in 1833. High dignitaries of the city, state, navy, and nation were present in goodly numbers. The press recorded the event most adequately. One selection tells us: [4]

'With the old 15 starred ensign of the United States still proudly flying at its stern, the United States Frigate Constitution was placed in drydock today at the Boston Navy Yard preparatory to being reconstructed.

'The throng about the dockside, in which were scores of high officials of state and nation, paid tribute with cheers and the singing of "The Star-Spangled Banner."

'At 11:40 o'clock, just after Curtis D. Wilbur, Secretary of the Navy, had concluded his address, Lieut. John Lord,[5] Constitution construction officer, standing at the frigate's starboard gangway, gave the order, "heave short." The huge windlass at the dock head started turning and as the towing hawser was brought up taut the national salute of 21 guns crashed out from the deck of a vessel close by.

'GOVERNOR REQUESTS SINGING

'While the moving of the ancient hulk into the dock was underway, Rear Admiral Philip Andrews, commandant of the First Naval District, and in charge of the ceremonies, announced that Governor Fuller had requested that the throng be asked to join in the singing of "The

[4] *Christian Science Monitor,* June 16, 1927.
[5] Lieutenant John A. Lord, C.C., U.S.N.

Star-Spangled Banner," and "the singing will be led from the reviewing platform," Admiral Andrews concluded as he signaled to the band to commence playing. Everybody stood at attention; even the divers who waited to slip into the dock from their equipment rafts clumsily arose in their cumbersome suits and faced the music.

'The ceremonies began with an address by Governor Fuller, after which were introduced Vice-Admiral Guy Burrage, commander of the European station, who returned on the Memphis last week with Colonel Lindbergh; the Rt. Rev. Charles Slattery, bishop of Massachusetts; Miss Letitia Humphries and Mrs. Susan Carson, great-grandaughters of Joshua Humphries, the designer of the Constitution; Mrs. Edith Nourse Rodgers, United States Congresswoman from Massachusetts, and Mayor Nichols. John L. Nicholson, grandson of the first commander of the Constitution, presented the frigate's first flag to Secretary Wilbur.'

The ceremonies at the dock were followed most appropriately by a spiritual recognition of the importance and solemnity of the event. A commemorative religious service was held in Old North Church. In delivering the principal address on "Our National Treasure" Bishop Slattery said:

'For more than a century and a quarter the battleship *Constitution* has been an eloquent reminder of the courage and devotion of the men who preserved the freedom of our country, which had recently been won. Now the ship is to be so far restored that it may more completely be a

"HER SHATTERED HULK."

"Old Ironsides" entering dry dock, June 16, 1927.

symbol of our thanksgiving for those distant heroes of our liberty.

'The world is prone to judge our Nation as commercial, interested only in the surging wealth which flows in upon our people, while the rest of the world is agonizing with the sorrowful aftermath of a great war.

'An event like the event of today tells the world that we do not consider our national treasures to be in the great modern buildings which tower 600 or 700 feet into the sky, nor in the uncounted millions of our commercial princes, nor even in our proud universities and rising cathedrals; but in old Bruton Parish Church in Williamsburg in Virginia; in the tomb of Washington hard by his home at Mt. Vernon, the simple tomb built with his own hands.

'We find our treasures in Independence Hall in Philadelphia; in this venerable North Church in Boston, where Paul Revere caught the sight of the lantern light which sent him forth on his midnight ride to start our endeavor for national freedom; and the good ship *Constitution,* which today takes on new life and will become, we trust, an inspiration to our children and our children's children.

'With such sacred and shining symbols of our earnest, God-fearing past, we kindle our faith in the future of our beloved country, and we pray the Heavenly Father to keep us simple, true, and loyal as our fathers were before us.

'It is good that this rededication of the *Constitution* should be associated with a religious service in this ancient shrine.

'We know today that the grateful restoration of this old

battleship is an act of supreme thanksgiving to God for glowing memories in our national history, and we pray that this remembrance shall continue through untold years.'

The work undertaken in dry dock alone involved in large part the rebuilding of the entire ship. There follows an account of some of the first work which was necessary after docking: [6]

'Since the frigate was docked a large amount of shoring has been installed, from the bottom of the dock, supporting the hull structure, this being essential in view of the decayed and weakened condition of the structure. A great deal of additional shoring has been installed internally since the transverse bulkheads and other supporting partitions have been removed.

'To lighten the hull, all the fittings have been removed. These will be restored again during the restoration period. An examination of the stern and overhang aft of the sternposts showed simply a mass of decayed live-oak framing, white-oak planking and yellow-pine ceiling. During the numerous repair periods in the past 130 years —the frigate was built in 1794–97—many jobs were done and now this decayed material has been removed, including short pieces of any kind of material installed or fitted at that time.

'To reproduce the stern of the Constitution an unusual feature has been employed, consisting of five harpins located transversely at the main rail and extending down

[6] *Boston Evening Transcript,* October 1, 1927.

below the counter. These harpins have been fitted to the contour of the stern, heavily shored and braced and secured by steel cables coming from all angles. This has permitted the removal of the whole stern framing, as well as the decayed part of the transom beams. The fashioned timbers giving the contour of the side of the ship at the stern have been removed. These were found to be in three pieces, as were nearly all other sections of the cant-frame. These have been entirely removed and new cant-frames in one piece reinstated and copper-fastened. All of the stern framing, as recently installed, is of grade A live-oak material, cut fifty or sixty years ago and submerged in Commodore Pond, Pensacola, Fla. This rare material was shipped here expressly for the restoration of Old Ironsides.

'Some of the old timbers removed by way of the transom beams were original material, which, because of its age, had become so hardened that it had to be chipped and bored out in small pieces. Several of the original copper bolts made by Paul Revere have been saved.

'Work on the vessel has been somewhat delayed because of the extreme difficulty in obtaining high grade white oak of unusual size for the purpose of removing Old Ironsides' keelsons, stem, aprons, solid waterways, etc. One piece for the keelson is a timber fifty-two feet long by nineteen and one-half inches square, and weighing several tons. This "stick" is lying alongside the dock now. It will form the after keelson timber of the lower section.

'Bow ports are being cut on the forward end and runways erected externally and internally for the receipt of the keelson timbers which will give a wonderful longitudinal strength and backbone to the vessel, and will permit her to have another long lease of life and also retain her pleasing lines.

'The stern post and apron of Old Ironsides is of live oak. Her stern and cutwaters, being of white oak and exceedingly decayed, have been removed. The bow of the Constitution at present resembles very closely a human face with the nose cut off.'

The restoration went on with great latitude and to splendid effect. As the months passed it became evident that, once more, the cost had been estimated at too low a figure. Although the drive for subscriptions and donations had "gone over the top," this top had not been set quite high enough. It was not possible as late as 1930 to fan back to life again the flame of enthusiasm which had brought in more than $600,000 months and years before. On March 4, 1930, Congress authorized and directed the Secretary of the Navy "to refit and restore the frigate Constitution, as far as may be practicable, to her original condition. For such purpose there is hereby authorized to be appropriated the sum of $300,000, or so much thereof as may be necessary, to be expended under the direction of the Secretary of the Navy, together with such sums as may have been or may be voluntarily contributed for such purpose."

Note that this bill does not contain any clause reading "but not for active service." It was decided to do a good job while about it and *restore her to her original condition.* More than enough money was now available and the reconstruction went on apace.

A few days after this bill was passed *"Old Ironsides"* was undocked—March 15, 1930. Many hours were permitted to elapse from the time the flooding of the dock was commenced until the ship was moved. The utmost care was taken at every stage of the flooding. She had been in dry dock for nearly three years, a most unusual period for a ship under any circumstances. There was no special ceremony this day but a considerable crowd attended, drawn by the announcements in the press. The Navy Yard band rendered a number of patriotic selections; but, while a tug moved the old but rejuvenated ship to the adjacent pier, her progress was greeted by a reverent silence on the part of one and all.

After undocking, more than a year's work still remained to be done before the *Constitution* was "restored to her original condition" *and fit for active service.* The first time she moved on the waters was on October 8, 1930, the occasion being the National Convention of the American Legion at Boston. She was towed by four tug boats around the harbor accompanied by five cruisers, six destroyers, and a submarine. At every hand she received recognition by the cheers of the multitudes and the whistles of steamboats while airplanes dipped over head and the *Memphis* fired a salute of twenty-one guns.

CHAPTER XXVIII

FROM DOWN EAST TO THE GREAT NORTHWEST

FINALLY the very comprehensive work was finished and *"Old Ironsides"* went into commission once more on July 1, 1931—one hundred and thirty-seven years after her keel was laid. A grand sight, she was ready to fulfill her mission of visiting all of our harbors that she is able to enter. She started almost immediately on her first little round, beginning with Portsmouth, N. H., and finishing at Yorktown, Va., for the sesquicentennial of Cornwallis' capitulation. Alas she was towed, though fully equipped to move under sail. A mine-sweeper is taking her from port to port with only a skeleton crew aboard, the Navy Department having deemed it impracticable to man and sail her.

She will be at Washington as an important feature of the bicentennial celebration commemorating the birth of the "Father of his Country." After this her cruise will be resumed. It is planned that, before its completion, an opportunity will have been given to the people of all of our ports to inspect the old ship and draw inspiration from her and her story. Not alone will our seacoast cities be thus favored. It is expected that *"Old Ironsides"* will not only travel along the shores of our Atlantic, Pacific, and Gulf states but will see the innermost bays of Puget Sound, ascend the Mississippi River, and enter the Great Lakes as well.

Here follows a list of the visits proposed for her for 1932, the latest that have been scheduled at the present writing: [1]

AT	FROM	TO
Key West, Fla.,	Dec. 31, 1931,	Jan. 4, 1932.
Pensacola, Fla.,	Jan. 7, 1932,	" 11, "
Mobile, Ala.,	" 11, "	" 15, "
Gulfport, Miss.,	" 15, "	" 19, "
Baton Rouge, La.,	" 21, "	" 27, "
New Orleans, La.,	" 28, "	Feb. 12, "
Corpus Christi, Tex.,	Feb. 16, "	" 23, "
Houston, Tex.,	" 24, "	Mar. 1, "
Galveston, Tex.,	Mar. 1, "	" 7, "
Beaumont, Tex.,	" 8, "	" 13, "
Port Arthur, Tex.,	" 13, "	" 18, "
Lake Charles, La.,	" 20, "	" 22, "
Tampa, Fla.,	" 26, "	" 30, "
Key West, Fla.,	April 2, "	April 5, "
Washington, D. C.,	" 14, "	. . . . .

Where will she lay up after all of her wanderings are over? Will it be Washington or Boston or some other haven? Either our National Capital or the place of her birth would seem to be first in line for the privilege. Wherever she may be, whatever may be her duties during

[1] See Appendix E for 1931 itinerary.

this her latest lease on life, one can be certain of one thing: the intangible returns—those of a higher nature—will alone recompense our people many fold for the dollars and the labours put into her timbers and her sinews.

FAREWELL [2]

'Her commanders have been brave and lucky men. Her officers have been gallant spirits. Her decks have never been soiled by the foot of a conqueror—nor has her ensign-peak been dishonored by an enemy's flag. Nobly has she fulfilled her youthful promise; gallantly has she withstood that flag whose meteor fold struck terror to the world. Many times has she been in the very jaws of the enemy, and as often has she glided away upon the gentle breath of the morning, with her drums beating, her colors flying, and her cannon frowning upon the astonished foe. Her course has been onward—the ends of the earth have seen her—the isles of the sea have rejoiced at her coming, and the tyrant's minion has dipped his blood-stained flag to her as she swept along on her ocean path, with her old sides echoing to "the anthem of the free."

'Long and pleasantly, old ship, have we travelled along in company; now amid the thunder of battle, and now amid the piping of the dreadful tempest; now hanging upon the blood-tinged wave, and now scudding like a flash of lightning along the breakers of a terror-spreading lee. Varied has been thy life—far and wide has spread thy fame—history delights to dwell upon thee, and memory has marked thee for ever. Upon thy anchor, hope,

[2] Jesse Erskine Dow, March 8, 1840.

"THE METEOR OF THE OCEAN AIR."

U. S. S. *Constitution* ready to leave Boston for tour of American ports, July 2, 1931. Her main truck rises more than 200 feet above the water.

angelic hope, makes her throne; fleetness rides upon thy yard-arm; terror perches upon thy cannon's rim, and victory flies upon thy bugle note.

'I see thee still in thy glorious beauty. I see thy star-glittering banner streaming proudly to the wind of heaven. I hear the ripple singing sweetly before, and behold the dark waves closing fearfully behind thee. The sea-eagle perches upon thy topmast—the sun's last ray of crimson splendor kisses the western billow, night closes her curtains upon the ocean, and thou art hid from view. Farewell, Old Ironsides.'

APPENDIX A

Ammunition Expenditure of U. S. S. *Constitution* in Battle with H. M. S. *Guerriere*

32–lb. round shot	236
24–lb. " "	300
18–lb. " "	10
32–lb. stand of grape	140
24–lb. " " "	120
32–lb. canister shot	60
24–lb. " "	40
24–lb. double head shot	47
Total rounds of shot	953
Pounds of gun powder	2,376

APPENDIX B

Cruise of the United States Ship Constitution, Com.^{re} J. D. Elliott.

In the Years 1835, 1836, 1837, and 1838.[1]

Departure	From	Arrival	At	distance run
March 2 1835	Boston	March 12 1835	New York	600
" 16 "	New York	April 10 "	Off Havre	4567
April 24 "	Off Havre	" 25 "	Cherbourg	147
May 3 "	Cherbourg	May 5 "	Havre	80
" 6 "	Havre	" 11 "	Plymouth Eng^d	691
" 16 "	Plymouth Eng^d	June 23 "	New York	4775
Augt 19 "	New York	Sept 11 "	Tangiers	3454
Sept 11 "	Tangiers	" 12 "	Gibraltar	30
" 13 "	Gibraltar	" 19 "	Mahon	835
Oct 10 "	Mahon Cruise	Oct 14 "	Off Mahon	571
Novr 1 "	Mahon	Novr 8 "	Athens	1110
Otho King of Greece & staff visited the Ship, also Prince Calacatroni				
Novr 16 "	Athens	Novr 18 "	Cira	150
Upwards of 200 orphan children accomp^d by Am^n & Eng^h missionaries on board				
Novr 19 "	Cira	Novr 20 "	Vourla Bay	212
" 21 "	Vourla Bay	" 22 "	Smyrna	28
Jany 5 1836	Smyrna	Jany 11 1836	Off Malta	704
" 12 "	Off Malta	" 28 "	Gibraltar	1565
Feby 2 "	Gibraltar	Feby 6 "	Off Tangiers	30
" 6 "	Off Tangiers	" 11 "	Lisbon	797
Prince of Saxe Coburg arrived & next day married Queen Don^a Maria 2^d				
April 13 "	Lisbon	April 18 "	Malaga	573
" 19 "	Malaga	" 20 "	Gibraltar	60
" 23 "	Gibraltar	" 29 "	Mahon	540
Thos D. Allen murdered John Nowlan on shore at Mahon.				
May 23 "	Mahon	May 25 "	Toulon	218
June 1 "	Toulon	June 2 "	Genoa	100
" 7 "	Genoa	" 9 "	Leghorn	87
" 19 "	Leghorn	" 22 "	Civita Vecchia	216
July 1 "	Civita Vecchia	July 3 "	Naples	153
Sentence on Thos D. Allen carried into effect on board the John Adams				
July 11 "	Naples	July 14 "	Palermo	168
" 19 "	Palermo	" 22 "	Messina	89
" 25 "	Messina	" 30 "	Corfu	554

[1] Jesse Erskine Dow.

Departure	From	Arrival	At	distance run

Sir Howard Douglass, Lord High Com:, the President & council of the Ionian Islands visited the Ship

Augᵗ 7 1836	Corfu	Augᵗ 12 1836	Milo	490
" 13 "	Milo	" 15 "	Napoli d'Romani	94
" 17 "	Napoli d'Romani	" 19 "	Athens	226
" 24 "	Athens	" 26 "	Suda (Candia	180

The Frigate United States arrived & relieved the Potomac at Athens

Augᵗ 30 "	Suda	Sept 4 "	Sidon	734
Sept 5 "	Sidon	" 6 "	Beirout	60
" 11 "	Beirout	" 12 "	Tripoli (Syria	76

Ibraham Pasha, Govr of the Coast of Syria visited the Ship

| Sept 17 " | Tripoli (Syria | Sept 20 " | Jaffa | 227 |
| " 29 " | Jaffa | Oct 2 " | Alexandria | 284 |

Mahomet Ali, viceroy of Egypt & suite visited the Ship

Oct 7 "	Alexandria	Oct 15 "	Off Tripoli (Africa	992
" 17 "	Off Tripoli (Africa	" 19 "	Tunis	547
" 21 "	Tunis	" 26 "	Mahon	601
Decr 18 "	Mahon	Decr 28 "	Cadiz	1146

Fell in with Engʰ Schr Perseverance dismasted took her in tow

| Decr 31 " | Cadiz | Jany 4 1837 | Lisbon | 416 |

The English, French, Danish & Belgium Ambassadors, Charge d' Affairs, Consuls and Admirals visited the Ship at Lisbon

Jany 26 1837	Lisbon	Jany 28 "	Gibraltar	297
" 31 "	Gibraltar	Feby 11 "	Mahon	901
April 23 "	Mahon	April 28 "	Marseilles	524

Genl Cass (Amn Minister to France) suite & family came on board

May 1 "	Marseilles	May 6 "	Genoa	522
" 7 "	Genoa	" 10 "	Leghorn	206
" 18 "	Leghorn	" 25 "	Civita Vecchia	572
" 28 "	Civita Vecchia	" 31 "	Palermo	275
June 2 "	Palermo	June 5 "	Malta	331
" 8 "	Malta	" 15 "	Athens	657

Their Majesties the King and Queen of Greece & retinue visited the Ship

June 24 "	Athens	June 24 "	Temple of Minerva	35
" " "	Temple of Minerva	" 26 "	Hydra	101
" 26 "	Hydra	" 27 "	Corinth	135
" 28 "	Corinth	" 29 "	Doro Passage	104
" 29 "	Doro Passage	" " "	Plains Marathon	58
" 30 "	Plains Marathon	July 4 "	Dardanelles	610
July 4 "	Dardanelles	" " "	Plains of Troy	30
" 6 "	Plains of Troy	" 13 "	Galipoli & Nagara	271
" 14 "	Galipoli & Nagara	" 16 "	Constantinople	260

Lord Ponsonby British Minister visited the Ship

July 22 "	Constantinople	July 23 "	Tenedos	180
" 24 "	Tenedos	" 25 "	Scio	122
" 25 "	Scio	" 27 "	Cira	95
" 28 "	Cira	" 28 "	Suda	139
" 29 "	SudaCandia	" 29 "	City of Candia	75

Departure	From	Arrival	At	distance run
July 30 1837	City of Candia	Augt 3 1837	Jaffa	596
Aug 4 "	Jaffa	" 5 "	Cesarea	33
" 5 "	Cesarea	" 6 "	Mount Carmel	58

Monastary on Mt Carmel, from here Elijah was taken up to Heaven

Departure	From	Arrival	At	distance run
Augt 6 "	Mount Carmel	Augt 7 "	Tyre	30
" 8 "	Tyre	" 8 "	Sidon	27
" " "	Sidon	" 11 "	Beirout	35

Here two ancient Sarcophagus or marble Tombs were found and brought on board Supposed age 1600 years

Departure	From	Arrival	At	distance run
Augt 27 "	Beirout	Augt 28 "	Tripoli (Syria	47
" 31 "	Tripoli (Syria	Sept 2 "	Beirout	162
Sept 3 "	Beirout	" 6 "	Limasol (Cyprus	205
" 7 "	Limasol (Cyprus	" 7 "	Larnaca "	42
" 9 "	Larnaca "	" 11 "	Jaffa	351
" 11 "	Jaffa	" 14 "	Alexandria	310
" 24 "	Alexandria	" 30 "	Larnaca (Cyprus	531
Oct 5 "	Larnaca (Cyprus	Oct 16 "	Off Malta	1353
" 17 "	Off Malta	" 24 "	Mahon	863
Feby 1 1838	Mahon	Feby 3 1838	Malta	560
March 8 "	Malta	March 12 "	Syracuse	312
" 13 "	Syracuse	" 19 "	Mahon	780
June 15 "	Mahon	June 23 "	Gibraltar	692
" 26 "	Gibraltar	" 29 "	Madeira	700
July 5 "	Madeira	July 31 "	Hampton Roads	3871
				46,635

APPENDIX C

ABSTRACT OF THE CONSTITUTION'S CRUISE IN THE PACIFIC[1]

Ports sailed from	Day of Month	Ports arrived at	Day of Month	Days at Sea	Distance Sailed	Days in Port
	1839.		1839.			
Norfolk,	April 10,	New York,	April 20,	10	982	30
New York,	May 20,	Vera Cruz,	June 16,	27	2600	2½
Vera Cruz,	June 20,	Havana,	July 3,	13	1421	2
Havana,	July 5,	Rio de Janeiro,	August 27,	53	7164	12
Rio de Janeiro,	Sept'r. 9,	Valparaiso,	Nov'r. 2,	54	5739	13
Valparaiso,	Nov'r. 15,	Callao,	Nov'r. 26,	11	1342	92
	1840		1840			
Callao,	Feb'y. 26,	Talcahuana,	March 15,	18	2294	10
Talcahuana,	March 25,	Callao,	April 4,	10	1469	32
Callao,	May 6,	Payta,	May 10,	4	498	7
Payta,	May 17,	Callao,	June 1,	15	1860	102
Callao,	Sept'r. 11,	Payta,	Sept'r. 15,	3½	489	1
Payta,	Sept'r. 16,	Puna,	Sept'r. 19,	4	228	12
Puna,	October 2,	Payta,	October 9,	7½	308	2
Payta,	October 12,	Callao,	October 31,	19	1990	31
Callao,	Dec'r. 2,	Valparaiso,	Dec'r. 31,	29	2739	28
	1841		1841			
Valparaiso,	Jan'y. 28,	Talcahuana,	Feb'y. 4,	7	489	31
Talcahuana,	March 8,	Valparaiso,	March 11,	2½	270	5
Valparaiso,	March 16,	Callao,	March 26,	10	1430	106
Callao,	July 11,	Rio de Janeiro,	August 28,	48	6696	16½
Rio de Janeiro,	Sept'r. 15,	Hampton Roads,	October 31,	46½	5743	
				392	45751	535

[1] *Life in a Man-of-War.*

APPENDIX D

NATIONALITIES OF BLUEJACKETS ON U. S. S.
Constitution IN DECEMBER, 1844

Native Born Americans	200
English	35
Irish	34
German	16
Swedish	14
Scotch	12
Dutch	11
Canadian	8
French	6
Danish	6
Welsh ..	5
Chinese	5
Hamburg	4
Russian	4
Norwegian	3
Portuguese	2
Italian	2
Prussian	2
West Indian	1
Bremen	1
Mahonese	1

Australian	1
Peruvian	1
Swiss	1
Unclassified	10
Total Bluejackets	385

The ship's company included also 32 officers, all of them Americans, and 40 Marines, making a total of 457 (before any deaths occurred).

APPENDIX E

1931 ITINERARY OF U. S. S. *Constitution*

AT	FROM		TO	
Boston, Mass.,	. . . . .		July	2
Portsmouth, N. H.,	July	3	"	9
Bar Harbor, Me.,	"	10	"	13
Bath, Me.,	"	13	"	16
Portland, Me.,	"	16	"	23
Gloucester, Mass.,	"	23	"	30
New Bedford, Mass.,	"	31	August	6
Providence, R. I.,	August	6	"	10
Newport, R. I.,	"	10	"	13
New London, Conn.,	"	13	"	20
Fort Pond Bay, N. Y.,	"	20	"	24
Oyster Bay, N. Y.,	"	24	"	27
New York, N. Y.,	"	29	September	8
Newark, N. J.,	September	8	"	14
Wilmington, Del.,	"	15	"	18
Philadelphia, Pa.,	"	18	October	1
Newport News, Va.,	October	3	"	9
Norfolk, Va.,	"	9	"	16
Yorktown, Va.,	"	16	"	23
Baltimore, Md.,	"	24	November	2
Annapolis, Md.,	November	2	"	6

1931 ITINERARY OF U. S. S. *Constitution (Cont.)*

AT	FROM		TO	
Washington, D. C.,	November	6	November	18
Wilmington, N. C.,	"	21	"	27
Charleston, S. C.,	"	28	December	4
Savannah, Ga.,	December	5	"	11
Brunswick, Ga.,	"	12	"	15
Jacksonville, Fla.,	"	16	"	21
Miami, Fla.,	"	23	"	30